UNITED STATES SINCE 1865

the text of this book is printed
on 100% recycled paper

"Driving the Last Spike" — The First Transcontinental Railroad

COLLEGE OUTLINE SERIES

UNITED STATES
SINCE 1865

JOHN A. KROUT
Formerly Vice President
Columbia University

Eighteenth Edition

BARNES & NOBLE BOOKS

A DIVISION OF HARPER & ROW, PUBLISHERS

New York, Hagerstown, San Francisco, London

First BARNES & NOBLE BOOKS edition published 1973.

LIBRARY OF CONGRESS CATALOG CARD NUMBER: 73–7140

STANDARD BOOK NUMBER: 06–460156–0

76 77 78 79 80   12 11 10 9 8 7 6 5 4

ABOUT THE AUTHOR

John A. Krout received his A.B. degree from the
University of Michigan and his A.M. and Ph.D.
degrees from Columbia University. From 1922
until his retirement in 1962 he served at Columbia
University successively as instructor in, to professor
of, history, Dean of Graduate Faculties, and Vice
President. He is a trustee of the Museum of the
City of New York and of the New York State
Historical Association, and belongs to numerous
other historical groups—among these being the
American Historical Association and the Society of
American Historians. He was a member by pres-
idential appointment of the Civil War Centennial
Commission. His published works include *The
Origins of Prohibition, Annals of American Sport,
American History for Colleges* (with D. S. Muz-
zey), *Approaches to American Social History*
(W. E. Lingelbach, editor), *The Completion of
Independence* (with D. R. Fox), *Great Issues in
American History,* and *United States to 1877* (a
companion College Outline).

PREFACE

In preparing this edition of *The United States Since 1865*, the author has tried to give appropriate emphasis to the events of the past quarter-century. He has sought to avoid the temptation to exaggerate the significance of contemporary trends. At the same time he has accorded recognition to the political, economic, and social changes becoming apparent in this atomic age, some of which may soon be guideposts on the road to the future.

Since chronology is the basic framework of history, a chronological arrangement determines the pattern of this Outline. At the same time, a topical sequence for all important subjects can easily be traced by the students through use of the comprehensive index.

The Bibliography lists general surveys with which every serious student of American history should become acquainted; it also provides selected readings for each chapter. The review questions and the maps have been prepared as aids to an understanding of the development of the American nation since 1865. Specimen mid-term and final examinations are included, with cross references to the pages on which information relating to each question may be found.

The author hopes that students will find the Outline useful not only in history courses but also as a comprehensive digest of historical material for college students interested in American literature and American government. It is an introduction to the subject as treated by the most reliable sources; and it will yield the largest returns when used in conjunction with the other writings to which it is a guide.

John A. Krout

TABLE OF CONTENTS

MAPS AND CHARTS

UNITED STATES SINCE 1865

CHAPTER I

BUILDING A NEW NATION

The sectional conflict between North and South, which reached its climax in 1861–1865, worked a revolution in the life of the American people in many respects more profound than that which accompanied the War for Independence. For two decades after the end of the Civil War, the South was the scene of bitter strife about its status in the Union and the plans for its rebuilding. From the Reconstruction period emerged new patterns of government, economy, and society that transformed the Northern, as well as the Southern, states.

RECONSTRUCTION'S UGLY SCARS

War always disfigures; and a civil war often alters the face of society so greatly that it is scarcely recognizable.

The Prostrate South. Confederate soldiers, returning to their former homes after Lee's surrender, found destruction, destitution, and hopelessness on every side.

THE STRICKEN LAND. From Virginia to Texas, farmhouses, barns, and mills had been burned; bridges and railroad tracks had been destroyed; towns had been looted and their inhabitants driven out. Business was at a standstill, save for speculative enterprises which preyed on people impoverished by war. Plantation owners had lost their slaves and much other property; their land was now greatly diminished in value; and they could not borrow the capital for agricultural equipment to replace slave labor.

SOCIAL CONFUSION. The war destroyed the whole structure of pre-war Southern society. The aristocratic planter, shorn of wealth and power in many sections, yielded reluctantly to the growing influence of bankers, merchants, and small farmers. The changing status of the

Negro, as he made the slow transition from slave to wage earner, created serious social tensions and economic difficulties.

POLITICAL UNCERTAINTY. The collapse of the Confederacy stopped all governmental processes in the South. Local and state governments had to be reorganized; the new state governments had to establish normal relations in the Federal Union. In Washington and throughout the North, political leaders differed sharply over what should be done and how it should be done. There were bitter quarrels among the statesmen of the dominant Republican party concerning the proper basis for political reconstruction.

Framing a Reconstruction Policy. Motives were so mixed, when legislators tried to formulate a program for the former Confederate states, that the voters of the nation were badly confused. Some congressmen were determined that Southerners must pay a heavy penalty for secession—an illegal act. By this crime, the Southern states had placed themselves outside the protection of the Constitution. They must now be treated as "conquered provinces" (which Congress had constitutional power to govern). But President Lincoln brushed aside the "conquered province" theory, though he knew it had support from such Republican leaders as Thaddeus Stevens and Benjamin Wade. Lincoln believed that the right to secede did not exist; therefore, despite the attempt to sever relations by force of arms, the Southern states had never left the Union but were merely "out of their proper practical relation" with it. This position was subsequently upheld by a Supreme Court decision (*Texas* v. *White,* 1869) that the Union was constitutionally indestructible.

LINCOLN'S TEN PER CENT PLAN. Convinced that he should aid the Southern people to resume quickly their former status in the Union, Lincoln (1) set up provisional governments in areas where Union armies were victorious; (2) issued a Proclamation of Amnesty and Reconstruction (1863) pardoning all (with a few exceptions*) who would swear allegiance to the government of the United States and accept "all acts of Congress passed during the existing rebellion with reference to slaves"; and (3) authorized the establishment of a new government for any state if one tenth of its qualified voters of 1860 would take the required loyalty oath.

CONGRESSIONAL OPPOSITION. Lincoln's moderate proposals ran into

---

* High Confederate officials and persons who had left United States military or government service to aid the Confederacy.

strong opposition among the congressional leaders of his own party. They feared that the President would "let the South off too easily" and that the former Confederate officials would return immediately to political power in their respective states. In July, 1864, Congress passed the drastic Wade-Davis Bill which (1) provided that a majority of white male citizens had to take a loyalty oath before a civil government could be organized in a seceded state and (2) excluded from the electorates of such states former Confederate office-holders and soldiers. Lincoln pocket-vetoed this bill; whereupon, Congressmen Wade and Davis issued a manifesto accusing him of "dictatorial usurpation."

THE "JOHNSON GOVERNMENTS." The assassination of President Lincoln (April 14, 1865) was a cruel blow to those who favored a policy of moderation. His unfinished work fell into the hands of Andrew Johnson, a War Democrat from Tennessee who had been elected on the Union (Republican) ticket with Lincoln in 1864. The new President felt that he was carrying forward his great predecessor's plan, but he had little skill in handling angry congressmen. Johnson granted amnesty to all former Confederates (except Southern leaders and large property-holders) who were willing to take an oath to "support, protect, and defend the Constitution." By successive proclamations he set up provisional governments in North Carolina, Mississippi, Texas, Georgia, Alabama, South Carolina, and Florida. He authorized the loyal white citizens to draft and ratify new constitutions and to elect state legislatures, which were to repeal ordinances of secession, repudiate the Confederate state debts, and ratify the Thirteenth Amendment.

DEFINING THE ISSUE. In December, 1865, Congress refused to seat the senators and representatives who had been elected by the "provisional" state governments set up under the Johnson plan. (Under Article I of the Constitution each house of Congress was empowered to judge the election and qualifications of its own members.) Instead, the Republicans in Congress, led by Thaddeus Stevens, created a Joint Committee on Reconstruction, with fifteen members, which was authorized to examine the whole question of political reconstruction and make new proposals for congressional action.

The "Radicals" Emerge. Opponents of the Johnson plan soon came to be called "Radicals" in the newspapers of this period. Their hostility to the President's policy was a curious blending of high moral purpose and partisan self-interest. While it is difficult to classify motives, contemporary records show that the following factors were important: (1) personal animosity toward President Johnson on the part of congressmen who thought that he was unworthy of his high office; (2) the fear of executive encroachment on the authority of Congress; (3) resentment over the speedy return of the ex-Confederates to political power in the South; (4) the determination of the Republican politicians to create a Republican party in the South; (5) the humanitarian desire to safeguard the interests of the Negro; (6) the hope of representatives of Northern business enterprise that the removal of Southern influence from Congress would result in a program of government aid to industry.

Freedmen's Bureau Bill (1866). In March, 1865, Congress had created the Freedmen's Bureau to protect and provide for the newly emancipated Negroes. Early in 1866 the national legislators passed a law extending the life of the Bureau indefinitely. Johnson vetoed this bill on the grounds that the states affected by it had not been represented in Congress when it was passed and that its provision for the military trial of civilians violated the Constitution. However, a later bill enlarging the powers of the Bureau was passed over Johnson's veto in July, 1866.

Civil Rights Bill (1866). In April, 1866, the President's opponents passed over his veto a Civil Rights Act, conferring citizenship upon the Negro and assuring him equality of treatment before the law. Johnson argued that the act invaded states' rights and would revive the spirit of rebellion.

Black Codes. In an attempt to cope with chaotic conditions and to ensure white supremacy, Southern states enacted "Black Codes." These laws conferred some rights of citizenship upon Negroes but narrowly restricted their economic and political activities. The immediate effect in the North was increased support for the Radical position.

CONGRESSIONAL PROPOSALS. As the quarrel with Johnson grew more violent, the Radical Republican faction insisted upon the political punishment of ex-Confederates. The basis of their attack took the form of a proposal to amend the Constitution.

The Fourteenth Amendment. In April, 1866, the Joint Committee on Reconstruction proposed the Fourteenth Amendment, which Congress promptly referred to the states for ratification. By its provisions: (1) citizenship was conferred on every person born or naturalized in the United States and state laws abridging civil rights

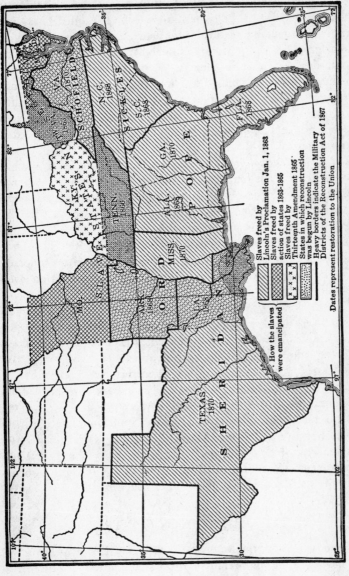

Emancipation and Restoration of Southern States

How the slaves were emancipated
Slaves freed by Lincoln's Proclamation Jan. 1, 1863
Slaves freed by action of states 1863-1865
Slaves freed by Thirteenth Amendment 1865
States in which reconstruction was begun by Lincoln
Heavy borders indicate the Military Districts of the Reconstruction Act of 1867
Dates represent restoration to the Union

were prohibited; (2) states which deprived the Negro of the ballot were to suffer a reduction of representation in Congress proportionate to the number denied the right to vote;* (3) ex-Confederates were barred from holding national and state offices if they had filled similar posts before the war (this disability could be removed by a two-thirds vote in each house); (4) the Confederate debt was repudiated and the validity of the United States debt affirmed. Tennessee quickly ratified the amendment and was readmitted to the Union (1866). All the other states of the Confederacy rejected this amendment upon the advice of Johnson, who considered it unconstitutional.

The Congressional Elections (1866). President Johnson and the Radical Republicans fought for control of Congress in the elections of 1866. The friends of the administration denounced the Fourteenth Amendment and urged a policy of conciliation toward the defeated South; but in many congressional districts the voters found that their only choice on the ballot was between a Radical Republican and a Democrat who had opposed Lincoln's wartime program. The result was never in doubt, and the Radicals scored an overwhelming victory.

The Reconstruction Acts (1867). After the election, Congress passed over the President's veto a Military Reconstruction Act (March 2, 1867), which was supplemented later in the year by acts outlining administrative and legal routines. This legislation provided that: (1) the ten states still unreconstructed were to be divided into five military districts with a major general in command of each; (2) constitutional conventions, elected by Negroes and loyal whites, were to frame constitutions providing for Negro suffrage; (3) these constitutions were to be acceptable to Congress; (4) qualified voters were to elect state legislatures pledged to ratify the Fourteenth Amendment; (5) with the ratification of the Fourteenth Amendment the states could apply for representation in Congress.

THE RADICALS IN CONTROL

The enactment of the Reconstruction Acts of 1867, which marked the beginning of the "reign of the Radicals," was far more significant than an attempt to punish Southern states for their failure

---

* This provision could have been carried out only with enforcement legislation, which Congress never enacted.

to ratify the Fourteenth Amendment. It indicated that the Republican party, which had been created as a political protest against the spread of slavery, was being transformed by the financial and business interests of the North.

Congress Challenges the President. The congressional leaders of the Radical faction were hindered by their inability to control the presidential office. Realizing that President Johnson was personally unpopular, they determined to humiliate him and thus remove any constitutional check on their policies.

ANDREW JOHNSON IMPEACHED. In the Tenure of Office Act (March 2, 1867), Congress forbade the President to remove federal officeholders, including members of his own cabinet, without the consent of the Senate. When Edwin M. Stanton, Secretary of War, who was in sympathy with the Radicals, refused to carry out a presidential order, Johnson dismissed him without the Senate's consent. The House of Representatives promptly impeached the President for "high crimes and misdemeanors."

THE TRIAL (MARCH 5–MAY 26, 1868). Johnson's trial, presided over by Chief Justice Salmon P. Chase, was a notable victory for the President's lawyers, who argued that the Tenure of Office Act was unconstitutional. In the final vote of the Senate, sitting as the jury, the Radicals failed by one vote (35 to 19) to secure the two-thirds majority required by the Constitution for conviction. Seven moderate Republicans voted with the Democrats to save the only American President ever impeached. Johnson's victory helped to preserve the authority and independence of the presidential office.

The Election of 1868. In the campaign of 1868 the Radicals within the Union (Republican) party emerged not only as the champions of a vigorous Reconstruction policy, but also as the defenders of Northern manufacturing, banking, and railroad interests against the agricultural leaders of the West and South.

THE UNION (REPUBLICAN) CONVENTION. The delegates to the national convention adopted a platform which endorsed congressional Reconstruction and demanded payment of the public debt in gold. The Radicals, having made sure that General Grant was one of their number, nominated him for President, and chose Schuyler Colfax of Indiana (Speaker of the House of Representatives) for Vice-President.

THE "OHIO IDEA." The Democratic party, seeking to recover its prewar strength, drafted a platform which denounced the congressional program of Reconstruction as unconstitutional and pledged support to the "Ohio Idea," a proposal that government bonds, whenever possible, should be paid in greenbacks (paper money) instead of gold. But Democratic support of this Western financial policy was weakened by the nomination of Governor Horatio Seymour of New York, who repudiated the greenback plank.

GRANT'S VICTORY. In the electoral college Grant defeated Seymour by 214 to 80 votes, but his 300,000 popular majority was made possible only by the 650,000 Negro votes cast for him in the Southern states under the military power of the federal government. The white voters had not endorsed the Radical Republican program.

THE SOUTH IN TRANSITION

The policy of military reconstruction, which was pushed vigorously by the Radicals, hastened changes in the economic and social life of the South and took political power from the upper classes that had been dominant before the Civil War.

The Changing Political Scene. After the registration of voters, under the terms of the Reconstruction Acts of 1867, there were 703,000 Negroes on the lists and only 627,000 whites.

THE "CARPETBAG GOVERNMENTS." The Negro vote was marshaled and controlled in many districts by ambitious but unprincipled whites. Negroes sat in most of the conventions which drafted the new state constitutions, although they comprised only about one-third of the total membership. Among the white legislators were Northerners who had come South with the expectation of achieving power and fortune ("carpetbaggers") and Southerners who sought political preferment and lucrative contracts by aiding the Radical program ("scalawags"). There were, however, in these governments a number of honest and able representatives, both white and black. Twenty-two Negroes went to Congress; among these ten had some college education and one, Robert B. Elliott, was a graduate of Eton and read five languages.

Some legislatures elected in the Southern states (1868–1869) indulged in extravagance and fraud which left an aftermath of public debts and burdensome taxes; but some Northern state legislatures of the period were also corrupt.

THE REFORMERS. There were in the Southern states some white

and Negro leaders who were determined to make life better for the average citizen in the South.

Toward Political Justice. Several Republican legislatures enacted laws providing for more courts and correcting legal abuses. Others authorized greater state support for hospitals and asylums. In almost every state an attempt was made to base representation in the legislature on electoral districts substantially equal in population.

Strengthening the Schools. Though fraud and theft tainted many of the appropriation bills passed by the carpetbag-Negro legislatures, many other expenditures were for worthy purposes. Notable were the efforts to build more schoolhouses and to provide better educational opportunities for both Negroes and whites. By 1876 nearly every state had constitutional provisions calling for the erection of tax-supported public schools, and some had more than tripled the number of pupils in the tax-supported schools as compared with 1860.

The Restoration of White Supremacy.

By 1868 most Southern states had been permitted to rejoin the Union. Ratification of the Fourteenth Amendment thereby obtained was announced in July, 1868. Virginia, Georgia, Mississippi, and Texas were not able to satisfy Congress until 1870, when they were readmitted on condition that their legislatures ratify the Fifteenth Amendment, which forbade any state to deny the suffrage on the grounds of "race, color, or previous condition of servitude."

THE KU KLUX KLAN. The Southern whites turned to nonpolitical methods in their efforts to undo the results of Radical Reconstruction. Secret societies—the Ku Klux Klan, the Knights of the White Camelia, the Boys of '76—were used as the instruments of a policy of terrorism designed to frighten the Negroes and compel them to renounce their new political power. The Klan, which became the most notorious of the organizations, was dominated in some districts by terrorists.

PEACEFUL COERCION. Southerners who disliked the violent tactics of the Klan and other secret societies turned to more subtle forms of coercion. Negroes were denied employment and were kept from the polls, not by force but by intimidation.

THE ENFORCEMENT ACTS. Southern resistance brought legislation for the enforcement of the congressional program. (1) An act of May, 1870, imposed heavy penalties for violations of the Fourteenth and Fifteenth Amendments; (2) an act of February, 1871, placed congressional elections under the control of the federal authorities; (3) the Ku Klux Act of the same year gave the President military powers to suppress violence in the Southern states. (In 1871 President Grant used these powers to subdue the Klan in South Carolina.)

THE RESTORATION OF THE CONSERVATIVES. In spite of the Fourteenth and Fifteenth Amendments and the "force acts" passed by Congress, the Radical Republicans lost ground in the South after 1870.

The General Amnesty Act. A combination of Democrats and moderate Republicans, who disliked the severity of military Reconstruction, pushed a bill through Congress in 1872 which restored to thousands of ex-Confederates their political privileges and hastened the collapse of the governments based on Negro votes. By 1876 only South Carolina, Florida, and Louisiana were still in the hands of the Radical Republicans.

The Withdrawal of Federal Troops. In 1877, as a result of the compromise between certain elements in the Republican Party and some leaders of the Southern Democrats (see p. 36), the federal government under President Hayes withdrew its troops from the South; the state governments still in Republican hands quickly fell to the Southern Democrats.

Supreme Court Decisions. In 1873 the Supreme Court, deciding cases that arose from a disputed grant of a state legislature to a slaughterhouse company, restricted the application of the Fourteenth Amendment. It held that this Amendment was not intended to protect civil rights in general but only United States citizenship rights. In 1875 Congress passed a Civil Rights Act that prohibited racial discrimination in public places. This act was never enforced, and in 1883 the Supreme Court declared it unconstitutional on the ground that the Thirteenth and Fourteenth Amendments did not prohibit acts of individual discrimination.

THE LEGACY OF RECONSTRUCTION

It is impossible to balance the good and the evil features in the congressional program of Reconstruction. It is even difficult to determine whether the policies of the federal government during the Reconstruction era were responsible for the political, economic, and social developments of the post-Civil War years in the former states of the Confederacy. Less vigorous Northern control might have resulted in similar political, economic, and social results.

Political Readjustments. The most obvious political consequence of congressional policies in the South was the adherence of the great majority of Southern whites to the Democratic party.

THE SOLID SOUTH. In the immediate postwar years most Southerners came to believe that the Republican party as a whole was the party of the Negro and the corrupt white man, who despised the South. As a result many areas in the former slave states knew only the one-party system. Whoever captured the Democratic nomination was virtually sure of winning. Between 1876 and 1928 the Republican party rarely carried any of the former Confederate states in a national election.

THE "BOURBONS." Within the one-party system, the leaders of the Democrats came to be known as "Bourbons." This faction consisted of some of the old planter class and many native whites who had made money during the Reconstruction period.

DISFRANCHISEMENT OF THE NEGRO. By ways which avoided violence, the Democratic leaders steadily reduced the number of Negroes who could meet the qualifications for the suffrage. Several devices were used: (1) literacy and educational tests which most Negroes could not pass; (2) poll taxes and other property requirements; (3) the application of the "grandfather" clause granting the suffrage only to those whose fathers or grandfathers had voted before 1867. The last device, of course, barred the Negroes and still made it possible for uneducated "poor whites" to vote.

Economic Rehabilitation. The political confusion of the postwar decade retarded all the Southern states in their efforts to promote the economic well-being of their citizens.

THE DISRUPTION OF THE PLANTATION SYSTEM. The revolutionary changes effected by the war compelled the landholders of the Southern states to reduce the size of their plantations. Some sold off surplus acres, but the majority preferred to try a plan of cultivation on shares, with tenants who were unable to pay a cash rental. Owner and tenant entered into a partnership, one furnishing land, the other labor.

THE RISE OF THE MERCHANT. The cash necessary to finance this partnership was generally supplied by merchants or bankers who took mortgages on the crops as security for loans. It proved to be an expensive system of rural credits. Interest rates were high; farmers were compelled to confine their production to staples like cotton and tobacco; and the small farmers became virtually tenants of the merchant-creditors.

INDUSTRIAL DEVELOPMENT. As the South of the great plantations disappeared, a new industrial order arose. The exploitation of coal, iron, phosphates, and lumber slowly gathered momentum. The less prosperous elements in the rural districts drifted into the towns to work in factories located where cheap water power was available. The increase in railroad mileage began to keep pace with the output of coal and pig iron and with the multiplication of cotton spindles.

Social Tensions. It is difficult to measure the effect of the Reconstruction years in the process of social readjustment throughout the South.

THE STATUS OF NEGROES. The brief period of political power which Negro voters enjoyed in the South under the Radical Republican regimes probably increased tension between the native whites and the freedmen.

Resentment Over the Excesses of Military Reconstruction. In many communities the bitterness engendered by imposed government and military occupation brought interracial conflicts that curbed the free development of the newly liberated Negro population.

Insecurity of Negro Workers. The breakup of the large plantations into smaller farms was by no means a social gain in every section of the South. Too often it meant that the freedman found it difficult to secure and hold a job. The Negroes who drifted into mill towns or who got employment in mines and factories found that their labor was exploited almost as vigorously as it had been during the years of slavery.

CLEAVAGES AMONG NATIVE WHITES. The small farmers, heavily in debt, and the tenants on larger plantations grew ever more hostile toward the "Bourbon" representatives of the old planter-aristocracy and the new merchant-capitalist groups.

The New South. The phrase "the New South" which Henry Grady of the *Atlanta Constitution* used to describe the efforts of Southerners to balance agriculture with new industries, told only part of the story at the close of the nineteenth century. There was a vigorous leadership trying to remake the South economically, but many critical problems remained: (1) the Southern economy had not escaped from control by Northern financiers; (2) Southern political leaders remained far more interested in sectional than in national problems; (3) too many white, as well as Negro, farmers still lived in poverty; (4) mindful of heavy losses during the war and Reconstruction years, most Southern voters refused to accept tax programs which would provide funds for the social services needed to rebuild from war's destruction.

REVIEW QUESTIONS

1. To what extent did Andrew Johnson follow Abraham Lincoln's policy in dealing with the reconstruction of the states that had formed the Confederacy?
2. How was the program of the congressional Radicals, as set forth in the Fourteenth Amendment, modified by the Reconstruction Acts of 1867?
3. In what sense was the election of 1868 a victory for the business and financial interests of the Northern states?
4. How do you explain the failure of the Radicals to secure a conviction in the impeachment proceedings against President Johnson?
5. If you had been a Southern planter during the years immediately following the collapse of the Confederacy, what economic problems would you have faced?
6. An eminent American historian has characterized the Civil War years as the period of a Second American Revolution. Do you see any justification for this statement?
7. What did Southern leaders have in mind when they wrote about the "New South"?
8. What did a Negro historian mean by referring to the period after the Civil War as "The Decades of Disappointment"?

Chapter II

AN EXPANDING ECONOMIC SYSTEM

While the planters of the South were being humbled during the war and the years of Reconstruction, foundations for a new economic order were established in the North and West. The land and resources of the trans-Mississippi West became available; the building of trancontinental railroads made it possible to transport people and goods from one end of the country to the other; and the "industrial revolution" created a manufacturing economy. As a result of these changes, cycles of prosperity and depression were accentuated and basic conflicts emerged between the interests of Eastern businessmen and Western farmers.

THE WESTERN ADVANCE

Several factors contributed to the conquest and settlement of the West: the skill of business interests possessed of abundant capital and an adequate labor supply; the courage and perseverance of the pioneers; and a government policy of support and encouragement.

Opening the Trans-Mississippi West. The domain of prairie, plateau, mountain, and desert beyond the Mississippi possessed remarkable resources. Before they could be utilized, however, the region had to be made safe and accessible for settlement.

THE VARIED RESOURCES. In topography and climate this American West offered a wide range of opportunities for large-scale farming, mining, ranching, and lumbering. The soils were generally fertile, and, wherever water was adequate, they could be made phenomenally productive.

OVERCOMING THE INDIANS. Complete utilization of the vast natural resources of the western regions was impossible as long as the nomadic Indian tribes (which relied for subsistence on the buffalo herds of the Great Plains) retained their former hunting grounds. These Plains Indians, probably numbering more than 225,000 at the close of the Civil War, were skilled fighters and often resisted the encroachments of the white man.

Frontier Hostilities. While some tribes, such as the Crow and Northern Arapaho, were generally friendly to the white man, the more militant Kiowas, southern Arapahoes, Cheyenne, and Comanches were determined to halt the advance of settlers into the Great Plains and intermountain valleys. Hundreds of skirmishes took place between United States troops and the "hostiles" during the decade after the Civil War. At times as many as 30,000 troops were in the field to protect emigrants moving along the Missouri River and westward.

The Collapse of the Sioux. The Sioux nation constituted one of the most difficult problems for the army commanders. It was large, powerful, and ably led. Its courageous campaign was slowly contained, however, and by 1880 the northern frontier was relatively quiet. The price had been high in money and in lives; the massacre of General George Custer's command on the Little Big Horn River (Montana) in 1876 shocked the government into a reconsideration of its Indian policy.

Exterminating the Buffalo. An important factor in the decline of militant resistance on the part of the Plains Indians was the slaughter of the buffalo herds by professional hunters and sportsmen. Buffalo hides and robes were in great demand during the quarter century after the Civil War. "Buffalo Bill" Cody claimed that he shot 4,280 in the northern herds within less than two years. By 1885 only a few straggling herds remained of the more than 15,000,000 that had roamed the Plains twenty years earlier. Though the species survived under governmental protection, the chief economic support of the nomadic Indians was gone.

FORMULATING· A NATIONAL POLICY FOR THE INDIANS. A more enlightened policy of dealing with the native American tribes was slowly taking shape. It was framed, however, only after the record had been liberally sprinkled with needless wars and massacres, fraudulent seizures of Indian lands, and speculations of dishonest agents. For many years the War Department, which advocated "extermination" worked at cross purposes to the Bureau of Indian Affairs (in the Interior Department), which at times supplied the Indians with hunting guns.

The Reservation System. As actual warfare between Indian warriors and United States troops diminished, the government forced the tribes onto reservations where they were almost completely dependent on the taxpayers' bounty, never adequate for their needs. The aim of the reservation policy was to assimilate the Indians to a farm economy. By 1885 there were 171 reservations in more than a score of states and territories. But the administration of the reservation system was notoriously corrupt. Government agents made fortunes by supplying Indians under their jurisdiction with shoddy goods, selling them forbidden liquor, and cheating them out of their rightful lands through fraudulent real estate deals. Meantime, traders, miners, ranchers, and railroad builders prodded the government into unwarranted encroachments on Indian reservations.

The Reform Movement. Humanitarians, inspired in part by Helen Hunt Jackson's portrayals of the degradation of the reservation Indian, tried to modify or to supplant the system. Among the reformers there was a sharp division between those who wanted to preserve old tribal customs and others who desired to hasten the "Americanization" of the Indian.

The Dawes Act (1887). At first, governmental action was confined to a program of increased appropriations for schools to train Indian youth in arts and crafts, in farming, and in animal husbandry. Congress partially accepted the philosophy that the Indian should be more adequately prepared for a place in American society when it passed the Dawes Act. This law modified the reservation system by granting 160 acres of land and United States citizenship to the heads of Indian families who would agree to abandon their tribal allegiance. These lands were made inalienable for a period of twenty-five years. The motives back of this legislation were twofold: the desire to encourage Indians to become assimilated into the nation and the willingness of the federal government to satisfy the land hunger of Western settlers.

The Burke Act (1906). Ranchers and farmers, seeking new homesteads in the trans-Mississippi West, profited more from the Dawes Act than did the Indians. The lands in the Indian Reservations not needed for allotment to former members of a tribe were opened to settlement. After some thirty years even the reformers admitted that title to private property and the rights of citizenship had not improved the status of many Indians. In the Burke Act there were new safeguards against exploitation of those who were making the transition from tribal membership to individual citizenship. Citizenship was not granted to Indians receiving allotments until they had completed a twenty-five-year probationary period.

Newer Trends in Policy. In 1924 citizenship was conferred upon all Indians. The philosophy underlying both the Dawes and Burke Acts was reversed in 1933, when the Indian Commissioner, John Collier, began to stress the government's interest in a revival of tribal arts, handicrafts, and customs. The individual might still seek a place outside the reservation, but the tribal Indian was encouraged to cherish the best traditions of his tribe. For most American Indians the most important decision was the choice which each had to make between life on the reservation and entrance into the larger society dominated by the white man. By 1970, most Indian leaders were determined that the affairs of the tribal Indians on their reservation should not be controlled by the federal government.

The Mining Frontier. One of the magnets pulling settlers westward through the Indian barriers and drawing squatters onto the lands over which nomadic tribes had long roamed was the discovery by venturesome prospectors of the rich mineral deposits beyond the Mississippi.

"BOOM AND BUST." During the third quarter of the nineteenth century the mineral resources of the American West were rapidly discovered and almost as rapidly exploited.

The "Strikes." In the speech of the period a new discovery was usually called a "strike." Gold had been found in California in 1849. More abundant deposits were revealed in Colorado's Pikes Peak district in 1858. The Comstock lode in Nevada (discovered in 1859) proved to be rich in both silver and gold. In 1874 gold was discovered in the Black Hills section of Dakota Territory. Gold-lead-silver mines were opened in the 1880's in the Coeur d'Alene district of Idaho territory.

The Mining Camps. Bret Harte and Mark Twain, among others, captured and preserved the mood and manner of the settlers who threw up the hastily built wooden towns that provided shelter and recreation for enthusiastic seekers of wealth. Here, dance halls and saloons, hotels and gambling houses were apt to be established earlier than schools or churches. Indeed, some of the "boom towns" had enjoyed a brief prosperity and had been largely abandoned before law and order were characteristic of the community.

Getting Out the Wealth. Some mining "booms," like the early one in Colorado, ended quickly. The resources of gold, silver, lead, copper, and other minerals were abundant; but it required more than enthusiasm and the techniques of panning or placer mining to get out the ore. In Montana and Idaho, as in Colorado and Nevada, the greatest wealth came after placer mining had been replaced by more elaborate processes, requiring heavy machinery and considerable capital. As a result, profits went more often to absentee capitalists than to resident prospectors and would-be miners.

THE IMPACT OF THE MINING FRONTIER. Despite the usual pattern of discovery-boom-bust, mining soon became the chief industry of the mountainous regions of the West. Upon it rested the economic structure of many communities. Before the pioneer days had ended, some of the more enduring influences of the mining frontier became evident: (1) it stimulated settlements which brought new states into the Union—Nevada (1864), Colorado (1876), Montana (1889), and Idaho and Wyoming (1890); (2) it provided gold and silver in such quantities that the volume of currency kept pace for a time with the increasing needs of business enterprise; (3) it offered new opportunities for the investment of capital accumulations in speculative, but often highly profitable, mining ventures; (4) it emphasized the need for the reorganization of the structure of American business so that larger amounts of capital could be used under the corporate form of investment; (5) it gave many settlers in new communities a chance to work out procedures of self-government necessary to combat violence and social anarchy; (6) it led to an increased demand for better transportation, which was met by the stage coach, the pony express, and, finally, the railroad.

The Transcontinental Thrust of the Railroads. Eastern business interests, Western mining companies, and the growing communities on the Pacific Coast enthusiastically sponsored plans to bind together distant parts of the nation with miles of steel rails. Inventions such as Pullman and refrigerator cars, air brakes, and signal devices greatly increased the economic potentiality of rail systems.

THE UNION PACIFIC AND CENTRAL PACIFIC. Even before the Civil War, Eastern merchants, notably Asa Whitney (whose investments were largely in the China trade by clipper ship), had campaigned for a transcontinental railroad. Opposition in Congress came chiefly from representatives of Southern districts which feared that such a railroad, over a northern route, would not benefit the South.

Governmental Aid. In 1862, while the South was unrepresented, Congress granted a national charter to the Union Pacific Company to construct a railroad from Nebraska to the eastern California border. The promoters of the company were to receive a right of way, free use of timber and minerals on the public lands, and a grant of ten square-mile sections of government land for every mile of track they constructed. (Two years later the land grants were doubled.) In addition, Congress agreed to loan the company $16,000 for every mile built across the plains, $32,000 for every mile in the plateau regions, and $48,000 for every mile in the mountains. At the same time similar terms were accorded the Central Pacific, a California corporation, formed to build a line eastward to meet the Union Pacific road.

Construction Methods. In 1867 the building of the transcontinental line began in earnest. The construction gangs (including thousands of Irish and Chinese immigrants) worked feverishly to overcome the difficulties inherent in spanning a region of desert wastes, wooded plateaus, and precipitous mountains. The promoters, whose ingenuity was tested in meeting engineering problems, were richly rewarded for their efforts. As we shall see later (p. 34), the principal stockholders of the Union Pacific formed the Crédit Mobilier (a construction company), in which capacity they took exorbitant profits for the actual building of the road. The two lines met near Ogden, Utah, in May, 1869, and the first transcontinental railroad was completed.

OTHER WESTERN RAILROADS. By 1890 twelve important rail systems had pushed into the region between the Mississippi and the Pacific Coast. They were organized by a few shrewd and powerful enterprisers, who frequently used unscrupulous methods to secure domination (see Chapter IV). Five new railroads, in addition to the Union Pacific, were transcontinental lines—the Great Northern (under James J. Hill); the Northern Pacific (first organized by Jay Cooke and taken over in 1881 by Henry Villard, a German immigrant); the Southern Pacific (organized by the controllers of the Central Pacific and taken over in 1879 by Jay Gould); the Atchison, Topeka and Santa Fe (under Cyrus K. Holliday); and the Chicago, Milwaukee, St. Paul and Pacific.

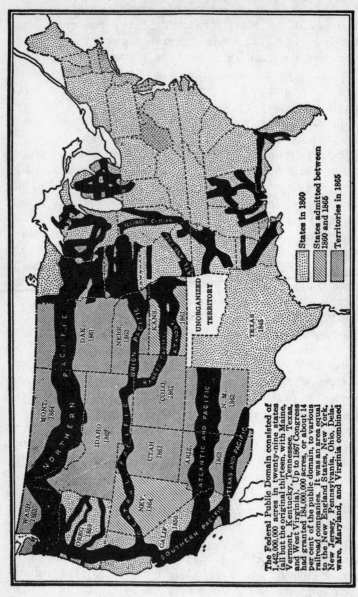

The Federal Public Domain consisted of 1,442,000,000 acres in twenty-nine states (all but the original thirteen, with Maine, Vermont, Kentucky, Tennessee, Texas, and West Virginia). Up to 1867 Congress had granted 184,000,000 acres, or about 14 per cent of the public domain, to various railroad companies. It was an area equal to the New England States, New York, New Jersey, Pennsylvania, Ohio, Delaware, Maryland, and Virginia combined

Political Organization of the West and Land Grants to Railroads

States in 1860

States admitted between 1860 and 1865

Territories in 1865

Patterns of Financing. The financial arrangements which made possible the building of the Union Pacific set the pattern for the early Western railroads. The capital for construction came from federal and state government loans, from private investments by Americans and Europeans, and from the sale of land.

Governmental Stimulus. So eager were many communities for rail facilities that cities and counties vied with states and the federal government to provide capital to railroad promoters. The aggregate of loans was supplemented by land grants from state and nation. More than 130,000,000 acres of the national domain and 55,000,000 acres owned by the states were granted to railroad corporations. For every $3.00 invested by private financiers, the public authorities advanced $2.00 for the building of the Western roads.

EFFECTS OF THE TRANSCONTINENTAL RAIL SYSTEMS. The completion of the transcontinental railroads had important effects on many aspects of American society.

Influence on Commerce and Industry. The trans-Mississippi roads slowly but surely created a national market within which raw materials, farm products, and manufactured goods could be freely interchanged. Western mining communities and frontier farms could supply urban centers of the East. Manufacturers were encouraged by the expanding market and easy access to raw materials to seek higher profits in mass production at lower costs per unit. Foreign trade also expanded rapidly. Within three years after the completion of the Union Pacific, exports and imports to China and Japan rose more than 100 per cent.

Influence on Population. The high cost of construction caused many railroad promoters to dispose of their land grants as rapidly as possible. Advertising homes for the industrious, at reasonable prices and along newly built rail lines, they sold off the land which the government had given them in large and small lots, thus stimulating the migration of ranchers, sheepherders, and farmers into the trans-Mississippi West. By advertising and sending agents abroad, railroad companies actively sought immigrants as workers and as land-purchasers. Large groups of Europeans and Orientals were thereby brought to the American West.

Influence on Politics. As American population moved further westward, new territories were organized to become states. In the federal government the influence of the new states was felt especially in the Senate (where each state, regardless of population, has two votes). The political revolt of the West against Eastern financiers and industrialists, which reached its climax in the Populist movement, is discussed in Chapter VI.

The Cattle Country. The westward thrust of rail facilities brought boom times to the Great Plains once the threat of Indian attack was removed. Ranchers discovered that the treeless grasslands were ideal for grazing livestock and rapidly exploited them.

THE "LONG DRIVE." After the Civil War, Texan longhorns were driven in ever larger herds to the "cow town" rail centers of Kansas and Nebraska for shipment. Soon the cattlemen discovered the advantage of fattening their stock on the free, open ranges of the northern plains, which were still part of the public domain. Colorado, Dakota, Wyoming, and Montana contained excellent pasturage. During the two decades after 1865 more than 285,000 cattle annually were fattened on the free pasturage and shipped to Eastern stockyards. At the peak, profits rose as high as 40 per cent.

DECLINE OF THE CATTLE INDUSTRY. The ten years prior to 1885 marked the heyday of the long drive, the cowboys, the open ranges, and the cattle barons. Boom times, however, did not survive: (1) the advance of the farmers' frontier, which meant the fencing of the former grazing lands; (2) the state legislation (Kansas and Colorado) providing for inspection and prohibiting the driving of Texas cattle across state lines; (3) the competition of the livestock grown on the farms of the Middle West; (4) the ability of the railroads and the commission men to dictate freight rates and prices; and (5) overexpansion of the cattle industry on a speculative basis. With the disappearance of the open range, Western ranching lost its most picturesque features.

The Advance of the Homesteader. The farmer, rather than the miner or the rancher, gradually became the dominant force in the "taming of the wild West." Government benefits, new inventions, and rail facilities opened the West to an agricultural population.

LAND POLICIES. In the disposal of its public lands, the United States had always been generous, but that generosity reached its zenith during the generation following the Civil War.

The Homestead Act (1862). This legislation provided that any citizen, or any alien who had declared his intention of becoming a citizen, might acquire 160 acres of surveyed land by residing on it for five years and paying a small entry fee. So rapid was the response to this invitation that by 1880 almost 20,000,000 acres had been entered by those who claimed to be homesteaders. Despite many fraudulent entries, most of this land was soon under cultivation by bona fide settlers.

Other Government Attempts to Create New Farmsteads. The Homestead Act was chiefly beneficial in bringing farmers into the forested and humid areas of the national domain. Its emphasis on the small-acreage farm proved a handicap to those who desired to cultivate the treeless and semiarid region of the Great Plains. Congress yielded to pressure from the exploiters of the trans-Mississippi West and passed the Timber Culture Act (1873) and the Desert Land Act (1877) to encourage the staking out of larger holdings by prospective homesteaders. The Timber Culture Act provided additional land allotments to persons who used a portion of their original allotments for tree-planting. The Desert Land Act authorized the sale of semiarid land at $1.25 an acre to persons who agreed to irrigate it. However, neither act contributed greatly to the westward advance of the farmers' frontier.

MEETING THE NEEDS OF THE PLAINS FARMERS. Many prospective settlers could not qualify under the terms of the Homestead Act, or found the land allotted by such legislation insufficient for large-scale agriculture on the Great Plains. They had other opportunities to secure land, though too often they were victimized by speculative interests. The land-grant railroads offered much of their land at reasonable rates, and the state governments, which had received generous allotments under the Morrill Land Grant Act (1862) for the endowment of agricultural and mechanical colleges, sold their acres on satisfactory terms. As a result, between 1870 and 1880 an area equal to that of Great Britain was brought under cultivation, and the agrarian frontier was pushed close to the limits of arable land.

New Methods and New Tools. To move homesteaders, or "nesters" as they were called, into the vast area of the Great Plains required more than congressional legislation. The open ranges of the cattle country had to be fenced, and neither deep furrows nor high hedges proved satisfactory substitutes for timber. After 1874 cheaper barbed wire provided the necessary fencing. At the same time, plows and mowers, more suitable to the Plains came on the market; but agriculture was not practicable in the semiarid sections until the twentieth century, when irrigation became widespread (see p. 108).

Cattlemen versus "Nesters." The ranchers viewed the farmers as their natural enemies. The fences, so necessary for an agricultural economy, broke the open ranges of West, and the farmers' search for water took from the grazing cattle easy access to customary water holes. The rivalry in some districts became open warfare in the 1880's. But the "nesters" had found their decisive weapon in cheap barbed wire (patented in 1874) which could be used to fence their homesteads from the open range.

Agrarian Immigrants. The bulk of the settlers in the "prairie states" and the Great Plains came from the older states. They were attracted to the West by cheap land, improved rail transportation, and the large crops that agricultural machinery made possible. Thousands more were foreign immigrants (primarily Germans and Scandinavians), who swelled the population of such states as Nebraska, Kansas, Iowa, Wisconsin, Minnesota, and the Dakotas.

CLOSING OF THE FRONTIER. In 1890, although much Western land still remained to be settled, the Census Bureau announced the end of a frontier line. The frontier was held by some historians, notably Frederick Jackson Turner, to be the greatest force in the shaping of American democracy. Others pointed out that the significance of the frontier as an economic "safety valve" was limited, since urban laborers had little opportunity to move West. The existence of free, open territory, with abundant natural resources, was perhaps most important in forming American tendencies to individualism, inventiveness, and expansionism. After 1890, the American West became a place for consolidation and conservation; expansion was henceforth sought overseas.

THE SHAPE OF INDUSTRIALIZATION

The phrase "industrial revolution" is a favorite one with historians, who use it most frequently to describe a prolonged, evolutionary process of industrialization. In the quarter-century after the Civil War, however, the rate of industrial change became much more rapid, and the entire population was affected by it.

Manufacturing. Three characteristics marked American manufacturing in the post-Civil War years: (1) the growth of mass production; (2) increased use of the corporate form of business organization; and (3) extension into new territories.

MASS PRODUCTION. The evolution from the small shop into the extensive factory was the result of a number of factors.

A National Market. The opening of the West brought the entire territory of the United States into a domestic market. Within this area the states were forbidden by the Constitution to tax imports or exports, and tariff barriers enacted by Congress protected many goods from foreign competition. The development of a far-flung transportation system put all parts of the market within reach of the industrial centers.

Abundant Resources. The discovery and utilization of the country's natural resources also aided the growth of industry. The mining frontier contributed gold, silver, lead, and copper. Large deposits of iron ore were found in Pennsylvania and in the Great Lakes region, where the Mesabi range was especially accessible. Oil was struck in Pennsylvania and in the Southwest. The great Northwestern forests were added to the sources of lumber. Coal, which became of vital importance to power production, could be mined in a number of states, especially in the Appalachian area.

Technical Improvements and Inventions. The records of the Patent Office tell an impressive story of how old businesses were revolutionized and new ones created by the invention and improvement of machinery and processes. The Bessemer process for making steel from cast iron was discovered in the 1850's by the Englishman Henry Bessemer and the American William Kelly. Thomas Edison and his laboratory associates were responsible for such significant inventions as the dynamo, the incandescent lamp, and the alkaline storage battery. Charles Goodyear's process for the vulcanization of rubber and Eli Whitney's system of interchangeable parts (though both had been invented earlier) came into widespread use after the Civil War. These and many other devices enabled manufacturers to produce goods more cheaply and in ever increasing quantities.

An Adequate Labor Supply. Following the Civil War, the supply of labor was augmented by veterans seeking jobs, by women and children (whose employment was not at this time restricted), and by persons attracted from farms to the new industrial centers. The largest source of factory labor, however, came from the millions of immigrants—Germans, Scandinavians, Russians, Poles, Bohemians, Hungarians, Italians, and Orientals—who came to the United States during the period between the Civil War and the First World War. Political unrest and religious persecutions abroad, inducements offered by American railroads and industries, and generally non-restrictive government immigration and emigration policies were factors that caused immigration to reach its peak in this period. Lacking skills or bargaining power, most of these immigrants had to work long hours for low wages.

Accumulation of Domestic and Foreign Capital. The growth of investment banking for the marketing of securities, war and post-war prosperity in the North, and the transfer of funds from commerce to industry (resulting from the decline of the merchant marine during the Civil War) made available increasing amounts of domestic capital. The fact that the United States imported more goods than it exported meant that foreign capital was also available, and large investments were made by Europeans in American railroads and other industries.

A Favorable Government Policy. As we shall see in Chapter IV, the laissez-faire attitude of the national government gave a relatively free hand to industrialists. In addition, the government often gave positive aid to industry by means of protective tariffs and subsidies.

CORPORATE ORGANIZATION. The form of business organization changed rapidly after 1850. The individual proprietorship and the partnership gave way to the corporation chartered under state laws. During the fifties and sixties the obvious advantages of the corporate form—relative permanence of the organization, limited liability of the stockholders, and adequate capital for the promoters—induced the industrialists to seek charters for their enterprises. Upon these foundations were later erected the elaborate structures designed to insure monopolistic control of particular industries.

TERRITORIAL EXTENSION OF MANUFACTURING. Although the states of the Northeast, which had first felt the impulse of the industrial revolution, still retained their primacy in manufactured commodities, industry rapidly expanded into other sections of the country. For example, the beginning of territorial shifts in the 1870's made Chicago the capital of the meat-packing domain, carried flour-milling from upstate New York to Minneapolis, and brought part of Pennsylvania's great iron and steel mills into Ohio and Illinois. In the 1880's manufacturing also began to occupy an important place in the economic life of the South, where textile, tobacco, and lumber industries benefited from cheap labor and accessibility to raw materials.

Transportation and Communication. Of paramount importance in the process of industrialization were the railroads, which united all sections of the country, bringing raw materials and foodstuffs to the industrial centers and carrying finished products to the domestic market and to ports of shipment for foreign trade.

BUILDING NEW LINES. Construction, in the Eastern states, which had gone forward rapidly in the decade of the fifties, was checked temporarily by the Civil War; but even before the cessation of hostilities, building had been resumed. Between 1865 and 1873 more than 30,000 miles of track were laid; and by 1880, despite the years of panic and depression after 1873, mileage in operation had reached 93,000. During the same period the railroad companies began to substitute steel for iron, to adopt the standard gauge for their tracks, to improve their engines, to introduce the air brake, perfected by George Westinghouse (1887), and beginning in 1865, to use Pullman cars.

THE RAILROADS EAST OF THE MISSISSIPPI. During the 1860's and 1870's the trend toward consolidation of the shorter rail lines established many of the nation's great rail systems (1) the New York Central, which Cornelius Vanderbilt organized in 1869; (2) the Pennsylvania, which reached Cleveland, Chicago, and St. Louis in 1871; (3) the Erie, which expanded its service even though it suffered much from financial rogues like Daniel Drew and Jay Gould; (4) the Baltimore and Ohio, which pushed steadily beyond the Ohio River toward Chicago; (5) The New York, New Haven and Hartford, which came to dominate New England; (6) the Illinois Central, which traversed the Mississippi Valley from Chicago to New Orleans and (7) the Atlantic Coast Line, formed out of more than one hundred small, independent roads. We have already noted (pp. 18–22) the opening of the important transcontinental lines.

TELEGRAPHIC COMMUNICATION. Operation of the railroads depended upon the telegraph. The wires in use throughout the country tripled within six years after the close of the Civil War. As the railroads and the telegraph united the remote sections of the nation, the trans-Atlantic cable, successfully laid in 1866 by Cyrus W. Field, brought all the nations of the world into closer contact with each other.

THE TELEPHONE. Among the interesting novelties exhibited at

the Centennial Exposition in Philadelphia in 1876 was the "lover's telegraph," which proved to be Alexander Graham Bell's early model of the telephone. Within a few years it had revolutionized business routine in the great cities and had become a familiar convenience in thousands of American homes.

The Rise of the City. One significant characteristic of industrial expansion was the growth of cities, both in size and in their influence on national thought and action.

EUROPEAN BUILDERS. The urban population grew rapidly as American resources and opportunities drew thousands of immigrants from Europe. Beginning in the 1880's "new immigrants" from eastern and southern Europe predominated. Many, notably the Jews, fleeing from political and religious persecution in the Old World, filled the factories and shops of America. They built railroads, dug mines, spanned rivers, and strung wires for telegraph and telephone. They also gave to the older American culture an awareness of Europe's treasures in art and architecture and music.

URBAN MIDDLE CLASS. Some of the foreign-born joined the native-born to swell the ranks of the middle class. They attained wealth through ingenious manipulation of investments in factories, banks, railroads, and mines. Their business methods were generally admired and widely imitated. Their power was recognized in all parts of the land, even if their standards of conduct and canons of taste left much to be desired. The term "Gilded Age" was used to describe the ostentatious, vulgar, and frequently corrupt ways of life that characterized the surface aspects of the postwar period.

MUNICIPAL PROBLEMS. While a majority of the business leaders were busy adding to their fortunes, acquiring town houses and country estates, and winning social recognition and prestige, a select minority grappled with the difficult problems presented by the disorderly growth of the cities. They strove mightily, if not always effectively, to provide satisfactory housing, transportation, fire protection, and policing. A few rare spirits persisted in attacking the squalor of the slum areas, or fought intemperance, disease, poverty, vice, and crime, which throve in the congested byways of the cities. Among the reformers were Henry George in politics; Joseph Pulitzer in journalism; Clara Barton in public nursing; Susan B. Anthony in temperance crusades; Frederick Olmstead in public archirecture; and William Graham Sumner in sociology.

URBAN INFLUENCES. If much of the city's population was drawn from the rural districts, the villages and farms also fell more and more under the influence of urban manners and standards. Despite the antagonism toward the city often manifested by the agrarians, they succumbed gradually to urban standardization in habits of thought as well as to uniform factory-made goods.

The Business Cycle.
In every part of the world where the process of industrialization was relatively rapid, speculative enterprises emphasized the fluctuations in the business cycle. Prosperous years were swallowed up in depression and panic. The United States had experienced depression periods in 1819, 1837, and 1857; but the collapse that followed the postwar "boom" years was more severe than usual, for it was on a wider front and in a more highly industrial economy.

THE PANIC OF 1873. The collapse of business prosperity in the United States was but a phase of the world depression resulting from: (1) a series of costly international conflicts, culminating in the Franco-Prussian War, (2) the too rapid expansion of railroads into central and eastern Europe, and (3) an inflation of national currencies which adversely affected international exchange. In America the panic terminated a period of increasing production of farm crops, raw materials, and manufactured goods; of excessive construction of railroads and public works; of inflated currency and rising prices which had persuaded investors to put their savings into speculative enterprises.

THE COLLAPSE OF THE CREDIT STRUCTURE. The insolvency of the Philadelphia banking and brokerage firm controlled by Jay Cooke (who had won fame and huge profits by helping the United States government sell its bonds during the war) precipitated the panic in September, 1873.

The Northern Pacific Syndicate. Cooke and his associates had formed a syndicate to finance the Northern Pacific Railroad. Their operations brought more capital into railroad building than the receipts from freight and passenger traffic warranted.

Commercial Failures and Declining Prices. The attempts of creditors to protect their loans threw some five thousand firms into bankruptcy within a year of the Jay Cooke failure. In September, 1873, the New York Stock Exchange was forced to close for ten days. In 1874 the bread lines lengthened, as three million men were thrown into the ranks of the unemployed. Prices fell and the farmer was forced to sell his grain and livestock below the cost of production.

PROPOSALS FOR INFLATION. Price levels remained low for several years after the crisis. As a result numerous proposals were discussed in an effort to secure an inflation of the currency which would artifically raise prices and stimulate trade. Many wanted the government to issue more "greenbacks" (the same type of paper money, in the form of promissory notes, that the Lincoln administration had used to finance the Civil War); others joined Western mine-owners in demanding that the "hard" money in circulation be increased by laws which would compel the government to coin silver (then being mined in large quantities) as freely as it coined gold. Both groups maintained that prosperity could be induced by cheapening the value of the dollar and thus lifting the value of the businessman's commodities, the farmer's crops, and the worker's labor. Labor organizations, as well as farm groups, gave strong support to inflation as the solution of the business cycle.

The Agrarian Reaction. The declining prices of agricultural commodities following 1873 brought into sharp focus the protests of the farm population, East and West, against what they feared would be the unfortunate consequences for them of the advance of industrialization. They insisted that new machines and new methods, more acres and larger markets, had not enabled agriculture to keep its proportionate share of the national income. They began to organize.

THE PATRONS OF HUSBANDRY. Popularly known as the Grange, the Patrons of Husbandry was a ritualistic society formed in 1867 by Oliver H. Kelley, a government clerk, who was eager to promote rural social activity as an antidote to the loneliness and monotony of farm life. The meetings of the local Granges soon became centers for the discussion of such agrarian problems as: (1) the declining prices of grain, resulting from the rapid increase in the production of agricultural products; (2) the exorbitant prices which the manufacturer, protected from foreign competition by the tariff, charged for farm implements and other finished goods; (3) the excessive rates demanded by the commission merchants for the storage and handling of grain; (4) railroad abuses such as high and discriminatory rates, "long-and-short haul" techniques to eliminate competition, rebates, pools, and political bribery (see Chapter IV); (5) the high interest on farm mortgages charged by most banks; (6) the heavy burden of taxation borne by farm lands and real estate generally, as compared with other forms of personal property; and (7) the lack of agrarian representation either in the state legislatures or in Congress.

THE CO-OPERATIVE MOVEMENT. The Grangers organized farmers' co-operatives in order to reduce the cost of the commodities which they purchased and to market more successfully the crops which they produced. In the decade of the seventies they were operating plow factories, harvester works, and retail stores as well as conducting grain elevators, packing plants, and loan and discount companies. Most of these co-operative ventures were wrecked on the rocks of inefficient management, internal dissension, and aggressive hostility of private competitors.

POLITICAL ACTION. By 1874 the Grangers reported more than 1,500,000 members, chiefly in the Midwestern grain-growing states.

The Granger Laws. Supporting third-party movements, under a variety of names (see p. 69), Grangers fought for control of the state legislatures and won notable triumphs. In Illinois they passed a law fixing the maximum railroad rates and maximum charges of elevator companies; in Wisconsin and Iowa they controlled the legislatures and enacted laws regulating freight rates; in Minnesota they formed a railroad commission to supervise public utilities, particularly railroads. Their political power in some of the prairie states enabled them to send delegates to Congress.

The Courts Intervene. When the Granger laws were tested in the state courts they were frequently declared to be unconstitutional, but in 1876 the Supreme Court of the United States in several cases decided the courts were not competent to review rates of railroads and other public utilities that had been fixed by state legislatures. In *Munn* v. *Illinois,* for example, the highest court upheld the state's right to establish maximum fees to be charged by grain elevators. Within a decade, however (see pp. 52–53), the federal judiciary modified its position concerning the competence of a state to regulate railroad traffic. By that time the agrarian protests had assumed political form.

REVIEW QUESTIONS

1. What factors were most important in determining the characteristics of large-scale industry in the United States after the Civil War? Why?

2. If you had been in a position to determine the policy of the government toward the Indians of the Great Plains, what changes would you have made in the policies which were actually applied?

3. To what extent are the grievances voiced by the Grangers still insistent problems of American agriculture? Was the Granger movement a failure?

4. Why is the debtor class in any community generally in favor of a policy of inflation of the currency?

5. How did the building of the Western railroads change the pattern of economic developments in the trans-Mississippi West?

6. What events during the remarkably prosperous years after the Civil War contributed to the industrial collapse in 1873?

7. What is meant by the "Ohio idea"?

8. Explain the decline of the cattle industry after 1885.

9. Why did the federal government attempt to stimulate the settlement of the trans-Mississippi West?

Chapter III

STALEMATE IN POLITICS

The professional politicians, interested in winning elections and dispensing patronage, were slow to face the new issues which arose out of economic changes. Since the most insistent national problems —regulation of corporations, control of interstate railroads, adjustment of labor disputes, and maintenance of a satisfactory monetary system—were apt to cut across party lines and impair party discipline, the political leaders either avoided them or dealt with them in evasive generalizations. Demand for reform met with response slowly and over strong opposition.

WANING PRESTIGE OF GOVERNMENT

The postwar administrations of the Republican party were marred by factional quarrels, political scandals, and lack of constructive leadership.

Grant in Command. President Grant was inclined to regard the presidential office as a gift bestowed upon him by the American people in gratitude for his military service to the nation during the Civil War. His naïveté and lack of political experience proved severe handicaps.

DECLINE IN POLITICAL STANDARDS. Business leaders sought and received favors from the government for a price; government officials betrayed the interests of their constituents; politicians shamelessly used public office as a source of private profit.

Grant's Advisers. The cabinet at first contained three men of outstanding ability: Hamilton Fish (State), J. D. Cox (Interior), and E. R. Hoar (Attorney General). However, Cox and Hoar soon retired in disgust, and the President came under the influence of such astute politicians as Roscoe Conkling and Benjamin F. Butler. The civil service was filled with Grant's friends and relatives and with the protégés of unimportant party workers.

The Gold Conspiracy. Neither by temperament nor by training was the President qualified to set a high standard of political ethics. Instead, his frank admiration for men of wealth involved him unwittingly in such scandals as that occasioned by the attempt of Jim Fisk and Jay Gould to corner the nation's gold supply. Grant was associated with the conspirators, who persuaded him to keep government gold off the market. On "Black Friday" (September 24, 1869) the administration took belated action to save the nation from economic collapse. Secretary of the Treasury Boutwell released four million dollars in gold, thereby driving down the price and ruining the speculators.

The Tweed Ring. Symptomatic of the conditions permeating political and business circles were the frauds committed against the city of New York by a gang of unscrupulous officials headed by William M. Tweed, boss of Tammany Hall. The persistent detective work sponsored by the *New York Times* and the striking cartoons of Thomas Nast in *Harper's Weekly* finally brought the destruction of the gang in 1871.

The Crédit Mobilier Scandal. Ugly rumors of graft and political corruption in connection with the Crédit Mobilier, which built the Union Pacific (see p. 19) were partially verified in 1872. A congressional investigation (1873) produced evidence that Oakes Ames, a congressman from Massachusetts, had placed shares of Crédit Mobilier stock among government officials in order to influence legislation. Schuyler Colfax, Vice-President during Grant's first term, was one of those who retired from public life, thoroughly discredited.

THE LIBERAL REPUBLICAN MOVEMENT. Some within the Republican Party, who were hostile to the policies and tactics of the Grant administration, strove to prevent the President's re-election in 1872.

The Missouri Liberals. The center of the anti-Grant movement was in Missouri, where such Republican leaders as Carl Schurz and B. Gratz Brown favored a more conciliatory attitude toward the ex-Confederates in the state and resented the dominance of the Radical Republicans in national affairs. The Missouri Liberals were especially critical of Grant's policy toward the South.

Nomination of Horace Greeley. The convention of Liberals, which met in Cincinnati in May, 1872, contained champions of various political reforms. Besides the opponents of radical Reconstruction, there were civil service reformers and advocates of lower tariff rates, as well as ardent crusaders against the corruption of the Grant regime. The delegates ignored such reformers as Charles Francis Adams and Lyman Trumbull and unwisely selected Horace Greeley, brilliant but eccentric editor of the *New York Tribune,* as the presidential nominee. Although Greeley had been a vitriolic critic of the Democrats, they accepted him as their standard-bearer, because a fusion with the Liberal Republicans was the only chance to defeat the nominee of the regular Republicans, President Grant.

The Election of 1872. Greeley's defeat was overwhelming. He carried only three border states (Missouri, Kentucky, and Maryland) and three Southern states (Georgia, Tennessee, and Texas). Major factors in Grant's victory were Greeley's personal unpopularity and the control of the South by the Republican party. The Liberal Republican movement, however, was not without results. It threw a sufficient scare into the administration to cause the President to advocate civil service reform, downward revision of the tariff, and modification of the Southern policy. Congress had already passed a general Amnesty Act in May, 1872 (see p. 10).

THE CLIMAX OF POLITICAL CORRUPTION. Despite these campaign promises, Grant was either unwilling or unable to put the political house in order, and his second administration was marked by a distressing series of governmental scandals.

The "Salary Grab." The country was incensed by the action of Congress (March, 1873) in voting generous salary increases which included a 50 per cent increase for senators and representatives, to be effective as of December, 1871. Public protest made the next Congress repeal this "back-pay steal."

The Sanborn Contracts. In May, 1874, it was discovered that Secretary of the Treasury Richardson had permitted J. D. Sanborn, a friend, to retain exorbitant commissions for collecting unpaid internal revenue taxes. Richardson resigned in order to escape a vote of censure by the House of Representatives.

The "District Ring." Despite the fact that Alexander Shepherd, governor of the District of Columbia, had enriched his friends through the "honest graft" of lucrative contracts, President Grant appointed him to the newly created commission for the District in 1874. The Senate indignantly refused to ratify the appointment.

The "Whiskey Ring." By ingenious detective work Secretary Bristow, who had succeeded Richardson in the Treasury Department, revealed the existence of a conspiracy, including Grant's private secretary, O. E. Babcock, to defraud the government of internal revenue taxes on whiskey.

The Belknap Scandal. In March, 1876, Secretary of War Belknap suddenly resigned in order to escape impeachment for having accepted bribes for several years to sell trading appointments in Indian territory.

The Disputed Election (1876). The Democrats nominated Samuel J. Tilden, governor of New York, who had won a national reputation by his successful prosecution of the corrupt "Tweed Ring" in his own state. The Republicans avoided several prominent leaders who had been too close to Grant and his associates, and chose as their nominee the conservative and upright governor of Ohio, Rutherford B. Hayes.

BALLOTS IN DOUBT. Tilden carried states with 184 votes in the electoral college, one short of the necessary majority. Hayes received 165 undisputed votes, but twenty electoral votes were in doubt. One Republican elector in Oregon was technically ineligible, while there were charges of fraud involving nineteen votes in South Carolina, Florida, and Louisiana. These Southern states were just passing from the control of carpetbaggers and Negroes into the hands of the native whites (see p. 10).

THE ELECTORAL COMMISSION. To avert any possibility of violence, Congress created a special commission of fifteen to pass judgment upon the disputed votes. Five from the Senate (three Republicans and two Democrats), five from the House (three Democrats and two Republicans), and five justices of the Supreme Court (three Republicans and two Democrats) were named to the Commission. (It had been expected that Justice David Davis, an independent, would be chosen by the other justices as the fifteenth member; but, having just been elected to the Senate, he was ineligible.) The decision was eight to seven (along straight party lines) on every disputed point in favor of the Republican candidate, Hayes. The country acquiesced in the decision after Southern Democratic leaders had received informal assurance from Republican politicians that federal troops would be removed from the South.

Revamping Republican Leadership. The narrow margin of Hayes' victory emphasized the demand of the reform wing of the

Republican party that unscrupulous leaders and workers be punished.

STALWARTS AND HALFBREEDS. Within the Republican ranks, quarrels between the Stalwarts (stanch supporters of the Grant regime, who looked to Roscoe Conkling of New York for leadership) and the Halfbreeds (who rallied around the standard of James G. Blaine of Maine) gave the reform element an occasional chance to determine party action. Factional strife, however, had more to do with political offices than with public policies.

HAYES' ADMINISTRATION. Though President Hayes was no crusading reformer, he worked hard to give the country an honest and efficient administration. In economic matters he was an adherent of sound money and a straightforward representative of the business interests of the nation.

The Cabinet. Unlike Grant's cabinet, Hayes' official advisers were unusually able men. The reformers were particularly pleased by the selection of William M. Evarts of New York (State), John Sherman of Ohio (Treasury), and Carl Schurz of Missouri (Interior). Hayes' conciliatory attitude toward the South was shown by his frequent consultation with Southern leaders and particularly his appointment of David Kay, a Tennessee Democrat, as Postmaster General.

Civil Service Reform. President Hayes cast his lot with the enemies of the spoils system. He issued an executive order forbidding financial assessments on federal officeholders for party purposes; he gave Carl Schurz a free hand to try the merit system in making appointments in the Interior Department; he named T. L. James, a champion of civil service reform, to the postmastership of New York City; and he removed Conkling's supporters Chester A. Arthur and A. B. Cornell from their posts in the New York Customhouse for violating a regulation against political campaigning by government employees.

Struggle with Congress. Hayes' relations with Congress were far from happy, for the Democrats controlled the House during his entire administration and the Senate from 1879 to 1881. In the House the Democratic majority set up the Potter Committee which investigated the presidential election of 1876 in order to embarrass the President. Hayes in turn vetoed congressional appropriation bills when the Democrats, attempting to repeal the Force Acts, attached objectionable "riders." No intelligent program of legislation was possible in this partisan quarreling.

CURBING THE INFLATIONISTS

The creditor class generally, and Eastern business interests particularly, supported strongly the anti-inflationist policies of both President Grant and President Hayes.

The Greenback Question. From the early years of the Civil War the trade of the country had been carried on largely through the medium of depreciated paper currency (greenbacks). Business and financial leaders advocated a policy of sound money which would gradually contract the volume of paper in circulation and redeem paper dollars at face value in gold. The process of retiring the greenbacks (deflation), which had been initiated in 1866, was stopped two years later by Grant's administration; the Republican platform of 1868 included this promise.

THE INFLATION BILL OF 1874. With the falling of prices, and the corresponding rise in the value of the dollar in terms of commodities, which marked the Panic of 1873, the farmers of the West, following the lead of the Grangers (see pp. 31–32), became active in a movement for cheaper currency. Congress passed a bill providing for the issuance of more greenbacks, but President Grant vetoed the measure.

RESUMPTION OF SPECIE PAYMENTS. In January, 1875, the Republicans passed the Resumption Act in an effort to reconcile the inflationist sentiment of the West with the sound-money policies of the East. (The Supreme Court had upheld the constitutionality of greenbacks in an 1871 decision that reversed an earlier ruling.) The Resumption Act provided that at least $300,000,000 of greenbacks should remain in circulation permanently but that after January 1, 1879, they should be redeemable at face value in gold. A gold reserve of $100,000,000 was set up so that these government notes could be redeemed in gold whenever they were presented to the Treasury. In 1878 Congress fixed the amount of greenbacks in circulation at $346,681,016, where it has remained ever since.

THE GREENBACK PARTY. The extreme inflationists answered the deflationary policy of the government by organizing the National Greenback party (1875). Three years later in the congressional elections they cast one million votes, but their strength quickly declined when the advocates of cheaper money decided that the free and unlimited coinage of silver would provide a more satisfactory currency than that which would result from a further issuance of greenbacks.

The Silver Controversy. Both the Republican and Democratic parties were divided over monetary policies. Westerners were apt to be more sympathetic than Easterners towards inflationary proposals; and debtors, regardless of party affiliation, were more determined than creditors to cheapen the value of the dollar.

THE BLAND-ALLISON ACT (1878). A combination of Western Republican and Southern Democratic votes carried through Congress a bill which authorized the Treasury Department to purchase between $2,000,000 and $4,000,000 worth of silver bullion each month at the market price and coin it into silver dollars. Hayes vetoed the bill on the ground that it substituted cheaper dollars in the payment of obligations contracted before 1878, but the measure was passed over his veto.

Declining Market Price of Silver. The Bland-Allison bill won bipartisan support in Congress because silver mineowners and others interested in the districts where silver was produced loudly demanded that "something be done for silver." They pointed out that the price of commercial silver had been sharply declining, that new deposits in Nevada were responsible for larger quantities on the market, and that the metal was no longer used as widely in European and Latin-American coinage systems.

The "Crime of 1873." The friends of silver insisted, some years after the event, that the chief reason for falling prices was the scarcity of "hard" money, and they traced this to the decision of the government (the Coinage Act of 1873) to drop the silver dollar from the list of official coins. They called for prompt action to increase the currency by coining more silver; the Bland-Allison Act was the first step in that direction.

THE DEFENSE OF SOUND MONEY. Probably a large majority of the nation's businessmen feared inflation—either by the issuance of greenbacks or the coinage of cheap silver. They worked to preserve a "sound money" policy that would base currency on actual gold reserves.

Resuming Specie Payments. In conformity with the Resumption Act of 1875, Secretary Sherman announced on January 1, 1879, that the Treasury would redeem greenbacks at face value in gold. This meant, in actual practice, that the nation was using a gold standard in maintaining the value of its currency.

Strain on the Gold Reserves. Though Treasury officials were fearful that the gold reserves would prove insufficient, the inflationists were restive because their demands had not been fully met. They wished to use both silver and gold as the basis of the currency, since they felt that commodities were still too low in price in terms of gold dollars. Temporarily halted, they had not been defeated (see Chapter VI).

THE PASSING OF THE REPUBLICAN STALWARTS

Factional rivalries within the dominant Republican party seemed more important to many professional politicians than the serious issues which should have been considered. In 1880, for example, the Stalwarts, led by Conkling of New York and Logan of Illinois, made a vigorous attempt to take over the control of the Republican organization.

Temporary Triumph of the Halfbreeds. President Hayes' refusal to seek renomination seemed to remove the chief obstacle in the way of the Stalwarts who were determined to force former President Grant on the party and the country for another term.

Republican Convention of 1880. In the Republican national convention a deadlock developed between Grant's Stalwart supporters and the Halfbreed friends of James G. Blaine. Not until the thirty-sixth ballot did Grant's opponents concentrate their strength and lead a stampede of delegates to the standard of Congressman James A. Garfield of Ohio. They then tried to pacify the Stalwarts by nominating their man, Chester A. Arthur of New York, for the vice-presidency.

The Garfield-Hancock Campaign. Early in the campaign Republicans were alarmed because the animosities of the convention days were not easily forgotten; but Grant and Conkling finally agreed to speak for Garfield and thus present a united front against the Democrats, who had nominated a gallant Civil War general, Winfield S. Hancock of Pennsylvania.

Personalities and Issues. At a moment when the voters needed guidance in deciding important economic and social questions, they received little help from the presidential candidates. In ability and achievement there was little difference between Garfild and Hancock, and both men were essentially conservative in their views on financial and other economic problems. Partisan strife and personal rivalries still held the center of the political stage.

The Influence of Blaine. As soon as Garfield had been elected (by 214 to 155 votes in the electoral college) he indicated that James G. Blaine, whom he appointed Secretary of State, would exercise a commanding influence in the new administration. The result was an unseemly quarrel between Senator Conkling and the President. When Garfield used the patronage in New York in such a way as to build a Garfield-Blaine machine, Conkling defied the administration. This controversy was still acute when the President was assassinated by James Guiteau, a disappointed supporter of Conkling's Stalwart faction.

Arthur's Administration. The assassination of Garfield elevated to the presidency Vice-President Chester A. Arthur, who quickly surprised those who had doubted that he would be equal to the tasks of the office. He refused to use his high office to reward his former "cronies," and he frowned upon the continuation of factional strife within the Republican party.

CABINET APPOINTMENTS. Gradually the new President reconstituted his official family so that the influence of Blaine's friends declined. Senator Frelinghuysen of New Jersey replaced Blaine in the State Department; C. J. Folger of New York became Secretary of the Treasury; but Robert T. Lincoln, son of the wartime President, was retained as Secretary of War.

REFORM OF THE CIVIL SERVICE. In his first message to Congress, Arthur indicated his willingness to co-operate with the legislators in breaking up the practice of using positions in the civil service as rewards to the victorious party.

Planning the Merit System. After the Civil War the idea that merit alone should be the test for public office slowly made headway in the following steps: (1) Congressman Jenckes of Rhode Island, a student of the civil service of Great Britain, introduced a bill into Congress (1865) calling for competitive examinations; (2) a commission appointed by Grant (1871) experimented futilely with examinations for certain positions; (3) Secretary Schurz effected important reforms in the Interior Department; (4) the National Civil Service Reform League, founded in 1881 by George William Curtis, served to unite the efforts of many publicists and political reformers.

The Pendleton Act (1883). The assassination of President Garfield, which seemed to be the result of factional quarrels over political appointments, shocked the country into a realization of the evils of the spoils system. Popular indignation became widespread as revelations of political jobbery and corruption marked the trial of Garfield's assassin. The result was the Pendleton Act, passed by a Congress in which the Republican majority supported the measure, hoping that it would safeguard Republican officeholders in the event of Democratic success the next year.

The purposes of the Pendleton Act were (1) to substitute merit for political influence in federal appointments and (2) to protect officeholders from financial assessments against their salaries for party campaign funds. The President was authorized to appoint a bipartisan commission of three to advise him in classifying the grades of service and in supervising competitive examinations to establish fitness of candidates for office. The Act also prohibited the collection of funds from federal employees for political purposes.

WATCHING CONGRESSIONAL APPROPRIATIONS. President Arthur warned against wasteful expenditure of government income even when it was alleged that federal funds were available.

The "Pork Barrel." As the government's receipts from high customs duties and internal revenue taxes piled up a surplus in the Treasury, congressmen yielded to the temptation to spend freely on public works in their respective districts. Between 1870 and 1880 such "pork-barrel" appropriations more than doubled.

Presidential Disapproval. Arthur courageously attacked unnecessary expenditures. When the Appropriation Bill of 1882 called for the use of $18,000,000 in river and harbor improvements of doubtful value, he vetoed the bill. Though it was passed over his veto, he won the applause of the country for his sensible action.

CHINESE EXCLUSION. Chinese immigration, which had increased rapidly after 1850, began to arouse hostility in the decade of the seventies.

The Burlingame Treaty (1868). Chinese laborers were welcomed on the Pacific coast, so long as they were needed for such work as the construction of the Central Pacific railroad. The Burlingame Treaty granted Chinese subjects unrestricted rights of immigration as well as equality of treatment with immigrants from other countries.

Demand for Exclusion. Shortly after 1870, as it became apparent that the Chinese were competing with American laborers, a movement developed in California for revision of the policy of free immigration. The Chinese were said to be socially unassimilable and to endanger American standards of living by virtue of their own low economic standards. Congress abrogated the Burlingame Treaty, but Hayes vetoed the measure and sent a commission to China to secure modification of the treaty, whereby Chinese immigration was regulated but not stopped.

Act of 1882. After President Arthur had vetoed an exclusion bill, Congress passed an act excluding Chinese laborers for a period of ten years. This exclusion was extended in 1892 and remained the policy of the government until amendment of immigration regulations in 1965.

THE RETURN OF THE DEMOCRATS

The election of 1884 brought a political upheaval which enabled the Democrats to secure the presidential office for the first time since the administration of James Buchanan (1857–1861).

The Independent Voters. Ever since the scandals of the Grant administrations the Republicans had been on the defensive. They could win only if they held the independent voters who since the Civil War had supported the Republican ticket. In 1884 defections from their own ranks also contributed to Republican defeat.

THE NOMINATION OF BLAINE. The Republican convention refused to grant the nomination to President Arthur, though he desired it and deserved it. Instead, the delegates, disregarding the small but vigorous reform element, yielded to the magnetism of Blaine and on the fourth ballot nominated him in a frenzy of rejoicing.

THE MUGWUMPS. The Republican reformers (nicknamed "mugwumps") in considerable numbers announced that they would bolt the ticket if the Democrats would name a candidate to whom they could give their support. The answer of the Democratic convention was the nomination of Grover Cleveland, who had won national acclaim as a courageous and efficient governor of New York.

THE ELECTION OF GROVER CLEVELAND. There were numerous reasons for the success of the Democrats in the campaign of 1884: (1) the belief, inspired by the revelations of the 1876 "Mulligan Letters," that Blaine had used his political position to further his private financial interests; (2) the refusal of many independent Republicans to support the party ticket; (3) hostility to Blaine on the part of some of the former Stalwarts; (4) the vote polled by the Prohibitionist candidate in the normally Republican counties of upstate New York; (5) the resentment of the Catholic voters, especially in the crucial state of New York, over the speech of Reverend S. D. Burchard, a Blaine supporter, who characterized the Democrats as the party of "Rum, Romanism, and Rebellion." Cleveland was stronger than his party, for he embodied the hopes of most political reformers, regardless of party affiliation.

Cleveland—An Independent President. Though Cleveland soon made it known that he regarded public office as a public trust, he had difficulty in persuading his associates that he was in earnest.

THE PATRONAGE. Cleveland was the ablest man to fill the presidential office since Abraham Lincoln, but he frequently was embarrassed in dealing with patronage matters and legislative problems by partisan pressure with which he had little sympathy.

The Cabinet. In choosing his official family, President Cleveland looked for men of ability, even if they had no experience in governmental office. Thomas F. Bayard of Delaware (State), William C. Whitney of New York (Navy), and L. Q. C. Lamar of Mississippi (Interior) were outstanding members of the cabinet.

The Civil Service. With the Democratic chieftains enjoying their first national victory in twenty-eight years and demanding that 100,000 federal jobs be given to faithful party workers, Cleveland reluctantly permitted some partisan removals to satisfy the demand. He showed his interest in reform, however, by adding almost 12,000 positions to the classified service on a merit basis.

Repeal of the Tenure of Office Act. When Cleveland removed a federal district attorney in Alabama, the Senate, invoking the Tenure of Office Act (see p. **77**) demanded that the President submit the papers relative to the removal. This Cleveland refused to do, insisting that the right of removal of federal officers was a purely executive function. The Senate censured the President, but in 1887 Congress repealed the Tenure of Office Act. (In 1926 the Supreme Court upheld the right of a President to remove an executive officer without the Senate's consent.)

THE PENSION CONTROVERSY. The mounting Treasury surplus enabled Congress to be generous in granting pensions to veterans of the Civil War who had served in the Union armies.

Arrears of Pension Act (1879). The modest appropriations for pensions, which had been granted to veterans disabled in war service, increased rapidly after the passage of the Arrears of Pensions Act. This law permitted the successful applicant to receive back-pensions from the date of his discharge from the army to the time of filing his claim. Soon pension agents and brokers were touring the country persuading veterans to file claims, and the pension roll by 1885 numbered 345,125.

Private Pension Bills. Claimants whose cases were not approved by the Bureau of Pensions were accustomed to turn to Congress, where willing legislators sponsored private bills, many of which were outrageous frauds. President Cleveland tried to investigate these private bills, and his researches led him to veto more than two hundred measures. Despite the charge that he was hostile to the veterans, Cleveland did his utmost to keep the pension list a roll of honor.

Dependent Pension Bill (1887). Congress abandoned the test of service-disability in the general Dependent Pension Bill, which provided that any ex-soldier who had served three months and was incapable of earning a livelihood could receive a pension, regardless of whether he had suffered disability in the war. Cleveland vetoed the measure on the ground that it would tend to "pauperize" the veterans and that it was too soon after the war for so comprehensive a pension policy.

THE LEGISLATIVE RECORD. Many of Cleveland's recommendations to Congress were either ignored by the legislators or blocked by the Republican leaders. He urged without success (1) the repeal of the Bland-Allison Act, (2) the revision of the tariff schedules, and (3) the husbanding of the diminishing acreage of public lands. Among the nonpartisan measures enacted were: (1) the Presidential Succession Act (in effect until 1947), fixing the line of succession to the presidency: the Vice-President, followed by heads of executive departments in order of rank; (2) the Electoral Count Act, authorizing the states to decide contests over presidential electors;* (3) the Dawes Act (see p. 16); and (4) an act establishing the Department of Agriculture. The most significant piece of legislation, the Interstate Commerce Act, was not, as we shall see in the next chapter, the result of Cleveland's leadership.

---

* If more than one result was submitted by opposing factions, the House and Senate, voting separately, were empowered to decide which to accept; if they disagreed, the returns certified by the state's governor were to be accepted.

REVIEW QUESTIONS

1. What evidence, if any, do you find to support the contention that the Grant administrations were dominated by the banking and business interests of the Eastern states?

2. Who were the Liberal Republicans of this period? How successful were they in securing action on the program which they sponsored?

3. How do you account for the fact that the professional politicians avoided the new issues engendered by the economic changes after the Civil War?

4. Discuss the political and economic forces responsible for the passage of the Bland-Allison Act of 1878. Why did President Hayes veto the measure?

5. Were there any differences based on economic theory or political principle between the Stalwarts and the Halfbreeds?

6. If you had been a voter in 1884 would you have cast your ballot for Blaine or Cleveland? Why?

7. Explain the contribution of each of the following to the cause of civil service reform: Thomas A. Jenckes, Carl Schurz, Chester A. Arthur, and George William Curtis.

8. Why has the Pendleton Act been called the "Magna Carta" of civil service reform?

9. Who were the "mugwumps"? Explain their attitude in the campaign of 1884.

10. Did the "return of the Democrats to power" cause any change in the economic policies of the government? What were its most obvious results in the realm of politics?

CHAPTER IV

PRIVATE ENTERPRISE AND PUBLIC REGULATION

The expansion of American business during the quarter-century after 1865 was probably accelerated by the fact that the dominant economic theory of the period was favorable to the free play of individual initiative. However, the monopolistic trend of large corporations and the abuses of railroad power—both of which the states were constitutionally unable to regulate—eventually forced federal action in the public interest. Another industrial problem, the financial imbalance caused by high protective tariffs, was more difficult to deal with because of congressional pressure to keep the rates up.

THE DECLINE OF ECONOMIC LIBERALISM

The principles of laissez faire, as formulated by Adam Smith, did not seem applicable to an industrialized, "big-business" economy.

Freedom of Competition. It was generally believed that freedom of competition in industry would insure fair prices for the consumer and would compel efficient methods on the part of the producer. But as competition in transportation and industry became more intense, businessmen, fearing its effect on profits, sought to limit it by combinations and concentrated control in ever larger corporations.

THE TREND TOWARD MONOPOLY. Various devices were used by the great corporations as they strove to secure a dominant position in their particular fields of production.

Pools. The pool, which was early used by the railroads, generally took the form of an agreement by which several supposedly competing firms established prices, regulated output, and divided markets. Such agreements were easily broken and often proved unsatisfactory.

Trusts. This form of combination first was tested in the organization of the Standard Oil Trust (1879). John D. Rockefeller's ingenious attorneys worked out a plan whereby a group of corporations, engaged in the refining and transporting of petroleum, entrusted their stocks to a small board of trustees, which was authorized to vote the stocks and control the combination. The original stockholders received "trust certificates" on which they were entitled to dividends from the earnings of the trust. As revised in 1882, the Standard Oil Trust included forty companies, the stock of which was held in trust by a board of nine men. The forty companies represented 90 per cent of the oil refineries and pipelines of the country. The Standard device was followed in modified form by groups which organized the "Sugar Trust," the "Beef Trust," the "Steel Trust," and a score of others.

Holding Companies. When some of the states prosecuted these trustees on the ground that they were restraining trade, industry began to abandon the trust device and experimented with the holding company. The latter agency was able to dominate a particular industry by: (1) purchasing the physical properties of competing plants, (2) securing control of companies through purchase of a majority of the capital stock, and (3) leasing facilities or patent rights which were essential to success. The holding company became important after 1889, as New Jersey, Delaware, West Virginia, and other states modified their corporation laws to permit the chartering of such combines.

THE STRENGTH OF INDIVIDUALISM. Most Americans during the last half of the nineteenth century seemed to believe that individual businessmen, through ingenuity and skill, were responsible for the industrial progress of the nation. They were inclined to admire the more prominent captains of industry—Carnegie, Gary, Harkness, Morgan, Rockefeller, Vanderbilt—and to excuse the sharp practices that businessmen too often condoned.

GOVERNMENTAL SUPPORT OF PRIVATE INITIATIVE. Although neither Republican nor Democratic politicians were willing to face important economic problems during the quarter century immediately following the war years, they seldom opposed the generosity of the government in its support of the nation's businessmen. This support took various forms: (1) government grants of land and financial loans to the railroad builders; (2) high tariff rates maintained to protect American industrialists against foreign competition; (3) banking and financial policies which benefited investors at the expense of other elements in the nation. Individual initiative often realized its objectives only with government support.

Laissez Faire or Economic Liberalism. Industrialists and other businessmen found a philosophy to their liking in the writing of the English economist, Adam Smith, and other classical economists.

THE ROLE OF GOVERNMENT. Economic liberalism emphasized the doctrine that the state was responsible for the protection of the individual's "life, liberty, and property," but that it should not interfere with individual initiative or enterprise. Government should maintain a hands-off, laissez-faire policy, said the French. In this country the philosophy was popularly summarized: "The government of business is no part of the business of government." We have seen in Chapter III how closely the political leaders followed this injunction.

THE CHALLENGE TO ECONOMIC LIBERALISM. An increasing number of voters during the 1880's and 1890's came to doubt the prevailing theory that government should abstain from meddling in business affairs. They vigorously questioned the assumption that the individual left to his own discretion would always adopt plans and procedures in the public interest. They insisted that there was a "public interest" which had to be protected against the "private interests."

THE CRITICS OF LAISSEZ FAIRE. Those who proposed governmental regulation of business, usually for the purpose of maintaining freedom of competition, represented various points of view: (1) the resentment of small business enterprises against the railroads and larger industrial corporations; (2) the complaints of consumers who discovered evidence of monopolistic price-fixing; (3) the criticisms of the methods employed by Standard Oil and other corporations to curb competition from independent companies; (4) the attacks upon monopoly by economists and publicists such as Henry George, Edward Bellamy, and H. D. Lloyd; (5) the propaganda of minor agrarian and labor parties in the Western and Southern states.

THE CONTROL OF THE RAILROADS

In spite of the obvious benefits resulting from the rapid extension of railroad lines into all parts of the country, protests against the methods of the owners of the transportation system constantly increased.

Popular Indictment of the Railroad Magnates. The charges against those responsible for the management of the great rail network included various aspects of the promotion, construction, and operation of the lines.

SPECULATIVE PROMOTION. Even the imaginative skill of James J. Hill on the Great Northern, or the efficiency of E. H. Harriman on the Illinois Central, could not obscure the fact that too many American railroads were constructed by speculators who knew little about the country's needs and paid scant attention to the law's requirements. They were guilty of: (1) promoting lines in regions where absence of competition enabled them to charge exorbitant rates; (2) unloading the securities of unsuccessful roads on the residents of the localities which the roads pretended to serve; (3) imposing an excessive capital burden on new projects by paying huge profits to themselves as directors of construction companies which laid the tracks.

FINANCIAL ABUSES. The practices of some owners and managers embraced a wide range of chicanery and dishonesty.

Fraudulent Sale of Securities. In some instances powerful railroad directors sold bonds and pocketed the proceeds, thus increasing the corporation's liabilities without adding to its assets. English investors were warned against putting their money into American companies that had sold more stock than the law permitted.

Manipulation of Securities in the Market. Jay Gould, Jim Fisk, and Daniel Drew were typical of some owners who used valuable railroad properties as devices for building up private fortunes through the unscrupulous manipulation of securities on the stock exchange. They knew little, and cared less, about managing a transportation system.

"Stock-Watering." Shippers complained that in prosperous years the railroad directors concealed excessive profits by the process of declaring stock dividends, which increased the outstanding capital stock of the enterprise without adding a dollar of new capital to the

existing investment. When traffic tended to fall off, the directors increased the freight rates with the plea that they had to earn enough to pay dividends on the total capital stock. The public realized that it paid high rates for service in order to return dividends on stock certificates which represented no real investment in the road. In 1883, for example, it was estimated that the roads of the country were carrying an indebtedness of $7,500,000,000 of which $2,000,000,000 was "water."

POLITICAL CORRUPTION. There was a growing concern during the 1870's and 1880's over the interference of powerful railroad lobbies with the course of state legislation. Pressure was exerted in various ways to secure favors from legislators or to block restrictive legislation. By the resort to: (1) extensive distribution of free passes among politicians and officeholders, (2) generous contributions to party campaign funds, and (3) outright bribery of legislators, the railroads gained "protection" but also incurred popular ill will.

UNFAIR RATE-MAKING. In the eyes of the shippers the greatest sins of the common carriers were their rate-making policies.

Pooling Agreements. In order to prevent rate wars and cutthroat competition, many of the roads entered into pooling agreements, which provided either for a distribution of territory among the members of the pool or for a pro rata division of the profits at the end of the fiscal year. Thus genuine competition among the roads was eliminated, and rates remained as high as traffic could bear.

Discrimination between Localities. The "long-and-short-haul evil" grew out of the tendency of the roads to favor shippers who resided at important terminal points where there was competition between lines. As a result, rates from one terminal point to another were low, while the shipper using way stations, where there was no competition between carriers, paid a proportionately higher rate for the same service. The same shipment could be sent from New York to Chicago at a lower rate than was charged for the shorter distance between Rochester, New York, and Toledo, Ohio.

Secret Rebates. The small shipper bitterly complained that his larger competitor was the recipient of favors from the railroads in the form of secret rebates, which brought freight costs far below the rates advertised by the roads in their published schedules. We shall see in our consideration of the growth of "big business" that this discriminatory practice was forced upon the carriers by the powerful industrial enterprises in their war on the independent producers.

State Regulations. Mounting protests finally brought attempts by several state legislatures to regulate the practices of the common carriers.

RAILROAD COMMISSIONS. In 1869 Massachusetts created the first commission with supervisory powers. Its record of correcting abuses through investigation and conference caused other Eastern states, notably New York and New Hampshire, to set up similar bodies to hear complaints and report discriminatory practices.

FIXING MAXIMUM RATES. The Western states, under the impulse of the Grangers and various agrarian parties (see p. 32), passed laws fixing maximum rates for the transportation of freight and passengers. Illinois set up a commission which was given power to prepare rate schedules; Wisconsin, Minnesota, and Iowa established carrying charges by direct legislative action; several other states adopted constitutional amendments empowering the legislature to deal with railroad abuses.

Judicial Review of State Legislation. The railroads appealed to the courts to protect them against state regulation, but the trend of the early decisions was against the carriers.

THE GRANGER CASES. During the 1870's the Supreme Court of the United States held that, when property becomes "clothed with a public interest," its owner must "submit to be controlled by the public for the common good."

Munn v. *Illinois*. In the autumn of 1876 the Court decided that an Illinois law fixing the maximum rates for the storage of grain in elevators did not deprive the warehouse owners of property rights without due process of law.

Peik v. *The Chicago and Northwestern Railroad*. In 1877 the Court, distinguishing between intrastate commerce and interstate commerce, maintained the right of Wisconsin to regulate railroad rates within the state even though such regulation might incidentally affect persons outside the state. A majority of the judges believed that the states should be permitted to handle their railroad problems without judicial interference "until such time as Congress should legislate on this matter."

THE WABASH RATE CASES. The principles established in the Granger cases were apparently reversed by the Supreme Court in 1886 when it handed down the decision in *Illinois* v. *Wabash, St.*

Louis and Pacific Railroad. A statute of Illinois which attempted to prevent rate discrimination by railroads that passed through its territory was held unconstitutional on the ground that the power of Congress over interstate commerce was exclusive. The effect of the decision was to limit the state's jurisdiction to intrastate commerce and to render ineffective most of the rate-making legislation of the previous fifteen years.

Congressional Action. For years before the Wabash decision crippled the power of the states over interstate commerce, Congress had been considering proposals for federal regulation of the railroads.

DEMAND FOR LEGISLATION. Every presidential campaign after 1868 had been marked by the demand of the minor parties that Congress regulate rates. The Labor Reform party (1872), the Prohibitionists (1876), the Greenbackers (1880), and the Greenback-Labor party (1884) cited the outstanding railroad abuses and called upon the national government to take action. Within the two major parties there was considerable sentiment favoring congressional legislation. The Windom Report (1874) to the Senate, the McCrary Bill (1874) passed by the House, and the Reagan Bill (1878), which the Senate refused to consider, all kept the issue alive.

THE CULLOM COMMITTEE INVESTIGATION. In 1885 the Senate appointed a special committee of five, headed by Senator Shelby M. Cullom of Illinois, to investigate the subject of federal control of interstate commerce. This committee, after protracted hearings in every section of the country, filed a two-thousand-page report which reached the conclusion that "upon no public question is public opinion so nearly unanimous as upon the proposition that Congress should undertake in some way the regulation of interstate commerce."

THE INTERSTATE COMMERCE ACT (1887). The congressional debates over the Cullom Report finally brought the first important attempt of the national government to control private business enterprise in the public interest.

Provisions of the Act. The Interstate Commerce Act forbade the railroads: (1) to grant special rates, secret rebates, or drawbacks; (2) to discriminate between persons, places, and commodities in rate-making; (3) to charge more for a short haul than for a long haul under the same conditions of traffic; (4) to form pooling agreements; (5) to deny the public the right to inspect schedules and rates. A bipartisan commission of five was created to supervise the accounting systems, rate schedules, and business methods of the roads, to hear complaints from shippers, and to assist the Attorney General in prosecuting offenses against the law in the federal courts.

Significance of the Act. Under the law even an able and conscientious Commission found its efforts ineffective for several reasons: (1) the inability to compel witnesses to testify; (2) the numerous appeals to the courts from Commission rulings; (3) the success of the railroad attorneys in winning their appeals from the Commission's orders; and (4) the tendency of the Supreme Court to interpret the Interstate Commerce Act in such a way as to restrict the Commission's control over discriminatory rates and the long-and-short-haul evil. For years the country waited for Congress to remedy the situation by further regulatory legislation, but that did not come until the administration of Theodore Roosevelt (see p. 106).

THE BATTLE OVER THE TARIFF

The passage of the Interstate Commerce Act, which marked the first serious attack on the philosophy of economic liberalism was quickly followed by a reconsideration of the government's policy of protecting American business from foreign competitors.

The Trend of Tariff Legislation. During the Civil War the Republican party had redeemed its campaign pledges by raising custom duties to protection levels, and those levels were maintained after the war emergency had passed.

TINKERING WITH THE SCHEDULES. Protection, justified at first to develop "infant industries" and then to compensate industry for increased internal revenue taxes, was generally accepted as an important factor in the growth of American industry. Such modification of rates as occurred in 1870, 1872, and 1875 was designed to meet sectional demands and protests without changing the protective principle.

ACT OF 1883. During the campaign of 1880 there was much talk of taking the tariff out of politics and revising schedules to meet the needs of domestic producers on a scientific basis. Two years later a tariff commission of nine members, after conducting a thorough investigation, surprised the country by recommending "a substantial reduction of tariff duties." Congress, however, ignored the sound advice of the experts and finally enacted (1883) a bill which was a caricature of genuine reform. The reductions in rates scarcely averaged 2 per cent in various schedules.

The Tariff in Fiscal Policy. Cleveland regarded the tariff question as one phase of the government's fiscal policy, which was accumulating treasury surpluses through an indefensible program of taxation.

SURPLUS REVENUE. From 1880 to 1890 the excess of government receipts over expenditures averaged $100,000,000 annually. This surplus was embarrassing because (1) it indicated that the taxpayers were bearing an unnecessary burden; (2) it reduced the amount of currency available for normal business needs; and (3) it was a constant temptation to Congress to make "pork-barrel" appropriations of doubtful public value.

CLEVELAND'S TARIFF MESSAGE (1887). President Cleveland was opposed to any wholesale increase in government expenditures in order to reduce the surplus; he feared the effect of paying off the public debt by purchasing government bonds before they fell due; and he believed that the internal revenue taxes had been sufficiently reduced. Consequently, the tariff remained as the obstacle in the way of tax reform. In his message to Congress in 1887 the President not only denounced the existing customs duties as "a vicious, inequitable, and illogical source of unnecessary taxation," but he also maintained that the protective principle was responsible for the growth of industrial combinations which increased prices by stifling competition.

CONTROVERSY IN CONGRESS. Presidential pressure persuaded the Democratic House to pass the Mills Bill, providing for drastic reduction of tariff rates, but the Republican Senate replied with the Aldrich Bill (1888), containing the elements of high protection.

THE MCKINLEY BILL (1890). The deadlock in Congress was broken after the Republicans had gained control of the House of Representatives as well as the Senate. The legislation was guided through the House in 1890 by William McKinley of Ohio, chairman of the Ways and Means Committee.

Protective Schedules. On the theory that prosperity flowed directly from protection, McKinley and his colleagues raised the level of duties to a new peak. Rates in the woolen goods, cotton goods, and steel products schedules were increased, while the protective principle was extended to some products of American farms, such as butter, wheat, eggs, and potatoes.

Sugar Subsidy. To satisfy the producers of raw sugar, as well as the American Sugar Refining Company, the legislators put raw sugar on the free list and granted a bounty of two cents a pound to domestic producers of raw sugar. This strategy also reduced revenues and thus decreased the treasury surplus.

Reciprocity. At the suggestion of Secretary Blaine, the Senate included reciprocity provisions in the tariff act. The President was empowered to impose duties on such commodities as coffee, tea, molasses, sugar, and hides, whenever the nations exporting these articles discriminated against the products of the United States. Blaine used this provision to negotiate several reciprocity agreements with Latin-American countries.

Opposition to Protection. As soon as the McKinley Bill became law, prices of protected commodities were raised by manufacturers, wholesalers, and retailers in anticipation of the effect of the protective schedules. The Democrats used this "increase in the cost of living" as an effective weapon against the Republicans in the congressional elections of 1890. The Democratic landslide was partly a result of repudiation by the electorate of the apparent effects of the protective tariff.

THE TRUST PROBLEM

President Cleveland failed to win strong support for his proposal that reduction of the tariff schedules was the best way to cope with the growing power of American corporations. Most voters were apparently willing to give businessmen the benefit of protective tariffs, though they opposed the trend toward monopoly.

The Antimonopoly Movement. As we have already noted (pp. 47–48), unrestrained competition had become so intense that businessmen had been compelled, so they said, to correct the "evils of competition" by mergers and consolidations.

THE ATTACK ON "BIGNESS." Many Americans were suspicious of all big corporations. They idealized earlier generations when producton was on a small scale and most business firms were partnerships or individual proprietorships. For them big corporations meant "trusts," and "trusts" meant the threat of monopoly control.

MONOPOLISTIC OFFENSES. Though most consumers appreciated the economies and cheaper prices made possible by large-scale production, they feared that most business managers were more interested in monopolistic control of prices than in quality production under conditions of maximum efficiency. During the 1880's popular magazines and sensational newspapers reported on the unfair practices of monopolistic corporations.

Producers' Complaints. Farmers complained that the power of the great corporations to determine prices often resulted in low prices for their produce, high transportation rates, and excessive charges for the manufactured goods they purchased. Small-scale businessmen accused their more powerful competitors of using unfair methods, based on monopoly, to force them out of business.

Consumers' Complaints. Impressed by the congressional investigations into the monopolistic methods of the great railroad systems, many consumers demanded equally searching examination of the way in which great corporations used their control of the market to charge exorbitant prices. They called upon the government to restore that freedom of trade which would permit the "law of supply and demand" to operate.

Antitrust Legislation. Since corporations received their charters from states, the early response to such demands came from the state legislatures. They did little more than apply the rules of the common law forbidding agreements or contracts in restraint of trade.

STATE ACTION. By 1890 fifteen states had defined in somewhat specific terms the various acts of corporations which would be punished as actions in restraint of trade. These laws were of little effect because (1) corporations chartered in states which had no restrictive legislation might trade across state lines, and (2) the federal courts had shown a tendency, ever since Roscoe Conkling's plea in *San Mateo County* v. *Southern Pacific Railroad* (1882), to interpret the Fourteenth Amendment in such a way as to protect corporations against any state legislation which might deprive them of "life, liberty, or property without due process of law." (Corporations were considered legal "persons.")

SHERMAN ACT (1890). So powerful was the popular sentiment against the "trusts" in 1889 that President Harrison recommended action by Congress, and the Republican leaders followed his recommendation. The Sherman Antitrust Act, reiterating one of the principles of the common law of England, declared illegal "every contract, combination in the form of trust or otherwise, or conspiracy, in restraint of trade or commerce among the several states, or with foreign nations." It authorized prosecutions by federal district attorneys and suits for damages by any person or corporation injured by a company in restraint of trade.

ENFORCEMENT AND THE COURTS. During the first eleven years of the law's enforcement the federal government was far from aggressive in filing bills in equity and securing criminal indictments. The inactivity of the federal prosecutors can be blamed wholly neither on the loose phrasing of the statute nor on the attitude of the courts. Though the Supreme Court in 1895 held (*U.S.* v. *E. C. Knight Co.*) that the control by the Sugar Trust of 95 per cent of the refining of sugar was not an illegal restraint on interstate trade, in subsequent decisions a majority of the Courts prepared the way for successful prosecutions. The administrations from Harrison through McKinley, however, did not want to undertake a vigorous campaign against the trusts.

REVIEW QUESTIONS

1. Discuss the relation of the Granger movement to the control of interstate commerce.
2. What constitutional safeguards did the legal counsel for the railroads invoke in order to nullify state regulatory enactments?
3. In what sense was the Supreme Court's decision in the Wabash rate case a reversal of the principles set forth in the opinion in *Peik* v. *The Chicago and Northwestern Railroad?*
4. How was the Interstate Commerce Commission frustrated in its efforts to carry out the purpose of the act of 1887?
5. Why did an accumulating surplus in the treasury of the United States constitute a financial problem of great importance for the government?
6. Explain Cleveland's reasons for demanding that Congress undertake a revision of the tariff schedules.
7. What difficulties did the Republican leaders have to overcome before they could redeem their campaign pledges concerning the tariff?
8. What features of the McKinley Bill were unusual in the history of American tariff-making?
9. What is meant by the "trust problem"?
10. To what extent did the Sherman Antitrust Act accomplish the purpose for which it was enacted?

CHAPTER V

THE STATUS OF THE INDUSTRIAL WORKER

By the 1860's the American workingman had learned that, so far as he was concerned, the most important effect of industrialization was the transformation of the skilled craftsman into a factory worker. The consequences of this change for the worker included: (1) the loss of the bargaining power that his skills and tools had given him; (2) the impersonality of employer-employee relations in the new corporations; and (3) the increased competition for jobs resulting from a nation-wide labor market and large-scale immigration. For unskilled laborers a working day of ten hours or more and weekly wages of $10.00 or less were common. Working conditions in factories, sweatshops, and mines were unhealthy and often dangerous. From the close of the Civil War to the outbreak of the First World War, American workers, in confused and fumbling fashion, strove to adjust themselves to the new industrial order and to organize effectively in order to improve their status.

OBJECTIVES AND ORGANIZATION OF THE LABOR MOVEMENT

As industrial producers formed ever larger business units, the factory workers tried to create organizations large and strong enough to bargain on equal terms with employers. In this they rarely succeeded, but their small local craft unions gave way to trade union organizations on a national scale.

National Labor Union (1866). The earliest attempt to bring the various craft unions into a single national organization was made by William H. Sylvis, leader of the iron molders' union. Some of his associates were friends of the wage earner rather than industrial workers themselves. As a result, they stressed general reforms and the philosophy of the labor movement, but often failed to win the confidence of the factory worker. In its program the National Labor Union demanded: (1) the establishment of a federal labor department; (2) abolition of contract-labor of aliens; (3) elimination of monopoly in industry; (4) the enactment of laws providing for the eight-hour day in factories. Its leaders entered politics as sponsors of the National Labor Reform party, which made a poor showing in 1872 and contributed to the disruption of the National Labor Union.

The Knights of Labor (1869). For fifteen years after the collapse of the National Labor Union the forces of labor were represented by the Noble Order of the Knights of Labor, a secret society formed by Uriah S. Stephens in 1869 among the garment cutters of Philadelphia.

CHARACTERISTICS. The Knights stressed: (1) industrial unionism rather than trade-unionism; (2) the inclusion of all workers in one great organization; (3) the formation of local assemblies on the basis of residence rather than the craft affiliation of the worker; and (4) the highly centralized control of the local assemblies by the General Assembly.

OBJECTIVES. In furthering industrial brotherhood the Knights pledged themselves "to secure for the workers the full enjoyment of the wealth they create, and sufficient leisure in which to develop their intellectual, moral, and social faculties." Their program included such specific objectives as: (1) the eight-hour day; (2) arbitration in industrial disputes; (3) equal pay for equal work for both sexes; (4) the prohibition of the labor of children under fourteen years of age; (5) the establishment of bureaus of labor statistics; (6) the enactment of safety and health codes for industry; (7) laws compelling employers to pay laborers weekly; (8) the recognition of the incorporation of labor unions; (9) the prohibition of contract foreign labor; (10) the abolition of national banks; (11) the imposition of an income tax; and (12) government ownership of railroads and telegraph lines.

METHODS. In politics the Knights fought aggressively for their program, but not until their influence was waning did they view favorably the idea of a labor party. The creation of producers' and consumers' co-operatives accomplished less than their idealistic leaders anticipated. Although arbitration was one of their main tenets, the Knights relied increasingly upon the strike and the boycott to win victories.

GROWTH AND DECLINE. The organization of the Knights expanded rapidly under the leadership of Terence V. Powderley and reached its greatest strength in 1886 when 5,892 locals reported 702,924 members. A series of unsuccessful strikes in 1886 marked the beginning of the Order's decline. Its complete collapse was hastened by: (1) the growing belief that many of the Knights favored violence in industrial disputes; (2) the hostility of the skilled workers toward an organization which minimized the interests of the trade-union; (3) the failure of most of the producers' co-operatives in which the Knights had invested funds; (4) the confusion of counsel among the leaders, many of whom were unsympathetic with the idealism of the social reformers within the organization; (5) the revolt against centralized control by many of the local assemblies; and (6) the inability of the Order to handle the large numbers of unskilled and transient workers.

The American Federation of Labor. The increasing dissatisfaction of skilled craftsmen with the aims and methods of the Knights of Labor resulted in the formation in 1881 of the Federation of Organized Trades and Labor Unions, changed in 1886 to the American Federation of Labor.

AIMS AND METHODS. Samuel Gompers and Adolph Strasser, who had revived the International Cigarmakers' Union, were influential in formulating the philosophy of the new Federation. Its structure was based upon the autonomy of the national craft union; the authority of the central body was strictly limited; and the membership was confined to those who belonged to "trades and labor unions." The specific objectives of the Federation were quite similar to those of the Knights, and for a time the two organizations co-operated. Gradually, however, the Federation leaders concentrated their efforts upon the campaign for shorter hours, higher wages, immigration restrictions, and improved conditions of employment within the various crafts. Their weapons came to be collective bargaining, the strike, and the boycott. Refusing to sponsor an American labor party or to ally with any one party, they used their political power to secure immediate objectives rather than to champion a comprehensive program of economic reorganization.

GROWTH AND ACCOMPLISHMENTS. Despite the presence of a small minority of Socialists, the American Federation remained conservative, and defended the capitalistic system while denouncing its imperfections. The achievements of the Federation included: (1) the development of strong national unions with full treasuries and effective schemes of sickness and unemployment benefits; (2) the establishment of the eight-hour day in several trades; (3) the recognition of labor's right of collective bargaining by an increasing number of employers; and (4) the slow but steady growth of labor's strength in the state legislatures and in Congress. The membership of the Federation increased from 190,000 in 1890 to 550,000 in 1900 and slightly more than 2,000,000 in 1914. Since the large majority of the nation's industrial workers did not belong to the AFL organization, its victories had little effect on American labor generally.

Labor's Objectives. During the half-century following the Civil War the labor movement was concerned with more than wages and hours. Among the principal aims were: (1) abolition of conspiracy laws, used to break up unions; (2) abolition of child labor and contract labor; (3) establishment of federal and state bureaus of labor; (4) recognition of the principle of collective bargaining; (5) compulsory arbitration; (6) workmen's compensation laws; (7) an eight-hour working day.

Problems within Labor's Ranks. If the leaders of labor were less successful than the captains of industry in mobilizing and leading their forces, it was because their task was more difficult. In their attempts to weld the nation's workers into a united and class-conscious group, they had to cope with (1) the ever increasing numbers of foreign-born workers, divided by language, religion, and national tradition; (2) the doctrinaire radicals enamored of theories for the reorganization of the social order; (3) the large number of underpaid women workers in certain crafts; and (4) the entrance of Negroes, both skilled and unskilled, into the ranks of labor.

Employer Attitudes. Most employers distrusted labor's attempts to organize and took active measures to prevent it. Among their weapons were: (1) the employment of company police and company spies; (2) "yellow-dog" contracts (which made the employee promise not to join a union); (3) the widespread use of injunctions to restrain unions from actions that would damage employers; (4) "black-listing" labor leaders; and (5) the importation of contract labor.

INDUSTRIAL WARFARE

In the unequal struggle between the employers, powerful and well organized, and the trade unions, weak and without experienced leaders, American workers resorted to the strike as their only effective weapon.

The Railroad Strike of 1877. Symptomatic of the extensive labor unrest in the seventies was the great railroad strike of 1877, which started when employees of the Baltimore and Ohio Railroad struck because of a reduction in wages. Soon most of the roads lying east of the Mississippi were involved. Rioting in Baltimore, Pittsburgh, and other cities was more than the local authorities could handle, and militia companies were called into action. Finally, President Hayes authorized the use of federal troops to restore law and order and to protect nonstriking workers who crossed the picket lines.

The Haymarket Riot (1886). Despite the failure of the workers to win the railroad strikes, industrial warfare grew more intense. Between 1884 and 1886, in "the great upheaval," the forces of labor launched a drive for the eight-hour day. In May of the latter year a mass meeting gathered in the Haymarket Square in Chicago to protest the death of four persons, killed when the police broke up a riot at the plant of the McCormick Harvester Company. While the Haymarket meeting was in progress, a bomb exploded, killing seven and injuring several others. Though the person who hurled the bomb was never identified, eight anarchists were convicted of inciting to riot and four were hanged. This Haymarket Square affair injured the cause of labor throughout the country, for many unjustly accused the Knights of Labor of condoning violence and affiliating with anarchists.

The Homestead Strike (1892). The wave of antilabor hysteria that followed the Haymarket Riot had scarcely subsided when violence flared at the Homestead (Pa.) plant of the Carnegie Steel Company, after failure to agree on a new wage scale. In an attempt to break the grip of the union, the company employed Pinkerton detectives as strikebreakers. In desperation the strikers fired on and killed several Pinkerton men. After the state militia had restored order, the strike was called off and the Amalgamated Association of Iron and Steel Workers, a relatively strong union, collapsed.

The Pullman Strike (1894). In the depression year, following the business collapse of 1893, the Pullman Palace Car Company sought to protect the profits of its stockholders by reducing the wages of its employees and laying off many workers who had long been on the company's payroll.

SYMPATHETIC BOYCOTT. When the Pullman employees called a strike, members of the American Railway Union tried to help the strikers by refusing to handle any trains carrying Pullman cars. As the boycott spread from Chicago over the Middle West and Far West, the Railroad Managers' Association fought back vigorously.

THE USE OF THE INJUNCTION. The lawyers for the Managers' Association secured action from the federal government in the form of a court injunction to prevent the strikers from interfering with the carrying of the United States mail. When the strikers ignored the court order, the government made two moves: (1) President Cleveland, over the protests of Governor Altgeld of Illinois, sent United States troops into the Chicago area to maintain order and (2) Attorney General Olney instructed federal attorneys to press charges against officers of the American Railway Union on the ground they were in contempt of court. Eugene V. Debs, president of the union, was sentenced to prison for six months for refusing to obey the injunction, and the strike collapsed. In the Debs case (1895) the Supreme Court denied a writ of *habeas corpus* for Debs, basing its decision of federal jurisdiction over interstate commerce and the mails.

EFFECTS OF INDUSTRIAL WARFARE

During the two decades after 1880, according to the reports of the Bureau of Labor, there were more than 23,798 strikes involving 6,610,000 workers. Almost half ended in failure while another 15 per cent ended in compromise. But more significant than these failures was the evidence that popular opinion was opposed to the tactics of union workers who resorted to the strike, the picket line, and the boycott. Most organized wage earners believed that the force of government usually entered labor disputes in support of the employers. In a sense they were correct, for political action in state or nation was apt to be based on popular distrust of the more violent aspects of labor's methods.

Judicial Restrictions on Labor. If labor leaders had long found it difficult to defend the union's right to bargain collectively, their task became much more difficult after the passage of the Sherman Antitrust Act (1890). That law, designed to prevent industrial combinations leading to monopoly, was quickly turned against trade unions as "combinations in restraint of trade." The federal courts repeatedly held that the Sherman Act was applicable to trade unions (e.g., the Danbury Hatters' case, 1908), and attorneys for employers used the Act to secure injunctions against strikes and labor boycotts.

Public Opinion toward Labor. Most Americans were quickly responsive to the individual workingman's grievances over long hours, low wages, and unsatisfactory working conditions, but they were suspicious of trade unions conducting a strong offensive against the employing class generally. Many people accepted the laissez-faire theory that collective bargaining could not determine wages, which were actually set by economic competition. Holding an individualistic view of society, they were suspicious of collective action that looked like "socialism" and they were slow to admit that labor could organize without resorting to violence, that it could win shorter hours and higher wages without defying the operation of economic laws. Not until the second quarter of the twentieth century did the labor movement enjoy a favorable climate of political opinion.

Labor Legislation. Despite the obstacles encountered by the labor movement, some of its objectives were enacted into law. An eight-hour day on public works was established in 1868 and an eight-hour day for all federal employees, in 1892. In 1882 a policy of Oriental exclusion was begun by a law suspending the immigration of Chinese laborers (see pp. 42–43). The Erdman Act of 1898 provided for arbitration of disputes involving interstate carriers. (It also outlawed the "yellow-dog" contract for interstate carriers, but this provision was later declared unconstitutional by the Supreme Court.) Though the Supreme Court generally held that state laws regulating employment were unconstitutional, it upheld such laws in special circumstances as valid exercises of state police power. Thus, in *Holden* v. *Hardy* (1898) a Utah law establishing maximum hours for miners was sustained, and in *Muller* v. *Oregon* (1908), an Oregon law establishing maximum hours for women was sustained. In 1907 Congress passed the Hours of Service Act, which limited the consecutive hours worked by railroad employees, in the interest of public safety.

REVIEW QUESTIONS

1. Contrast the organization, methods, and objectives of the Knights of Labor with those of the American Federation of Labor.
2. How do you account for the failure of the leaders of American labor to sponsor the formation of an American labor party?
3. Why was the policy of the American Federation of Labor essentially hostile to European radicalism?
4. What influence, if any, did the labor disturbances of 1885–1886 have upon the American labor movement?
5. If you had been a citizen of Illinois in 1894, would you have supported President Cleveland or Governor Altgeld in the dispute over the use of federal troops in the Chicago area?
6. Why was the policy of the federal government in the Pullman Strike so bitterly resented by many labor leaders?
7. Do you consider justifiable the use of injunctions in labor disputes?
8. Why did employers' associations fight so hard against the use of the boycott by trade unions?

Chapter VI

THE WEST IN REVOLT

Growing dissatisfaction with the failure of the major political parties to develop a responsible leadership and to face national economic issues culminated in the Populist revolt of the 1890's. Though the conservative forces won the important 1896 election, the demands of farmers and laborers thereafter had to be reckoned with, and many were eventually accepted by both Republicans and Democrats.

THE AGRARIAN CRUSADE

The political power of the industrialists was seriously threatened during the decade of the nineties as the farmers of the West and South, joined by many wage earners of the East, launched a frontal attack against the bulwarks of big business.

The Farmers' Grievances. Fundamental in the discontent of American farmers was the fact that they seldom believed they were receiving a share of the national income commensurate with their great contributions to the nation's life.

THE NATURAL AND SOCIAL ENVIRONMENT. During the last half of the nineteenth century most farmers in the United States lived either along the frontiers of settlement or in comparative isolation on small farmsteads in more populous areas.

Monotony and Hardship. From seedtime to harvest the average American farmer was a hard worker in the fields, and his leisure was usually as monotonous as his toil. Independent he was, but he was too often isolated, and he was denied conveniences and advantages which his fellow-countrymen in small towns and cities took for granted.

The Struggle Against Nature. Always the farmer has been the recipient of nature's bounty and the victim of its uncertainties. In a peculiar way this was the fate of Western farmers in the post-Civil War generation. Many ambitious tillers of the soil had pushed into areas where the average annual rainfall was insufficient for farming without irrigation. For some years in the early 1880's rainfall on the Western plains was abnormally heavy, but for a decade after 1886 an extended drought ruined thousands who had gambled that the rains would continue.

ECONOMIC SITUATION. As in the days of the early Granger movement (see pp. 31–32) the farmer complained bitterly of the low prices of his grain, cotton, or livestock and the high prices of the machines and implements which he had to buy.

Financial Costs. Operating as an individual proprietor, constantly in need of credit, the farmer grew more and more indignant that he had to pay high interest rates for the bank loans, which he secured only on disadvantageous terms; that he was charged excessive freight rates in comparison with industrial shippers; and that his taxes were higher in proportion to his ability to pay than the taxes of the financier and the factory owner. He also objected to economic discrimination created by the tariff; he bought protected products and sold unprotected ones.

Competing Producers. Most American farmers failed to realize that the increased production of new farms, cultivated more efficiently with better machines (such as the gang plow, disc harrow, grain binder, and threshing machine), was partly responsible for declining farm prices. Furthermore, they minimized the growing competition of Canadian, Russian, and Argentine wheat farmers. A majority felt that the only solution of their financial problems lay in a cheapening of the purchasing power of the dollar through inflation of the currency. Thus a bushel of wheat or a bale of cotton would rise in value.

Farm Ownership. As a result of the farmer's unfavorable economic situation, mortgage foreclosures increased greatly during this period. There were eleven thousand foreclosures in Kansas from 1889 to 1893. Farm tenancy also increased as farms became larger, more specialized, and more dependent on capital. Especially prevalent in the South were sharecropping (whereby the landlord furnished tenants with land, equipment, and shelter in return for most of the proceeds from the crops) and the crop-lien system (whereby the farmer pledged his crop to a merchant in return for supplies).

Politics of Dissent. The grievances of the farmers and the industrial workers resulted in the formation of numerous minor parties during the last quarter of the nineteenth century.

THE GREENBACKERS. Though the forces of discontent won occasional local victories, they never were united under one banner. Their only common demand seemed to be for inflation of the currency as a means of increasing the prices of the farmer's commodities and the laborer's services. The Greenback party in 1876 nominated Peter Cooper, a New York philanthropist who believed in an inflationary policy; two years later the Greenbackers merged with the National Labor Reform party and the "Greenback Labor" combine sent fourteen representatives to Congress; in 1880, 1884, and 1888 they nominated presidential candidates but never polled more than 310,000 votes. Some of their leaders, like James B. Weaver of Iowa, however, achieved greater success under the Populist banner.

THE POPULISTS. The political climax of agrarian discontent of the 1870's and 1880's was the organization of the People's Party of America, or the Populists, in which were enrolled many who had seen service as Grangers, Greenbackers, Laborites, and in the inflationist ranks of the two major parties.

Attempts to Form a National Party. During the decade of the 1880's there was a phenomenal growth, in the Western and Southern states, of powerful agrarian organizations such as the Farmers' Union, the Agricultural Wheel, the Northwestern Alliance, the Southern Alliance, and the National Farmers' Alliance and Industrial Union. Such colorful leaders emerged as "Pitchfork Ben" Tillman, of South Carolina; "Sockless Jerry" Simpson and Mary Lease, of Kansas; Thomas Watson, of Georgia; and Ignatius Donnelly, of Minnesota. Among the various groups there was agreement concerning objectives but dissension over tactics and procedure. The chief difficulty arose over conflicting views concerning (1) the desirability of forming a third national party; (2) the advisability of cooperating with the representatives of the industrial wage earners; and (3) the role of Negro farmers throughout the Southern states in the movement. (Fear of Negro political power caused withdrawal of the Southern Alliance.)

Platform of the Populists. A series of conventions beginning in 1889 worked out the broad outlines of a political program for the formal organization of the People's Party at St. Louis on February

22, 1892. At Omaha on the following July 4, the new party announced its platform. The program of economic reform called for: (1) free and unlimited coinage of silver and gold at the ratio of sixteen to one; (2) increase of the currency in circulation to $50.00 per capita; (3) enactment of a graduated income tax; (4) reduction of state and national taxes; (5) the establishment of postal savings banks by the government; (6) government ownership and operation of railroads, telegraph, and telephone lines; (7) prohibition of alien ownership of land; (8) the appropriation by the government of all land held by railroads and other corporations in excess of their actual needs; (9) use of government funds to facilitate marketing of farm products and to extend short-term rural credits. As an invitation to the wage earners the Populists resolved that they favored: (1) restriction of undesirable immigration; (2) the eight-hour day for governmental employees; (3) the abolition of the Pinkerton detective system, which had figured in the Homestead strike. The political reforms included: (1) single terms for the President and Vice-President; (2) popular election of senators; (3) adoption by the states of the initiative and referendum; (4) the Australian secret ballot.

The Campaign of 1892. The Populists put their first ticket in the field in 1892, nominating James B. Weaver of Iowa, a former Greenbacker, for President and James G. Field of Virginia for Vice-President. Weaver's popular vote was 1,041,600. He received the entire electoral vote of Kansas, Colorado, Idaho, and Nevada, and one vote in the states of North Dakota and Oregon, making a total of twenty-two. In South Carolina the Populists captured the Democratic organization, while in several other states of the Solid South they co-operated with the Republicans in an effort to defeat the dominant Democrats. In the Middle West, third-party strategy dictated an alliance with the Democrats against the dominant Republicans, but the Populists were no more sympathetic toward Grover Cleveland, who was elected, than toward Benjamin Harrison, who was defeated.

THE CONSERVATIVE REACTION

While the agrarian forces, with their labor allies, were organizing the discontented voters, the two major parties were trying to make enough concessions to keep their ranks solid against the agrarian crusade.

The Republican Revival. Strategists in the Republican party tried hard to convince the nation that they were the protectors of American manufacturers, laborers, and farmers against the cheap labor and cheap goods of Europe.

THE CAMPAIGN OF 1888. In the presidential election of 1887 the issue was largely set by President Cleveland's demand for downward revision of the tariff (see p. 55).

The Candidates. The Democrats renominated President Cleveland by acclamation, in spite of the opposition of the Tammany Hall delegation. His Republican opponent was Benjamin Harrison of Indiana, nominated after Blaine declined to become a candidate. Harrison, the grandson of President William Henry Harrison, was a corporation attorney, conservative in opinion and dignified in demeanor. He had the enthusiastic support of the business interests.

The Issues. To a remarkable degree the protective tariff overshadowed other issues, and party lines held relatively firm. The Democrats were placed on the defensive by the aggressive and well-financed Republican campaign. Cleveland was accused, without justification, of being a free-trader whose tariff policy would benefit British manufacturers at the expense of American industrialists. The Republicans also made a strong appeal to Union veterans, whom Cleveland had antagonized by his pension policy (see pp. 44–45) and by an order for the return of captured Confederate battle flags. Neither candidate faced squarely the dissent of the farmer and the industrial worker.

The Result. Though President Cleveland had a popular plurality of more than 100,000 votes, he lost such pivotal states as New York and Indiana, where the Republicans mobilized the strength of the industrialists behind their ticket. Harrison won the electoral college by 233 to 168.

THE ADMINISTATION OF HARRISON. The new Republican President, who was an able lawyer but an inept political leader, leaned heavily on three prominent Republicans: James G. Blaine of Maine, who became Secretary of State once more; Thomas B. Reed of Maine, who was Speaker of the House of Representatives and William McKinley of Ohio, chairman of the House Committee on Ways and Means.

The Reed Rules. By parliamentary tactics, permissible under the existing rules of the House of Representatives, the Democratic minority tried to obstruct the President's legislative program. Speaker Reed promptly used methods which were considered arbitrary by the Democrats, to speed up legislative processes, and after a sharp controversy among the House members, the Reed Rules were accepted as standard procedure. They provided (1) that actual attendance should be the basis for determination of a quorum and (2) that the Speaker should entertain no dilatory motions.

The Civil Service. Harrison's support of the merit system was purely nominal during the first years of his administration. Wholesale removals of officeholders in the postal service brought protests even from some Republican leaders. Late in 1892 the President, already defeated for re-election, added a few offices to the classified service.

The "Billion Dollar Congress." Despite Harrison's plea that the problem of the surplus be solved by a reduction in taxation, the Republican leaders in Congress actually dissipated the surplus through greatly increased expenditures. The appropriations of the Fifty-first Congress, which exceeded $1,000,000,000, included: (1) the return to the Northern states of the direct tax collected during the Civil War; (2) an extensive program of river and harbor improvements; (3) additional sums for the construction of a steel navy, which had been started in 1883; and (4) a dependent pension bill (1890), which almost doubled the annual costs of pensions.

The Legislation of 1890. The attempt of the Republican protectionists to increase tariff schedules was delayed in Congress because it became entangled with other legislation. Western Republicans, who wanted inflation, demanded that their party expand the coinage of silver. To preserve party harmony and to insure the passage of the tariff act, the Republican managers accepted the Sherman Silver Purchase Act, which authorized the government to purchase 4,500,000 ounces of silver each month and to issue treasury notes, redeemable in gold or silver, against this silver bullion. As a result of this compromise with the Western members of the party, a high protective tariff act (the McKinley Bill) was passed (see p. 55).

The Re-election of Grover Cleveland (1892). As we have already noted, the dramatic feature of the presidential election of

1892 was the emergence of the Populists as a minor but strong party of protest (see p. 70). Nevertheless, the overwhelming majority of voters, except in Kansas, Colorado, the Dakotas, Idaho, and Nevada, remained loyal to one of the two major parties.

REPUBLICAN WEAKNESS. In the congressional elections (November, 1890) the Republicans had lost control of the House (235 Democrats, 88 Republicans) and even William McKinley went down to defeat in his Ohio district. This reversal foreshadowed trouble for the administration in 1892. Many factors contributed to the embarrassment of the Republicans: (1) resentment over higher prices following the high tariff of 1890; (2) hostility of reformers to Harrison's neglect of the merit system in his appointments; (3) disappointment of both inflationists and sound-money men with the compromise in the Sherman Silver Act (1890); (4) disgust with the Republican attempt to force federal control of elections on the Southern states (a federal election bill passed the House but did not come to a vote in the Senate); and (5) most important of all, the damaging charge that the administration had wasted the Treasury surplus at a time when many people feared that a business depression was starting.

RENOMINATION OF HARRISON. At the Republican convention in 1892, Blaine, whose record as Secretary of State had commanded general admiration, permitted his name to be presented for the presidential nomination. Nevertheless, Harrison, though he was unpopular among the party workers who considered him too reserved and unsympathetic, controlled enough delegates to win the nomination on the first ballot. Whitelaw Reid, editor of the *New York Tribune,* was named Vice-President.

CLEVELAND'S POLITICAL COMEBACK. Without Cleveland's knowledge, William C. Whitney and other Eastern bankers and businessmen lined up state delegations, pledged to the former President. In a surprising manifestation of party unity, he received the two-thirds majority required for nomination on the first ballot. The Middle Western faction of the party was recognized in the naming of Adlai E. Stevenson of Illinois for the vice-presidency.

THE DEMOCRATIC VICTORY. Though the two major parties differed on the tariff issue, with the Republicans supporting highly protective schedules, there was slight difference in their platforms or in the statements of the candidates on any other issue. The Democrats won a complete victory, capturing the presidency and control of both Senate and House of Representatives for the first time since Buchanan's election thirty-six years earlier. The Populists, however, had received almost 10 per cent of the popular vote, and constituted a force to be reckoned with.

THE FINANCIERS FACE A DILEMMA

During Cleveland's second administration the hostility of the West and South toward the industrial East grew more intense as a result of a severe business depression and the policies of the government in financial matters.

The Panic of 1893. Cleveland had scarcely been inaugurated (March 4, 1893) before the country was in the grip of a panic comparable to that of 1873.

CAUSES. As in the case of previous depressions the fundamental causes of the crisis of 1893 were obscure, but certain factors gave warning of the coming storm: (1) There had been an excessive conversion of liquid capital into fixed forms, often for purely speculative purposes; (2) governmental expenditures had mounted, while income remained stationary, until the Treasury surplus was changed to a deficit; (3) confidence in the government's ability to meet its obligations in gold waned as a result of the additional burden placed upon the gold reserve fund by the Sherman Silver Purchase Act of 1890; (4) the tendency to hoard gold increased as European investors began to sell their American securities in order to secure it, and as foreign business houses demanded the settlement of trade balances in gold; (5) the fears of the business community became acute in April, 1893, when the gold reserve in the Treasury fell for the first time below the $100,000,000 mark.

BUSINESS FAILURES. The panic, precipitated by the failure of the National Cordage Company early in May, was one of the most severe the country had ever experienced. Within two months nineteen national banks and a large number of state banks in the Southern and Western states had suspended operations. Between May and October, 1893, more than 8,000 business houses failed, and 156 railroads fell into the hands of receivers.

UNEMPLOYMENT—COXEY'S ARMY (1894). By the spring of 1894 unemployment had grown acute; bands of men and boys roamed the countryside. Some, organized as "armies," sought relief from state and national governments. One such army under the leadership of "General" Jacob Coxey, of Ohio, marched to Washington to present its petition for inflation of the currency and a government program of public works, but its appeal became a fiasco when the members of the army were arrested for walking on the grass of a Capitol lawn.

Cleveland's Financial Policies. Despite the demand from the South and West for a more abundant currency, President Cleveland was a determined foe of inflation. He insisted that the government meet its obligations in gold, that the federal budget be balanced by reduction of expenditures, and that tariff barriers be lowered to promote trade revival.

REPEAL OF THE SILVER PURCHASE ACT. The President informed a special session of Congress (August, 1893) that the panic was directly traceable to the fear that the country was going to substitute silver for gold as its monetary base. This fear seemed justified because of the generous purchases of silver under the Sherman Act and the drain on the gold reserve as Treasury notes, issued to buy silver, were presented at the Treasury for redemption in gold. Cleveland called for prompt repeal of the Sherman Act. With the aid of the Eastern Republicans the President won, but he incurred the bitter animosity of the Western and Southern contingents in his own party.

DOWNWARD REVISION OF TARIFF SCHEDULES. As a result of the battle over the repeal of the Sherman Act, Congress was in a bitter mood when it turned (December, 1893) to consider the Cleveland recommendations for tariff reform.

The Wilson Bill. The Wilson Bill, which passed the House, provided for: (1) the inclusion of raw materials like iron ore, coal, lumber, wool, and sugar in the free list; (2) the reduction of the duties in such schedules as cotton and woolen goods, iron and steel products, and silks and linens; (3) the repeal of the bounty granted under the McKinley Tariff to the domestic producers of raw sugar; and (4) imposition of a tax of 2 per cent on incomes of $4,000 or over in order to make up the loss in revenue from the reduced duties.

The Wilson-Gorman Tariff (1894). The Senate accepted 634 amendments to the Wilson Bill and the resulting Wilson-Gorman Tariff bore marked resemblance in many of its schedules to the McKinley Tariff. President Cleveland denounced the action of the protectionists in the Senate and refused to sign the act, but it became law without his signature. Within a year the Supreme Court held that its income tax provision was unconstitutional (*Pollock Farmers' Loan and Trust Company*).

MAINTAINING THE GOVERNMENT'S CREDIT. Cleveland's determination to meet governmental obligations in gold compelled him to watch closely the Treasury's gold reserves.

The Dwindling Gold Reserve. The greenbacks and the Treasury notes of 1890, which were redeemable in gold, constituted an endless drain upon the gold reserve. Once presented for redemption this paper currency could not be cancelled but was put back into circulation. Therefore, bankers and businessmen used it to draw sums from the Treasury whenever they needed gold. When the Treasury undertook to maintain its reserves by selling bonds to the public for gold, the subscribers paid gold, received their bonds, and then could present greenbacks or the notes of 1890 for redemption, which immediately drew out the gold that had just been paid into the Treasury. Cleveland tried to break this endless circle.

The Morgan Contract. In February, 1895, with the reserve standing at only $41,340,181, President Cleveland reached an agreement with J. P. Morgan and a financial syndicate whereby the bankers were to furnish the government with 3,500,000 ounces of gold for which they were to receive 4 per cent thirty-year bonds. During the operation of the contract the syndicate promised to secure the gold, without drawing any amounts from the Treasury reserves. Cleveland was bitterly denounced for appealing to the "Wall Street interests" and confessing that private bankers could accomplish, with profit, what the United States government seemed powerless to do.

The Currency Issue. Among both Democrats and Republicans, especially in the Western and Southern states and in many rural communities of the East, there was strong opposition to Cleveland's policies on the ground that his attempt to maintain the gold reserve was indirectly a decision that the currency should not be increased in amount. The inflationists, whatever their party affiliation, were insistent that the currency supply was inadequate and was responsible for falling prices and declining wages. They were not alarmed at the dwindling gold reserve, but they were angered that Cleveland and his associates would not increase the currency in circulation by coining more silver so that both gold and silver could supply the monetary needs of the nation.

THE FARMERS IN RETREAT

The political battle for the control of the government in 1896 was the most momentous since the election of Abraham Lincoln in 1860. The farmers of the West and South and the industrial workers of the Eastern states made a strong bid for power against the business and financial interests.

The High Hopes of the Populists. The country was in a sullen mood in the spring of 1896. The plight of the farmer was still acute; unemployment or declining wages was the lot of the wage earners; business enterprise had not yet recovered from the depression of 1893. The Populists viewed with high hopes these evidences of economic unrest and the consequent crumbling of old party lines throughout the West and South. Having increased their total vote by 40 per cent in the congressional elections of 1894, they looked forward to 1896 as a year of national victory, for they expected the Democratic and Republican parties to remain under the control of conservative leaders committed to a policy of sound currency based on the gold standard.

The Strength of the Republican Conservatives. The Populists were correct so far as the Republican party was concerned. Its Western wing was committed to the solution of the monetary question through the free coinage of silver, but control of the party was in the hands of Eastern bankers and industrialists.

"Big Business" Dominant. No Republican leader was more influential in 1896 than Mark Hanna, the Cleveland capitalist whose career in Ohio politics had demonstrated the intensity of his conviction that there should be a close union between "big business" and the Republican party. He was determined that his close friend, Governor William McKinley of Ohio, should be the presidential nominee, and that the platform should pledge maintenance of the gold standard.

The Republican Platform. Hanna adroitly handled a threatened revolt on the part of the free-silver men of the West. In the end a gold plank was adopted and only thirty-four delegates, led by Senator Teller of Colorado, bolted the convention. The platform also contained planks favoring: (1) a protective tariff; (2) generous pensions for Union veterans; (3) enlargement of the navy; (4)

American control of the Hawaiian Islands; and (5) federal arbitration of labor disputes involving interstate commerce.

McKINLEY'S NOMINATION. So effectively had Hanna lined up the Republican delegates that the convention required only one ballot to nominate William McKinley for President. The nominee was a veteran of the Civil War, who had served fourteen years in Congress, where he had become the leading champion of the protective tariff. As late as 1890 he had been a "silverite," but he finally "repented" of his heresy and agreed with the Eastern financial interests that only the gold standard could correct the nation's monetary ills.

Democratic Confusion. The smooth functioning of the Republican machine under Hanna's expert manipulation contrasted sharply with the confusion within the Democratic organization. The Western and Southern Democrats, particularly in the rural districts, were openly in revolt against the Cleveland administration.

A VICTORY FOR THE SILVERITES. The Democratic convention held in Chicago in July, 1896, was dominated by the supporters of silver coinage. The Cleveland administration was repudiated. The platform, adopted after spirited debate, demanded the "free and unlimited coinage of both gold and silver at the present legal ratio of sixteen to one." Other planks included: (1) opposition to the issuance of paper money by national banks; (2) criticism of the Supreme Court for its decision against the constitutionality of the income tax; (3) demand that tariff schedules be imposed merely to provide governmental revenue; (4) denunciation of "government by injunction" in labor disputes; and (5) the demand for enlargement of the powers of the Interstate Commerce Commission.

BRYAN, CRUSADER FOR INFLATION. In the Nebraska delegation was a young lawyer, more gifted as a political leader. William Jennings Bryan had made himself known as a campaigner for inflation. His impassioned plea for silver coinage, culminating in the famous "cross of gold" peroration, stirred the delegates so deeply that on the fifth ballot he was nominated. As a conciliatory gesture to the East, Arthur Sewall, a Maine banker, was named for the vice-presidency.

THE POPULIST DILEMMA. The Chicago platform was an open invitation to the Populists to join the Democratic ranks. Such a fusion was opposed by some of the most devoted Populist leaders, but the rank and file, eager for victory, nominated Bryan for Presi-

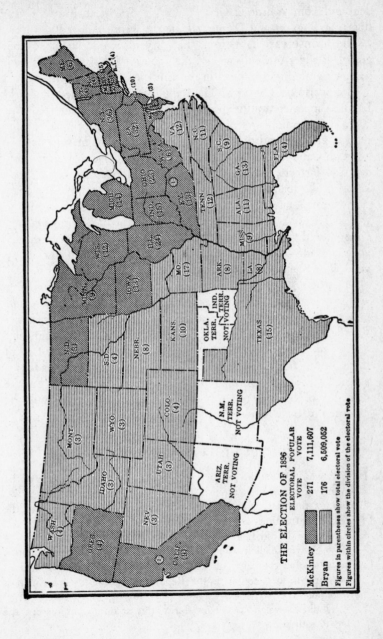

THE ELECTION OF 1896

	ELECTORAL VOTE	POPULAR VOTE
McKinley	271	7,111,607
Bryan	176	6,509,052

Figures in parentheses show total electoral vote

Figures within circles show the division of the electoral vote

dent and Tom Watson of Georgia for Vice-President. In twenty-six states the Populist and Democratic tickets were combined.

The Conservatives Win. When Bryan vigorously carried the gospel of silver into all parts of the country, the class hatreds and sectional animosities implicit in the struggle became evident.

THE SECTIONAL CLEAVAGE. The Republicans, astutely led by Mark Hanna, appealed to the propertied classes and emphasized the "dangerous radicalism" of the Democrats. Their candidate, Mc-Kinley, gracious and dignified, received delegations of voters at his home in Canton, Ohio. Bryan frankly spoke to the masses of debt-harassed farmers, poorly paid industrial workers and small shop-keepers. The balloting in November showed that McKinley had carried every state east of the Mississippi and north of the Ohio, as well as Kentucky, West Virginia, Iowa, Minnesota, North Dakota, Oregon, and California. The fact that the season was an especially good one for farmers is said to have caused Bryan to lose many votes. The South and most of the West were Bryan's country.

THE MEANING OF THE ELECTION OF 1896. The decisive Republican victory meant: (1) the defeat, for the moment, of the farmers and industrial workers in their greatest struggle with the industrialists; (2) the continuing dominance of business interests in governmental affairs; and (3) the triumph of conservative financiers of the East in the realm of fiscal and monetary policy. The agrarian crusade, for a time had been transformed into a battle over the currency, but the demands of farmers and laborers within fifteen years would be espoused by both Republicans and Democrats.

REVIEW QUESTIONS

1. Why was it difficult to organize the agrarian and labor elements of the country as an effective political party?
2. Discuss the basic grievances of the farmers at the opening of the decade of the nineties.
3. What remedy did Populism suggest for the farmer's plight?
4. How do you explain the fact that some newspaper commentators described the campaign of 1892 as a contest between "tweedledum and tweedledee," so far as the Republican and Democratic parties were concerned?
5. Why did Cleveland's policies during his second term disrupt the Democratic party?

6. If you had been a Populist leader in 1896 would you have advocated union with the Democrats? Why?

7. What philosophy of government was exemplified by Marcus A. Hanna?

8. How do you explain William Jennings Bryan's nomination by the Democrats in 1896?

9. The campaign of 1896 was far more significant than a mere party battle over free silver. Discuss.

Chapter VII

THE PATH TOWARD EMPIRE

For some time after the Civil War the United States attempted to pursue its traditional policy of isolationism. However, the forces that had transformed the nation into an industrial economy and a world power were also at work to make it an empire. Gradually Americans turned their attention from internal events to active participation in international affairs and overseas expansion. By the close of the nineteenth century this course had given rise to political conflicts at home between those who favored and those who opposed it; to tensions with rival powers, culminating in the Spanish-American War; and to basic constitutional issues as to how the new territories should be governed.

POLITICAL DIPLOMACY IN ACTION

During the three decades following the Civil War the United States had no purposeful foreign policy. Its relations with other nations were largely accidental or else were determined by events in domestic politics.

Isolation—Myth or Reality? American isolation was a state of mind, but to the generation of Americans between 1865 and 1900 it was reality. Though the people were aware of the importance of foreign markets for the products of their farms and factories, they were little concerned with the stakes of European diplomacy. In 1898 McKinley could refer to the years preceding his administration as "the period of exclusiveness."

Political Diplomats. Remoteness from the main currents of world affairs was revealed in the activities of the thirteen Secretaries of State who served between 1865 and 1898. With the possible exceptions of William H. Seward and Hamilton Fish, they were all politicians much more concerned with the political scene at home than with diplomatic developments abroad. Unimaginative they may have been, and inclined to be aggressive in particular controversies, but they practiced a statecraft that was straightforward and peaceful in its objectives.

THE FOREIGN SERVICE. American ambassadors and ministers in foreign capitals, though too often chosen because of their wealth or their conspicuous services to the party in office, were occasionally men of ability. So inconsequential, however, were the stakes of diplomacy that few of them had a chance to distinguish themselves. The changing administrations were more concerned with the work of consular agents, who were charged with the promotion of exports and imports.

TRADITIONAL ATTITUDES IN FOREIGN RELATIONS. From the pre-Civil War period two traditional policies persisted in American foreign policy—from adherence to the principles of the Monroe Doctrine and the expansion of American commercial interests in the Pacific.

Enforcing the Monroe Doctrine in Mexico. Near the close of the Civil War, Napoleon III, in flagrant violation of the Monroe Doctrine, had placed Archduke Maximilian of Austria upon an unstable Mexican throne. Secretary of State Seward had vainly protested; but with the conclusion of hostilities the United States government ordered General Sheridan's troops to take up positions along the Rio Grande. Though war seemed imminent, Seward scored a diplomatic victory when Napoleon's troubles in Europe caused him to withdraw French troops (1867). Without French support Maximilian lost his throne and was executed by his former subjects. Thus the attempt of a European power to intervene in the affairs of an independent American nation was thwarted.

Defining a Pacific Policy. Secretary Seward deserves credit for stating clearly the traditional basis of this country's commercial interests in the Pacific. In 1867 he found Russia eager to get rid of its outpost on the North American continent, and he persuaded Congress to purchase Alaska for $7,200,000. This rich base, Seward hoped, would start the United States on an expansionist policy. He also arranged for the United States to annex the Midway Islands (1868) and to acquire rights to a canal route across Nicaragua. At the same time he urged eventual acquisition of the Hawaiian Islands.

Anglo-American Misunderstandings. The attitude of Great Britain toward the United States government during the Civil War left a legacy of bitterness; relations between the two nations were far from friendly during the last quarter of the nineteenth century.

BASES OF ANTI-BRITISH SENTIMENT. American ill will toward Great Britain may be attributed to several influences: (1) the tradition, growing out of the Revolution and the War of 1812, which was perpetuated by many American publicists and historians, that the English nation had been and still was the most powerful enemy; (2) the fact that the governing classes in England had apparently desired the disruption of the Union during the Civil War; (3) the belief of many politicians that the best way to cultivate the Irish-American vote was to "twist the British lion's tail"; and (4) the resentment against the patronizing, or critical, attitude of many English commentators on things American.

THE "ALABAMA" CLAIMS. Great Britain's failure during the Civil War to enforce strictly its neutrality laws had made possible the construction in British shipyards of ships which were destined to fly the Confederate flag. The damages inflicted upon American shipping by these cruisers, the most famous of which was the *Alabama,* came to be known as the *Alabama* claims. Secretary Seward was ignored by the British government when he pressed for a diplomatic settlement.

Fenian Uprising. The British government, however, changed its attitude late in 1865, as it watched the United States deal effectively with the Fenians, Irish-American champions of Ireland's independence, who used the United States as a base for sporadic raids into Canada. The State Department was so vigilant in suppressing these violations of Canada's frontiers, that British statesmen finally announced their willingness to respond by settling all outstanding differences between Canada, Great Britain, and the United States.

The Treaty of Washington (1871). Negotiations extended over several years. In 1868 Reverdy Johnson, then ambassador in London, reached an agreement with Lord Clarendon, providing for an international commission to adjudicate the claims of both nations, but the Senate refused to ratify the agreement. Three years later the Secretary of State, Hamilton Fish, was more successful, and the Senate ratified the Treaty of Washington which authorized: (1) submission of the *Alabama* claims to an international tribunal; (2) settlement by arbitration of the disputed boundary through Vancouver Sound; and (3) a new arrangement concerning the New-foundland fisheries.

The Geneva Award (*1872*). Meeting at Geneva, Switzerland, the members of the tribunal, created under the Treaty of Washington, refused to accept the indirect claims for damages by British-built Confederate ships; but it awarded direct damages of $15,500,000, which the British government promptly paid.

THE NORTHEASTERN FISHERIES DISPUTE. The perennial quarrels over fishing rights in North Atlantic waters were temporarily quieted by the Treaty of Washington, but in 1885, when the fisheries clauses in the Treaty were terminated, Canada began seizing American ships in Canadian waters. In response an angry Congress authorized President Cleveland to close American ports to Canadian ships and goods. After the election of 1888, anti-British sentiment subsided; and the State Department finally worked out an informal agreement which remained in effect until the vexatious legal questions were settled in the Anglo-American Convention of 1912.

BERING SEA CONTROVERSY. During Cleveland's first administration the United States, in an attempt to protect the herds of seals in the Bering Sea and Alaskan waters, arbitrarily seized Canadian ships, contending that the Bering Sea was not open to the ships of all nations. After Secretary Blaine and Lord Salisbury had exchanged acrimonious diplomatic notes, Blaine finally agreed to submit the dispute to arbitration. In 1893 an international tribunal ruled against the United States on every point of law, though it recommended joint protection of the seal herds by Canada and the United States.

VENEZUELAN BOUNDARY ADJUSTMENT. Of all the Anglo-American disputes of this period the controversy over the Venezuelan boundary brought the United States and Great Britain closest to the brink of war.

Claims of British Guiana. The line of demarcation between the South American republic of Venezuela and the British colony of Guiana came into lively dispute in the 1880's, when gold and other precious minerals were discovered just beyond the boundary which England had been inclined to accept. Three times (1886, 1890, 1894) the United States offered its good offices as mediator, but the offers were received with distrust and suspicion in both England and Venezuela.

The Olney Doctrine. Finally, in 1895, when it appeared that Great Britain was using the boundary controversy to acquire additional territory, Secretary of State Olney sent several sharp notes to London in which he asserted: (1) that the United States was bound under the Monroe Doctrine to protect the territorial integrity of Venezuela; (2) that the United States was practically sovereign on this continent and that its fiat was law upon the subjects to which it confined its interposition; and (3) that peaceful arbitration was the only way to settle the boundary line. When Lord Salisbury denied the applicability of the Monroe Doctrine and refused to submit the disputed boundary to arbitration, President Cleveland asked Congress to approve the appointment of a commission to draw the boundary line which it would be the duty of the United States to defend against any possible British aggression. This stirring message roused the country, though Lord Salisbury was right in branding the Olney doctrine as a completely novel interpretation of the Monroe Doctrine.

The Victory for Arbitration. The war spirit, stirred up by President Cleveland's message to Congress, subsided when it became evident that responsible leaders in Congress and in Parliament desired peace. Representatives of Britain and the United States signed a treaty (1897) providing for an arbitral tribunal to settle the disputed boundary. Its decision (1899) was largely a victory for Great Britain; and Venezuela regretted its reliance on American support.

Inter-American Relations. One of the most serious defects in American foreign policy during the last quarter of the nineteenth century was the failure to establish enduring friendship with the independent republics of Latin America.

MEDIATION UNDER THE MONROE DOCTRINE. For a half-century after the Mexican War (1846–1848) the interest of the United States in the nations south of the Rio Grande was based upon the Monroe Doctrine, that is, a desire to prevent interference by European governments in the affairs of any American country.

Intervention in Boundary Disputes. Since peace was often threatened by quarrels over international boundaries, the United States frequently offered its services as an impartial mediator. (1) In 1876 the government arbitrated a dispute between Argentina and Paraguay; (2) in 1880 its good offices were accepted by Colombia and Chile in all controversies which they could not settle by direct negotiation; (3) the following year it helped Mexico and Guatemala, as well as Chile and Argentina, settle boundary disputes; (4) at the same time the United States intervened in the quarrel between Chile and Peru over the provinces of Tacna-Arica and earned the ill will of the latter nation by its efforts for compromise; and (5) the State Department tried hard to settle the War of the Pacific (1881) which involved Bolivia, Chile, and Peru.

Latin-American Reactions. In the hands of United States diplomats the Monroe Doctrine could be a two-edged sword. Gratitude over such protection as the Doctrine provided against European interference in American affairs was often overshadowed by Latin-American resentment against the manner in which the United States assumed a position of superiority.

BLAINE's PAN-AMERICAN POLICY. No Secretary of State since the days of Henry Clay worked harder than James G. Blaine to promote the interests of the United States in Latin America. But much of Blaine's effort was nullified by his aggressive insistence that commercial contracts be worked out along the lines laid down by the State Department.

The First Pan-American Congress (1889). During his brief secretaryship under Garfield, Blaine had arranged for a conference of the American nations at Washington, but his successor, F. T. Frelinghuysen, abandoned the project. Later, under President Harrison, Secretary Blaine presided over the deliberations of the first Pan-American Congress. He gained little satisfaction from it, however, as the delegates refused to approve his proposals for a customs union and tariff reciprocity. The sole tangible result of the Congress was the establishment of the Bureau of American Republics (Pan-American Union) to facilitate the interchange of commercial information.

The Chilean Controversy (1891). Under Secretary Blaine's direction the State Department was eager to maintain order in the republics of Latin America. When its minister in Chile, Patrick Egan, assumed a truculent attitude toward the new government which had seized power by force, Blaine supported him. Later in the year Blaine used a brawl between Chilean and American sailors in Valparaiso as a pretext for a tone of belligerency which brought the United States to the verge of war with a determined Chilean government. While Blaine secured apologies from Chile, his attitude created an unfortunate impression of United States aggressiveness among Latin-Americans.

THE LURE OF THE PACIFIC

As late as 1890 most citizens of the United States were little interested in the relations of their government with foreign nations, but a change in popular sentiment was already becoming evident. It was particularly noticeable in the favorable reaction throughout the nation to American expansion in the Pacific area.

Emergence of the New Imperialism. Many forces gave strength to the American desire to acquire territory beyond continental borders, which grew rapidly during the last decade of the nineteenth century.

MARINERS AND MISSIONARIES. Though many Americans failed to realize it, there was much in the new reaching out for overseas possessions that was traditional. In the Pacific, for example, it was in large part the result of ideas and attitudes that had been fixed in the days of the whalers and the clipper ships and the early nineteenth century trade of New England with the Orient. And it was shot through with the zeal of Christian missionaries who longed to reform the Far East in the image of their own gospel. Mariners and missionaries, indeed, were American pioneers in Samoa, Hawaii, and other Pacific islands.

THE SETTLEMENT OF THE WEST. The Western advance on the American continent ended with the closing of the frontier in the 1890's. Habits of expansion and pioneering were then transferred overseas. The settlement of the West also led to a greater economic and military interest in the Pacific region.

THE SEARCH FOR MARKETS. Expansion into the Pacific was spurred by the growing industrialization of the United States. Every decade after 1870 revealed the increase in its exports and, what was more important, the steady rise in the proportion of manufactured goods in the totals of its foreign trade. As the industrial system took shape, the need for markets gave added impetus to the demand that American political control over areas in the Pacific be strengthened.

THE IMPORTANCE OF SEA POWER. Though the United States had never maintained a large standing army, the people had long cherished the high tradition of the American navy. Naval strength, however, was allowed to decline after the Civil War, and a new steel navy was not constructed until the late 1880's. The Naval Act of 1890 marked the acceptance by the government of the concept of a navy capable of meeting any potential foe on the Atlantic or the Pacific. The new policy was being put into effect in the very years that Americans in large numbers were reading Captain Alfred Mahan's books and articles on the importance of sea power and its relation to commercial expansion.

The Samoan Islands. An early example of the changed attitude of many Americans toward overseas imperialism was the peaceful penetration of the Samoan Islands. Contacts with the islanders, first stimulated by the China trade, passed through several stages.

TRADING CONCESSIONS. Casual relations established by seamen and traders led in 1872 to the negotiation of a treaty granting the United States a naval station which the Senate failed to ratify. Six years later, however, a Samoan proposal that the United States establish a protectorate over the islands resulted in an agreement (1878) that gave American ships most-favored-nation rights in the harbor of Pago Pago and the opportunity to establish a naval base.

POLITICAL CONTROL. At the same time Germany and Great Britain received commercial privileges in Samoa, and the three nations entered into a competition for favored treatment by Samoans, which was not always friendly. This rivalry aroused a nationalistic spirit in the United States which was only partially satisfied in 1889, when the three nations established a condominium over Samoan affairs. Ten years later, after the Spanish-American War had been won, the United States permitted Germany to take over many of the islands, but retained the most important, Tutuila, with the fine harbor of Pago Pago (1899) as an American possession.

Hawaii. Acquisition of the Hawaiian Islands (1898) was the result of forces similar to those which brought to the United States colonial responsibilities in Samoa.

EARLY CONTACTS. As early as 1820 New England missionaries had established themselves on several of Hawaii's islands, where their descendants were joined by Yankee ship captains, traders with the Orient, and sailors on the whaling ships, who steadily augmented the American population in the islands.

THE SUGAR PLANTERS. Within a generation, sugar became the chief interest of Americans in Hawaii. The sugar planters, a majority of whom were Americans, worked indefatigably for closer relations with the United States. In 1875 they secured a treaty of reciprocity between the United States and the islands which greatly stimulated their sugar trade. However, the McKinley Tariff of 1890 removed the duty on imported sugar and provided for a bounty of two cents a pound on domestic sugar. Thus the Hawaiian planters lost their favored position and looked to annexation as their best prospect.

OVERTHROW OF THE HAWAIIAN MONARCHY (1893). The American faction in the Hawaiian Islands, led by the great planters and financed by American capital, staged a successful revolt against Queen Liliuokalani in 1893.

Intervention by Force. The government of Queen Liliuokalani was determined in its opposition to foreigners, and the American minority became alarmed when the queen proclaimed that Hawaii was for the Hawaiians. The revolution of the foreign elements was quickly accomplished after the American minister, John L. Stevens, gave his support to the temporary government of the revolutionists and had American marines landed to preserve order.

Cleveland's Rejection of Annexation. President Harrison, who favored annexation, left office before a treaty could be acted upon. The incoming President, Cleveland, withdrew the annexation treaty from the Senate and appointed anti-imperialist James H. Blount special commissioner to investigate the situation. After receiving Blount's report, Cleveland attempted to restore the government of Queen Liliuokalani on the condition that she pardon the revolutionists. The queen refused to do this, and the revolutionary government continued in power. On July 4, 1894, this government proclaimed the Republic of Hawaii, and the following month it was recognized by the United States.

Victory of the Annexationists. When McKinley became President (1897), sentiment in favor of annexation was running strong. Acquisition of the Hawaiian Republic, said the expansionists, was imperative because: (1) it might otherwise fall under the control of a foreign power; (2) it would provide badly needed naval bases in the Pacific; and (3) it offered opportunities for commercial expansion and for investment of American capital. These arguments were reinforced in the minds of many citizens by the belief that it was the manifest destiny of the United States to control the Pacific and that the nation had a duty to bring the Christian gospel and American democratic institutions to the native populations in that area. A Japanese protest against annexation also spurred on the move, and the war with Spain gave it added impetus. These considerations brought annexation of Hawaii by a joint resolution of Congress, which President McKinley signed on July 7, 1898.

WAR WITH SPAIN

The Spanish-American War caused the American people to move rapidly along the path of empire already clearly defined by the more enthusiastic expansionists in the United States.

The Cuban Situation. During the second half of the nineteenth century the United States frequently showed its concern over the fate of Cuba, its close neighbor, which was Spain's chief possession in the Caribbean.

CUBAN POLICIES. Early in the century the American government had expressed fear lest the sovereignty of Spain in the island should be replaced by that of a more formidable European power. For a decade after 1850 there was much discussion of the acquisition of Cuba either by purchase or seizure. Finally, in the last quarter of the century, as American commercial contacts and financial investments increased, the government was inclined to support any policy which gave promise of maintaining stable political and economic conditions in the island.

The Ten Years' War (1868–1878). This prolonged revolt of the Cubans against Spanish authority not only brought devastation to large areas in the island, but also pushed the United States to the verge of war with Spain, because of Spanish charges that Americans were aiding the rebels in violation of international law. Despite Spanish mistreatment of American citizens in Cuba and execution of Americans taken from a filibustering ship (the *Virginius*), the United States at this time had no desire for war. The close of the war in 1878 left the Cuban leaders resentful over unfulfilled promises of the Spanish government and sent many of them to the United States, where they carried on propaganda for Cuban independence.

Cuban War of Independence (1895). Continuing discontent in Cuba flared into revolt when declining prices of sugar and tobacco, partly induced by American customs duties under the Wilson-Gorman Tariff, brought widespread economic depression to the island. Nevertheless, the wealthier classes in Cuba and most Americans with investments in the island were opposed to the rebels' demand for independence.

SPANISH "RECONCENTRATION" POLICY. Unable to cope with the guerrilla tactics of the revolutionary forces, which were terrorizing the countryside, Governor-General Weyler tried to confine military operations within a limited area and to concentrate the civilian population in camps closely supervised by Spanish troops. Though Weyler's policy was misrepresented in sensational newspapers in this country, he probably deserved the sobriquet of "butcher" for the brutal effects of his concentration camps on noncombatants. Equally brutal, however, were the tactics of the insurgents as they tried to "fight fire with fire" and embarked on a campaign of destruction.

American Demand for Military Intervention. The United States government endeavored to maintain a policy of strict neutrality, but an increasing majority of its citizens openly voiced their sympathy for the Cuban revolutionaries.

CLEVELAND'S ATTITUDE. During the closing months of his administration, President Cleveland strove to maintain genuine neutrality and to persuade the Spanish government that the grant of Cuban autonomy was the surest means of establishing peace and political stability. He feared, however, that the demand for intervention would compel his successor, McKinley, to act.

THE WAR FACTION. American intervention in the Cuban situation was not desired by those who had the largest financial interests in the island, since they believed that Spain could eventually restore peace and order. The groups most enthusiastic for a war to secure Cuban independence included: (1) humanitarians who believed that Spanish policy, as exemplified by Weyler, had been not only dictatorial but also "brutal and inhuman"; (2) certain jingoes who felt that war was the highroad to commercial and industrial prosperity; (3) partisan politicians who hoped that a successful struggle with Spain would quicken patriotic support of the McKinley administration; (4) a few public officials, like Roosevelt and Lodge, nationalistic in spirit, who were eager to have the United States assume its place as a world power; and (5) a powerful portion of the sensational press, which was fattening its circulation by publishing exaggerated stories of Spanish "atrocities" and erroneous accounts of events in Cuba.

The de Lôme Letter. The war faction was strengthened on February 9, 1898, when Hearst's *New York Journal* published a letter which the Spanish minister, Dupuy de Lôme, had written to a friend in Cuba. The letter contained slurs against President McKinley which aroused widespread indignation. De Lôme promptly resigned.

The Sinking of the Maine. On February 15 the battleship *Maine,* which had been sent to Havana to be ready in case Americans there needed protection, was sunk at her moorings with the loss of 260 officers and men. Though it was impossible to determine whether the sinking had been the work of Spanish loyalists or Cuban insurgents, or was entirely accidental, the war faction immediately made "Remember the *Maine*" a slogan.

McKINLEY'S DECISION. Although he was truly desirous of averting war, President McKinley realized that a "peace at any price" policy might split his party and wreck his administration. Therefore, on April 11, 1898, he sent a message to Congress charging that the Spanish government was unable to suppress the Cuban rebellion and yet was unwilling to grant an armistice. Spain had actually yielded to McKinley's demands between the time that he wrote his message and the date that he sent it to Congress; nevertheless, the pressure for war was so great not only in Congress but throughout the nation that he could no longer resist it. The war resolution (April 20, 1898) contained the so-called Teller amendment, which pledged the United States to withdraw from Cuba as soon as its independence and political stability had been established.

Collapse of the Spanish Empire. In spite of serious blunders by military and civilian authorities, the United States won the Spanish War with relative ease.

PREPARATION FOR HOSTILITIES. During the thirty years following the Civil War the United States government had been negligent of its military establishment, since no powerful foe seemed to threaten the nation. The American people paid the price of this lack of preparedness in the Spanish War.

The Navy. Fortunately, the brunt of the conflict fell upon the navy, which was better prepared than any other part of the military establishment. It was the first test of the new steel ships, construction of which had been going forward since 1883. In addition to the Atlantic Fleet under Admiral Sampson, the Flying Squadron under Commodore Schley and the Asiatic Squadron under Commodore Dewey, the Navy Department had put into service more than one hundred auxiliary ships acquired during the spring of 1898. Thirty million dollars had been expended, the personnel of officers and men had been doubled, and contracts had been placed for munitions and supplies.

The Army. In contrast, the Army was ill-prepared for the conflict. For a generation Congress had been miserly in its appropriations for the War Department. Furthermore, too many high officials in the Department had been political appointees rather than men trained in the technical and administrative skills which the military service required. As a result, when war broke out the normal processes of the War Department broke down. It could not double the size of the regular army and train two hundred thousand volunteers with the speed and efficiency that war demanded. The record made distressing reading for Americans, who slowly learned that spoiled food, inferior guns and ammunition, lack of proper clothing, and insufficient medical service both in camp and in the field accounted for a heavier loss of life than did the actual fighting on the battlefield.

WAR ON TWO FRONTS. With the outbreak of war Spain became vulnerable not only in her Caribbean colonies, but also in her Pacific possessions.

The Philippine Campaign. The first blow for Cuban independence was struck not in Atlantic waters but in the far-distant Philippines. Commodore George Dewey's squadron (which was in Asiatic waters as a result of Assistant Navy Secretary Theodore Roosevelt's orders) steamed from Hong Kong to Manila and destroyed the Spanish fleet in Manila Bay. Dewey was compelled to wait from May 1 until August 13 for reinforcements which enabled the American troops to capture the city of Manila.

The Blockade of Cuba. Meanwhile, Admiral Sampson and Commodore Schley had established an effective blockade of all Cuban ports. They were not able, however, to prevent Admiral Cervera, with the most important Spanish fleet, from taking a position under the batteries of Santiago harbor. Lieutenant Hobson's attempt to sink the collier *Merrimac* across the mouth of the harbor failed, and the fleet waited for the arrival of American troops before beginning the Cuban campaign in earnest.

Santiago. The campaign against Santiago was brief and decisive. Its two phases were (1) the operations of the American expeditionary forces to the north and east of the city and (2) the destruction of Cervera's fleet. On June 14, 1898, seventeen thousand troops under command of General W. R. Shafter embarked at Tampa, Florida.

Within three weeks General J. F. Kent's division had taken San Juan Hill; General H. W. Lawton's division had reached El Caney; and General Wheeler's dismounted cavalry, with the Rough Riders,* had stormed Kettle Hill. Admiral Cervera, learning that the Americans controlled the heights above Santiago, made a desperate effort to escape. His entire fleet was destroyed, while the American

The West Indies

casualties were one killed and sixteen wounded. On July 17 Santiago surrendered.

The "Conquest" of Puerto Rico. After the termination of the Santiago campaign, General N. A. Miles undertook to conquer Puerto Rico. So feeble was the military resistance in the island that Mr. Dooley, the creation of American humorist Finley Peter Dunne, described the "campaign" as "Gin'ral Miles' Gran' Picnic an' Moonlight Excursion." It was cut short in August, 1898, by the peace protocol.

THE PEACE OF PARIS. The terms of the treaty with Spain revealed to the American people how far and how fast they had traveled along the road of empire-building.

---

* A volunteer cavalry group, organized and led by Theodore Roosevelt, who had resigned from the Navy Department to become an army colonel.

Negotiations. Through the good offices of the French government a peace protocol was signed by the United States and Spain calling for a conference at Paris on October 1, 1898. McKinley named a delegation of five (Secretary of State W. R. Day, Whitelaw Reid, publisher of the *New York Tribune,* and Senators C. K. Davis, W. P. Frye, and George Gray). The payment of the Cuban debt and the status of the Philippines caused the most serious disagreement among the negotiators.

Treaty Provisions. McKinley had decided that the country favored the retention of the Philippines and that humanitarian, as well as economic, considerations justified it. The chief clauses of the treaty which was finally signed on December 10 were: (1) the grant of Cuban independence and assumption of the Cuban debt by Spain; (2) the cession to the United States of Puerto Rico, Guam, and the Philippines; (3) the payment by the United States of $20,000,000 for the Philippines. This overseas expansion was the result of many motives: the desire to increase the national prestige, to promote new business enterprises, to tap the expanding trade with the Orient, to frustrate the designs of Germany in the Pacific, and to "uplift and civilize" the population of the islands.

Ratification. President McKinley encountered great difficulty in persuading the Senate to ratify the treaty. A few Republicans, led by Senator Hoar of Massachusetts, denounced any attempt to subjugate and rule distant Oriental possessions. The Democrats sought to make political capital out of the debate over ratification. Though he was opposed to overseas expansion, Bryan persuaded some Democratic senators to vote for ratification, because he believed that this would make the new imperialism a clear-cut issue in the presidential campaign of 1900. Thus the administration got the treaty ratified with the aid of Democratic votes.

THE DAY OF THE IMPERIALIST

As a consequence of its war with Spain the United States began to play a more vigorous part upon the world stage than at any previous period in its history.

John Hay's Foreign Policy. Among champions of overseas expansion was John Hay, who succeeded William R. Day as Secretary of State in 1898. Eager to see his country play a major role in world affairs, he was particularly concerned with the maintenance of a stable balance of power in the Far East for the benefit of American traders and investors.

FIRST HAGUE CONFERENCE. The international conference, which met at The Hague in 1899 at the invitation of Czar Nicholas II of Russia, gave Hay a chance to demonstrate the active interest of the United States. The American delegation, led by Andrew D. White, deserved credit for creating a tribunal for the adjudication of international disputes, which came to be known as the Hague Court.

POLICY IN THE FAR EAST. Alarmed by the activity of the European powers in carving out "spheres of influence" in China, Secretary Hay formulated a plan to safeguard American commercial interests and to prevent the dismemberment of the Chinese Empire.

The "Open Door" (1899–1900). Hay asked Great Britain, Germany, Russia, France, Italy, and Japan to agree to the principle of the "open door" (previously suggested by Great Britain) that no nation would interfere with the commercial and transportation rights of other nations within its special "sphere of influence." Reluctantly, the European powers agreed to Hay's doctrine of equality of opportunity in China, thus insuring to American traders equal treatment with the nationals of the countries which had previously received concessions from the Chinese government.

The Boxer Rebellion (1900). The "open door" was almost slammed shut for all non-Chinese by the patriotic society of Chinese known as the Boxers. Strongly antiforeign, the Boxers attacked the foreign settlement in Peking. At Secretary Hay's insistence the United States assumed the lead in organizing an international relief force which fought its way to Peking in time to save the majority of foreigners besieged in the legations. When some European nations desired to partition China, Hay's suggestions again prevailed in favor of restrictions on Chinese sovereignty which, however, maintained the country's administrative and territorial integrity.

Imperialists versus Anti-Imperialists. Many Americans attributed the emergence of the United States as a world power to the desire of the government to imitate the imperialistic policies of the European nations.

THE ANTI-IMPERIALISTS. Even before the treaty of Paris was signed, an Anti-Imperialist League had been organized in Boston (November, 1898). Its members, led by Charles Francis Adams, William Graham Sumner, and Carl Schurz, denounced the acquisition of colonial possessions as a policy which would conflict with democratic principles, impose heavy burdens upon the national treasury, and compel Americans to conquer millions of people hostile to their rule. The literature of protest sent out by the Anti-Imperialists was generally inspired by the Eastern "intellectuals."

THE CAMPAIGN OF 1900. Imperialism became the paramount issue in the political battle for the presidency in 1900.

McKinley and Roosevelt. The Republicans renominated McKinley with great enthusiasm; drafted Theodore Roosevelt against his wishes for the vice-presidency; and praised the administration for its successful conduct of a "righteous war" and for its courageous assumption of a "moral duty" in the Philippines.

The Democrats. William Jennings Bryan, nominated by acclamation, endeavored to spread the gospel of anti-imperialism. Denunciation of the trusts, condemnation of high protection, and support of free silver received less attention from the Democratic candidate than his demand that the country repudiate the course of empire upon which the Republicans had entered.

Endorsement of McKinley. Bryan's cause was hopeless. The country was enjoying heightened prestige abroad and widespread prosperity at home. The electorate was ready to assume the burdens imposed by the new possessions and to reward the party which had brought a revival of commercial and industrial activity. Bryan carried only four states outside the Solid South and received 155 electoral votes to 292 for McKinley.

Governing an Empire. The organization and administration of the colonial empire raised serious political, economic, and constitutional problems which required immediate attention, even if their final settlement had to be postponed.

THE INSULAR CASES. A vital question concerning the status of island dependencies was this: Does the Constitution follow the flag? The Supreme Court gave an involved answer in a series of cases concerning the application of American tariff laws in distant possessions. These so-called Insular cases (1901, 1902, 1903) laid down the principle that the Constitution is theoretically in force wherever the United States exerts its political control, but the "fundamental" provisions of the Constitution do not limit the power of Congress to legislate for colonial territories on "procedural" rights of citizenship (e.g., trial by jury). In effect, Congress was virtually free to govern the insular possessions as it saw fit.

PUERTO RICO. During the first half of the nineteenth century, the

United States tried to lead the people of Puerto Rico toward self-government and stable economic conditions.

Movement for Self-Government. Under the Foraker Act (1900) Puerto Rico occupied a position midway between that of a colony and a territory, with a governor and council appointed by the President of the United States. In 1917 Congress passed the Jones Act, which conferred citizenship on all Puerto Ricans, replaced the council with an elective senate, and provided for a number of civil rights. Some thirty years later (1947) the voters of Puerto Rico received the right to elect their own Governor and Congress by universal suffrage. Five years after this legislation, President Truman signed a joint resolution of Congress which approved a new constitution for the island, under which it became a free commonwealth voluntarily associated with the United States.

Economic Conditions. As they moved toward self-government, the Puerto Ricans tried to improve their standard of living. Largely dependent on the market in the United States for its great crop, sugar, the island could not produce sufficient foodstuffs and commodities for its rapidly growing population. During the 1950's the Puerto Rican government made a determined effort, with American assistance, to increase agricultural output and stimulate new industries. It was hoped that such policies would not only promote material prosperity but would provide support for a better school program for the island's children and cultural opportunities for the population generally.

THE PHILIPPINES. The most extensive and severe test of American colonial policy and administration was made in the Philippine Islands.

Aguinaldo's Insurrection. Emilio Aguinaldo, who had revolted against Spanish control of the islands in 1896, co-operated with the American forces two years later in the hope that he would be installed as president of a new Philippine Republic. When he realized that the United States would keep the islands, he organized an insurrection which was ruthlessly suppressed by the United States army in 1902.

Establishment of Civil Government. Meanwhile, two presidential commissions had reported on political conditions in the Philippines. The second commission, under the leadership of Judge William Howard Taft, laid the foundations of civil government, and in 1901 Taft was named governor-general. The following year Congress

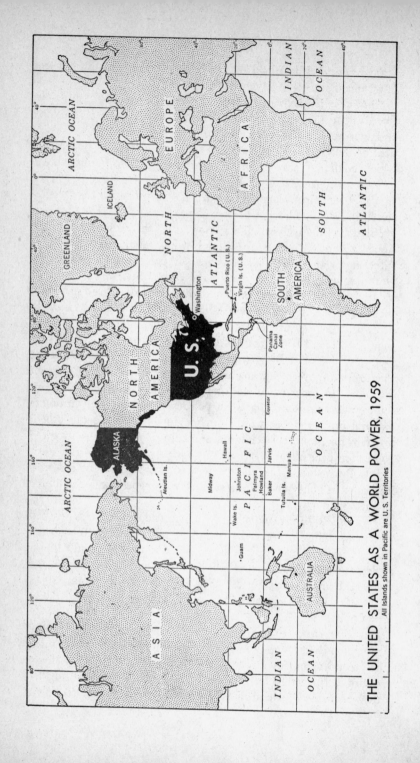

THE UNITED STATES AS A WORLD POWER, 1959

All Islands shown in Pacific are U. S. Territories

passed the Organic Act which outlined the conditions under which the Filipinos were to be admitted to greater participation in their own government. It provided for a popular assembly and a bill of rights. In 1907, after Governor Taft's advisers had prepared the way, elections were held for the assembly which was to share with the appointed council the legislative power.

The Jones Act (1916). In this act the Democrats moved toward that "ultimate independence" which their platforms had stressed since 1900. The appointive council was replaced by an elective senate, thus enabling the Filipinos to control both houses of the legislative body. Five of the administrative departments were to be filled by competent natives. Only the governor-general and the vice-governor were to be Americans.

The Independence Movement. The Jones Act and the liberal administration of Francis B. Harrison (1913–1921) gave impetus to the demand for immediate independence. Despite the reports of the Wood-Forbes Commission (1921) and the Thompson Committee (1926) that the islands were not yet ready for self-government, the agitation for independence continued both in the islands and in the United States. Those who opposed control by Americans on the ground that they were denying liberty to the Filipinos were joined by others who argued; (1) that American financial investments in the islands had been disappointing; (2) that duty-free sugar from the Philippines was competing with American-grown sugar on an unfair basis; (3) that possession of the islands had not enabled the United States to increase its trade with the Orient; and (4) that they constituted a liability rather than an asset, from the angle of national defense.

The Tydings-McDuffie Bill (1934–1946). Although the Hoover administration was opposed to "cutting the Philippines adrift," sentiment for independence in Congress grew rapidly. In January, 1933, the legislators passed over the President's veto the Hawes-Cutting Act providing for Philippine independence after a twelve-year probationary period. The Philippine legislature refused to ratify this measure but finally accepted (May, 1934) the Tydings-McDuffie Bill, which fixed 1946 as the date for the severance of economic ties between the islands and the United States. In 1935 Manuel Quezon became president of the Philippine Commonwealth inaugurating the transition toward independent status. Despite the Japanese invasion during the Second World War, there was no delay in putting the terms of the Tydings-McDuffie Bill into effect. In April, 1946, General Manuel Roxas became the first president of the completely independent Republic of the Philippines.

RELATIONS WITH CUBA. Although the United States withdrew its military forces from Cuba as soon as peace and order had been established, it imposed upon the island certain conditions which in effect would have kept it under American control.

The Platt Amendment. After a United States military government under General Leonard Wood had started Cuba along new paths, a convention of Cuban delegates wrote a constitution (1901). They were compelled to insert a provision included by Congress in the Army Appropriation Bill and called the Platt Amendment: (1) that Cuba would make no international agreements impairing its sovereignty without the consent of the United States; (2) that it would contract no debts unless the interest could be met out of current revenues; (3) that it would accept the intervention of the United States whenever necessary to preserve the independence or political stability of the island; and (4) that it would grant two naval bases to the United States. These provisions were not abrogated by the United States until 1934.

Military Interventions. While the Platt Amendment was in force the United States intervened several times in Cuban affairs: (1) in 1906 to quiet political protests against the existing provisional government; (2) in 1912 to quell disorders which had grown out of race riots in one of the provinces; and (3) in 1917 to supervise Cuban elections. On other occasions diplomatic pressure was sufficient to bring compliance with American wishes.

Economic Penetration. After the Spanish-American War, commercial contacts between Cuba and the United States increased rapidly, and Americans came to control the sugar industry and the railroad systems of the island republic. Thus, Cuba, though politically independent, became a better example of American economic imperialism than either Puerto Rico or the Philippines had been while they were completely under United States political control.

REVIEW QUESTIONS

1. Why did the United States encounter difficulty in settling the *Alabama* claims with Great Britain?
2. Was the action of Napoleon III in Mexico a violation of the Monroe Doctrine? Explain.

3. What were the objectives of Blaine's policy toward Latin America? Did he accomplish his purpose?

4. How do you explain the developing interest of the United States in the Pacific after the Civil War?

5. What relation did Secretary Olney seek to establish between the Monroe Doctrine and Great Britain's quarrel with Venezuela?

6. Was President Cleveland justified in manifesting a belligerent attitude toward Great Britain during the Venezuelan crisis? Why?

7. What is meant by "imperialism"? Did American "imperialism" at the close of the nineteenth century differ in any respect from that of the European powers?

8. Why did the United States intervene in Cuba? To what extent did economic motives affect our national attitude?

9. Who were the Anti-Imperialists? Explain the nature of their protest against imperialism.

10. Did the Platt Amendment make Cuba a protectorate of the United States? Justify your answer.

CHAPTER VIII

THE ERA OF THEODORE ROOSEVELT

The period which Theodore Roosevelt made memorable was a time of vigorous effort to remodel the structure of government, to democratize its processes, and to make it an arbiter of social justice. In foreign policy it was marked by aggressive actions of the United States to expand its role as a world power.

THE SEARCH FOR SOCIAL JUSTICE

For almost eight years the personality of Theodore Roosevelt gave a new meaning to the office of President of the United States. The significance of his influence lay in his unusual ability to arouse his fellow-countrymen to an awareness of their civic duties rather than in any measurable progress made under his leadership toward the ideal of social justice.

Presidential Leadership. The assassination of President McKinley by a crazed anarchist in the autumn of 1901 threw the conservative Republican leaders into a panic. They feared that the young and dynamic Vice-President, now elevated to the presidency, might put into effect his "progressive" ideas.

ROOSEVELT'S PROGRAM. The new President's first message to Congress, calculated to quiet the fears of his party associates, was nevertheless a blueprint of far-reaching reforms. He called for: (1) greater control of corporations by the federal government; (2) more authority for the Interstate Commerce Commission; (3) conservation of natural resources; (4) extension of the merit system in the civil service; (5) construction of an isthmian canal; and (6) a vigorous foreign policy. Implicit in all of his recommendations was his theory that the President should be the leader in the formulation of governmental policies.

THE COAL STRIKE (1902). In defining the government's relation to business enterprise, Roosevelt manifested a lively concern that there should be a "square deal" for all—capital, labor, and the public. This concern prompted his actions in the anthracite coal strike.

The Miners' Grievances. For many years the miners in the anthracite districts of eastern Pennsylvania, unable to effect a satisfactory organization to protect their interests, had been exploited by the mine operators. Their grievances included: (1) long hours and low wages; (2) the policy of compelling them to live in company houses and to trade at company stores; (3) the compulsion to produce 3,000 pounds to a "ton"; and (4) the refusal of the operators to recognize the union and collective bargaining. When the mine-owners refused to arbitrate, the miners went on strike (May 15, 1902), and the strike dragged on until autumn of that year.

The White House Conference. Waiving the question of his constitutional prerogative, President Roosevelt invited John Mitchell, president of the United Mine Workers, and the mineowners to confer with him. But the President's attempt to mediate failed completely, as the mineowners still refused to make any concessions.

The Strike Settlement. Roosevelt quietly exerted pressure in financial circles, and he also threatened to use federal troops to run the mines. He persuaded the operators to agree to his plan for an arbitral board to review the questions in dispute. The decision of this arbitral board granted a 10 per cent wage increase and a nine-hour day but did not recognize the union. It became the basis of industrial peace in the anthracite districts for fifteen years.

HANDLING THE TRUSTS. Although Roosevelt felt that governmental regulation of industry was preferable to any program of "smashing the trusts," he was determined to put teeth into the Sherman Antitrust Law, which had never been vigorously enforced.

The Northern Securities Case. The first gun in the fight against illegal combinations was fired when Attorney General P. C. Knox filed suit against the Northern Securities Company, a holding company which controlled (1) the Northern Pacific, (2) the Great Northern, and (3) the Chicago, Burlington and Quincy railroads. The President, who announced that the largest corporation, like the humblest citizen, would be compelled to obey the law, was pleased that the government won its case in the lower federal courts and that the Supreme Court upheld the decision (1904).

Federal Legislation. Congress failed to undertake a comprehensive modification of the Sherman Act, which Roosevelt urged, but it passed several measures designed to facilitate enforcement of the antitrust laws. (1) The Expedition Act gave precedence on the dockets of the federal courts to cases arising from the Sherman Act or the Interstate Commerce Act. (2) The Bureau of Corporations (in the Department of Commerce and Labor) was created and was empowered to conduct industrial investigations. (3) A special fund of $500,000 was appropriated for prosecutions of business combinations.

Federal Prosecutions. During Roosevelt's administrations the Department of Justice obtained twenty-five indictments and brought eighteen bills in equity against the trusts. The most important of the judicial decisions were: (1) the injunction forbidding the members of the Beef Trust to engage in certain practices designed to restrain competition (1905); (2) the suit that resulted in the dissolution of the Standard Oil Company of New Jersey, a holding company which had a monopoly of oil refining (1906–1911); the order dissolving the American Tobacco Company as an illegal combination (1907–1911). In the course of its decisions under the Sherman Antitrust Act, the Supreme Court formulated the "rule of reason": that only "unreasonable" combinations in restraint of trade were prohibited.

THE RAILROAD PROBLEM. Extension of the powers of the Interstate Commerce Commission, which had been crippled by judicial limitation of its functions, was Roosevelt's constant recommendation in connection with the regulation of the railroads.

The Elkins Act (1903). This act struck at the continuance of the practice of secret rebates which had been declared illegal in 1887 by the Interstate Commerce Act. The recipient, as well as the grantor, of the rebate, was made liable to prosecution, and the agent or official of the railroad was held liable for any deviation from regular published rates.

The Hepburn Act (1906). This piece of legislation fell short of conferring upon the Interstate Commerce Commission the absolute power to fix rates, but it represented a great advance toward government regulation of the railroads. The act (1) increased the membership of the Commission from five to seven; (2) extended its authority over express companies, pipelines, ferries, and terminals; (3) gave the Commission power to reduce unreasonable and discriminatory rates, subject to judicial review; (4) placed the burden of proof upon the carrier rather than the Commission in all legal disputes; (5) forbade the railroads to transport commodities in the production of which they were themselves interested; and (6) established a uniform system of accounting to be used by the common carriers. The Hepburn Act made the Commission an effective agency for the first time since its creation in 1887.

Judicial Decisions. After the passage of the Hepburn Act the federal courts showed an increasing disposition to strengthen the Commission. In 1910 the Supreme Court laid down the principle that the common carriers could expect protection from the courts only if they could prove "beyond any reasonable doubt" that their property was being confiscated. At the same time the judiciary refused to sanction extreme penalties imposed upon railroads or shippers found guilty of violating the law. In 1907 Judge K. M. Landis' decision imposing a fine of $29,240,000 on the Standard Oil Company of Indiana for accepting railroad rebates was set aside by the higher courts.

The Mann-Elkins Act (1910). In 1910 the progressives in Congress corrected certain defects in the Hepburn Act. The Mann-Elkins Bill, as finally signed by President Taft, (1) extended the Commission's authority to include telephone, telegraph, cable, and wireless companies; (2) empowered the Commission to institute proceedings on its own responsibility against carriers who violated the law; (3) authorized the Commission to suspend all new rates until it was satisfied of their reasonableness; and (4) created a new Commerce Court (abolished in 1913) to expedite the handling of rate cases.

The Physical Valuation Act (1913). The progressive Republicans, under the leadership of Senator La Follette, finally persuaded Congress to order the Interstate Commerce Commission to make a study of the physical valuation of the railroads in order to provide a basis for fixing rates which would represent a *reasonable return on actual investment.* The Commission's study of valuation was not completed until 1921.

CONSERVATION. No part of Roosevelt's program was carried forward more energetically or more successfully than his campaign for the conservation of natural resources.

Exposing National Waste. Roosevelt's outstanding achievement in the conservation movement was the widespread public interest which he aroused by his efforts to stop the squandering of the natural resources. The generosity of the government in transferring the public domain to private ownership had resulted in wasteful exploitation of America's riches of lumber, coal, petroleum, natural gas, and minerals. Roosevelt, aided by such associates as Gifford Pinchot and James R. Garfield, undertook to educate the electorate and thus to secure legislative action.

Irrigation. The Newlands Act (1902), recommended by Roosevelt, appropriated most of the money received from the sale of public lands in the West and Southwest for the construction of irrigation projects. By 1907 twenty-eight projects in fourteen states were under way.

National Parks and Forests. Roosevelt was not the originator of the campaign for national parks, but he gave vigorous support to those who were trying to preserve regions of great natural beauty and to prevent the forests from being destroyed. He set aside 148,000,000 acres as timber reserves and withdrew from sale all public lands containing minerals until such time as Congress might safeguard the resources by proper forms of lease.

Internal Waterways. Conservation included also the utilization of the system of internal waterways in order to facilitate transportation, to promote irrigation projects, and to develop water-power sites. The Internal Waterways Commission, appointed by Roosevelt, suggested that the President summon a conference of the governors of all the states to discuss the fundamental questions relating to conservation.

National Conservation Commission (1908). The result of the White House Conference of 1908 was the appointment by Roosevelt of a National Conservation Commission, with Gifford Pinchot as chairman, and the creation of thirty-six state boards which cooperated with the national body.

The "Muckrakers." A group of enthusiastic popular writers, whom Roosevelt named the "Muckrakers" because of their preoccupation with scandalous conditions in business and politics, exerted a powerful influence in stirring public opinion to the point of action. The President's crusade for social justice was aided by the work of such journalists and novelists as Upton Sinclair (*The Jungle*), Ida Tarbell (*History of the Standard Oil Company*), Lincoln Steffens (*The Shame of the Cities*), Ray Stannard Baker ("The Railroads on Trial"), and Frank Norris (*The Octopus*), even if the President did not always recognize his indebtedness. One can trace to the "Muckrakers" and their efforts such federal legislation as the Meat Inspection Act and the Pure Food and Drug Act (1906). They were also largely responsible for the government's suit against the Beef Trust and the proceedings against the subsidiaries of the American Sugar Refining Company for defrauding the government of customs duties.

GOVERNMENT BY THE PEOPLE

Reformers of the Roosevelt era also endeavored to make government organization and processes more democratic and to enact legislation that would directly benefit the people.

Direct Government. The accusation that American legislative bodies were unrepresentative and dominated by privileged interests led to a demand that the popular will be translated more directly into governmental action.

THE INITIATIVE AND REFERENDUM. These devices, first adopted by South Dakota in 1898, permit a certain percentage of the electorate to initiate by petition measures which the state legislature or the people may vote upon. Likewise, a certain percentage of the electorate may have a law, which has passed the legislature, referred to the voters for acceptance or rejection. Twenty-two states have at various times tested the initiative and referendum.

THE RECALL. This plan to make public officials more responsive to public opinion, first used in Los Angeles in 1903, permits the voters to remove an official from office before the expiration of the regular term for which he has been elected or appointed. Its use in connection with the recall of judges, as provided in Arizona's constitution, aroused bitter controversy, but there have been few examples of summary removal.

DIRECT PRIMARIES. The system of direct primaries, introduced in Wisconsin by Robert M. La Follette in 1903, represents an attempt to give the voters a chance to name candidates, as well as to choose between candidates, for public office. By 1933 some form of the direct primary was used in all but six of the states. But the promises of the reformers that the power of the political boss would be broken and that the character of candidates for public office would be improved were overoptimistic.

POPULAR ELECTION OF SENATORS. The champions of direct government were particularly insistent in their demand for popular election of United States senators. Charging that election by the state legislatures resulted in a Senate controlled by an alliance between predatory wealth and unscrupulous politicians, they persuaded state after state to permit the voters to express a senatorial preference at the polls which the legislature was bound to accept. At the same time the reformers worked hard to secure a constitutional amendment. Not until 1911 did the Senate finally capitulate and join the House in passing a resolution (which was ratified by three-fourths of the states in 1913 and became the Seventeenth Amendment) providing for direct popular election of the upper house of Congress.

Municipal Reforms. Probably no part of the program of the political progressives was more valuable than their attack upon the structure and administration of city government.

COMMISSION PLAN. The notorious failure of municipal government in the United States was attributed in part to the anachronistic mayor-and-council system. In 1900 Galveston, Texas, experimented with a new form of government—the commission plan. All municipal functions were vested in a small commission—usually five— each commissioner being responsible for the management of a department. By 1914 more than four hundred of the smaller cities of the country had tried the plan, some with such indifferent results that they abandoned it.

THE CITY MANAGER. In 1914 Dayton, Ohio, introduced the city-manager type of municipal organization, in which the politically responsible commission appoints a business manager to run the city as if it were a going business concern. As in the case of the commission plan, the results have not been uniformly satisfactory. Both new types, however, have done much to arouse the electorate to an appreciation of the problems of municipal government.

Woman-Suffrage Movement. The Progressive era was marked by a notable extension of the suffrage, as state followed state in granting the ballot to women.

STATE ACTION. The pioneer advocates of women's rights in the decade of the forties had started a suffrage movement which began to bear fruit after the Civil War. The discussion of the civil and political status of the Negro; the equalitarian philosophy of the Far Western frontier; the entrance of women into factories, trades, and professions; and the opening of the doors of institutions of higher learning to women—all gave impetus to the campaign for sex equality and for woman suffrage. Wyoming, the first suffrage state, was admitted to the Union in 1890; by 1912 Colorado, Utah, Idaho, Washington, Kansas, Arizona, California, and Oregon had granted the ballot to women.

THE NINETEENTH AMENDMENT (1920). Many of the feminists believed that an amendment to the Constitution was the royal road to equal political privileges with men. Susan B. Anthony proposed such an amendment as early as 1869; nine years later it was introduced in Congress. There it languished for forty-one years, until 1919, when Congress passed the amendment and referred it to the states. Ratification came in August, 1920, in time to permit the women of the nation to vote in the presidential election of that year. This result was a testimonial to the effective work of such leaders as Susan B. Anthony, Elizabeth Cady Stanton, Ann Howard Shaw, and Carrie Chapman Catt.

State and Municipal Welfare Action. The progressives were responsible for a good deal of state welfare legislation passed during this period. A number of states enacted laws regulating wages, hours, and working conditions; restricting the labor of women and children; providing for workmen's compensation; granting public aid to mothers with dependent children and the needy aged; and setting safety and health standards for industry. Progressive reforms in the cities included the establishment of settlement houses, slum clearance, and recreation facilities.

The Challenge of Socialism. Although the history of Socialism in the United States dates from the formation of Marx's First International in 1864, the Socialists attracted little attention until the opening years of the present century.

SOCIALIST PARTY OF AMERICA (1901). The remnants of the Socialist Labor party, established in 1876, and the following of Eugene V. Debs in the Social Democratic party (1897) united to form the Socialist party. The party set for its ultimate goal the Marxian principle of public ownership and control of the means of production and distribution. It also advocated such preliminary steps as reduction of the hours of labor, unemployment insurance, labor codes, government ownership of railroads, telegraph and telephone companies, and other public utilities, adoption of the initiative, referendum, recall, and proportional representation. It denounced the programs of the progressive as futile "bourgeois tinkering." The Socialist vote in presidential elections was most significant in 1912, when Debs polled 897,011 votes. In 1920, with woman suffrage, he secured

919,799 votes; but after 1928 (though the party was under the able leadership of Norman Thomas), its strength declined.

THE I.W.W. (1905). The Industrial Workers of the World (I.W.W.) was sponsored by an extremist faction among the Socialists and leaders of the revolutionary labor unions. It insisted that the "workers of the world, organized as a class, take possession of the earth and the machinery of production and abolish the wage system." Spurning the middle-class reformers and moderate Socialists alike, the I.W.W. championed direct action—the mass strike, sabotage, and violence. Its appeal was chiefly to foreign-born migratory laborers in the mines, lumber camps, and harvest fields of the Far West. Various states proceeded against it, and the federal government in 1918 imprisoned its most influential leaders for opposition to the war. By 1925 the membership, which never numbered more than 60,000, had disintegrated.

THE DAY OF THE PROGRESSIVES

Within both political parties, but particularly among the Republicans, those who championed political and economic reforms were known as "progressives." Many of them, regardless of party, looked to Theodore Roosevelt for inspiration.

Republican Politics. Popular support of Roosevelt's policies enabled him to wield unusual political power throughout his term of office.

THE ELECTION OF 1904. Having served three and one-half years of McKinley's term, Roosevelt was eager for an election in his own right. For a time he feared that the reactionary Republicans would refuse him the nomination and would name Mark Hanna. But Hanna's death in the spring of 1904 removed all possibility of opposition, and Roosevelt was nominated by acclamation at the Republican convention. The Democrats, turning aside from the "radicalism" of Bryan and ignoring the claims of William Randolph Hearst, selected a conservative New York jurist, Alton B. Parker, as their standard-bearer. The issue of the campaign was really the policies of Theodore Roosevelt. The President was re-elected by an electoral vote of 336 to 140 for Parker. He carried every state outside the Solid South.

CHOOSING ROOSEVELT'S SUCCESSOR. At the end of his second term Roosevelt could have been nominated again had he permitted his friends to carry out their plans. Instead, he directed all his political power toward the selection of William H. Taft, Secretary of War, as his successor. The convention of 1908 was a Roosevelt convention. The delegates were wildly enthusiastic over the President, and at his behest nominated Taft and adopted a platform which had been written at the White House. Bryan, once more dominant in Democratic circles, was unable to make any headway in the campaign against Roosevelt's trusted lieutenant. Indeed, there was much in the Republican platform which met with the approval of the Democratic leader. Bryan's electoral vote of 162 to 321 for Taft indicated, however, that the Nebraskan had regained some of the ground lost by Parker four years earlier.

Taft and the Reformers. Less dynamic than Roosevelt, and much more conservative in temperament, President Taft nevertheless sympathized with the political reformers of his day and approved of many of their objectives. But he frequently questioned their methods and criticized the haste with which they tried to put their progressive ideas into effect.

Roosevelt's Successor. Taft's task was twofold: (1) to carry forward in his own right the policies which his predecessor had so effectively dramatized; and (2) to reconcile the progressives (insurgents) and the conservatives (standpatters) within the Republican party. The President's legal training and judicial temperament made it impossible for him to assume the role which Roosevelt had played successfully in the reform movement. His official advisers, with two exceptions, were lawyers, who emphasized the legal limitations on the presidential prerogative and the difficulties of the progressive program. As a result, Taft seemed to be inclined to restrain the zealous reformers rather than to convert the conservatives to the cause of political reform.

Payne-Aldrich Tariff (1909). The first significant test of Taft's leadership came with the attempt to revise the tariff in the special session of 1909.

Protests against Protection. The protective duties of the Dingley Tariff, which had seemed reasonable in 1897 to the Republican party, became the object of vigorous attack as the prices of manufactured goods advanced more rapidly than the wages of labor. In 1907 Roosevelt admitted that the tariff schedules needed revision, and the following year Taft promised that he would interpret the Republican platform on the tariff to mean downward revision of rates.

Congressional Tariff-Making. Neither the Payne Bill, as it passed the House, nor the completed Payne-Aldrich Bill, with the Senate amendments, was a redemption of the party pledge. The measure was fought unsuccessfully by the Republican insurgents, ably led by La Follette, Dolliver, Bristow, and Beveridge. The schedules were not altered in any important particular; the levels of the Dingley Tariff were generally maintained or raised.

Taft's Attitude. The President, eager to preserve party harmony, tried to persuade the insurgents to accept the Payne-Aldrich Bill as a party measure. His assertion that the bill was "the best tariff ever passed by the Republican party" put the progressives immediately on their guard against the President.

BALLINGER-PINCHOT CONTROVERSY. This quarrel over the conservation program convinced many of Roosevelt's friends that Taft was not willing to continue the policies initiated by his predecessor.

Ballinger's Plans. The ardent supporters of conservation were apprehensive over the plans of Richard A. Ballinger, whom Taft had promoted from Superintendent of the General Land Office to Secretary of the Interior. The new Secretary concluded that Roosevelt had exceeded his legal powers in reserving certain public lands, and he opened them once more to private leasing. In addition he restored to private operation water-power sites in Wyoming and Montana, and he approved the so-called Cunningham claims of the Guggenheim-Morgan syndicate to valuable coal lands in Alaska. For these acts he was severely criticized in published articles by L. R. Glavis of the Public Land Office and Gifford Pinchot, Chief Forester.

Pinchot's Dismissal. Taft, distressed by the publicity attending this quarrel in administration circles, dismissed Glavis immediately and removed Pinchot after the forestry official carried his charges to Congress. Pinchot was quick to rally Roosevelt's friends and persuade them that Taft was a traitor to the former President's conception of conservation. The accusation was unjust to Taft, but he had to bear the brunt of the public antagonism to Ballinger, who was permitted to resign in 1911.

CONGRESSIONAL INSURGENTS. Although Taft was not directly involved in the warfare between conservatives and progressives in Congress, the revolt of the Republican insurgents against Speaker Cannon's rule clearly indicated the President's inability to control the party.

"Cannonism." As Speaker of the House of Representatives, Joseph

G. Cannon exercised enormous power in connection with the legislative process: (1) he controlled the Committee on Rules, which determined the routine procedure of the House; (2) he appointed all committees and designated their chairmen; and (3) he had the power to recognize members who desired to speak from the floor and therefore could guide the course of debate. Cannon wielded these considerable powers in such fashion as to aid the conservatives and embarrass the progressives.

The Revolt of 1910. The insurgent Republicans rose in revolt against Cannon's dictatorial tactics in the spring of 1910. Aided by the Democratic minority, they passed a resolution (introduced by George W. Norris, of Nebraska) which deprived the Speaker of his control over the Rules Committee. The following year the Democrats, now in the majority, denied the Speaker the right to appoint standing committees, thus establishing "representative government" in the House.

CANADIAN RECIPROCITY. The antagonism to President Taft on the part of the progressives, notably the Western insurgents, was accentuated by his ill-fated plan for reciprocity with Canada.

Agreement of 1911. A reciprocity agreement was negotiated with Canada which provided for (1) free trade in primary foodstuffs, such as grain, vegetables, and eggs; (2) mutual reduction of tariff duties on secondary food products, like flour and meats; and (3) a slight decrease in the duties on manufactured goods. Despite the bitter opposition of the Western agrarian interests, who feared the competition of Canadian produce, the President succeeded in persuading Congress to approve the reciprocity agreement.

Canada's Reaction. Taft's victory was fruitless, for the reciprocity issues caused a dissolution of the Canadian Parliament and the overwhelming defeat of Sir Wilfred Laurier, who had negotiated the agreement. Many Canadians interpreted Taft's interest in reciprocity as the first move in an American policy to bring Canada within the political and economic control of the United States.

LEGISLATIVE ACHIEVEMENTS. The record of the Taft administration for progressive measures and policies compares favorably with that of the Roosevelt administration. In listing the achievements of Taft's four years in office his friends included: (1) the Mann-Elkins Act (see p. 106); (2) the eight-hour day for workers on government contracts; (3) the establishment of the postal savings system and the parcel post; (4) the creation of a separate Department of Labor

(1913); (5) the passage of the Sixteenth and Seventeenth Amendments to the Constitution; (6) the extension of the merit system to new branches of the civil service; (7) the vigorous prosecution of illegal combinations in restraint of trade; and (8) legislation reserving additional public land from private exploitation.

The Election of 1912. From the standpoint of party politics the election of 1912 was of unusual significance; from the standpoint of the crusade for social justice it was confusing and indecisive.

THE REPUBLICAN SCHISM. More than a year before the presidential election the insurgent Republicans tried to mobilize the progressive sentiment of the country.

Progressive Republican League. This organization, sponsored by several Republican senators in January, 1911, announced the political program of Progressivism: (1) direct election of United States senators; (2) direct primaries; (3) direct election of delegates to national nominating conventions; (4) state adoption of the initiative, referendum, and recall; and (5) a national corrupt-practices act.

Robert M. La Follette. At first the League merely advocated progressive principles, but in October it indicated that Robert M. La Follette of Wisconsin was its candidate for the Republican nomination against President Taft. La Follette, who had won national fame by his successful battle against the power of the great corporations in his own state, promptly started a vigorous campaign to arouse the voters from their lethargy.

Roosevelt's Attitude. Although former President Roosevelt had been supporting the insurgent Republican ever since his return from Africa in 1910, he refused to join the Progressive Republican League or to support La Follette. After weeks of indecision he agreed to become a candidate for the Republican nomination. Then came an unseemly scramble for delegates between Taft and Roosevelt, with La Follette trying to salvage something from the wreck of his high hopes.

TAFT'S NOMINATION. Wherever the Republican delegates were chosen by state conventions or were hand-picked by the "bosses," President Taft had the advantage, but in those states which permitted the voters to express their preference for the nominee, Roosevelt was clearly the choice. The national convention was controlled by the administration forces and proceeded amidst great confusion to grant Taft another nomination.

THE FORMATION OF THE PROGRESSIVE PARTY. Roosevelt charged that the nomination had been "stolen" from him by irregular tactics. With evangelical fervor his followers undertook the task of forming a new party. On August 5, 1912, the Progressive party held its first convention in Chicago, where two months earlier its hero had been rejected by the Republicans. Roosevelt was nominated by acclamation, while Hiram Johnson of California was named for the vice-presidency. The schism in the Republican ranks was complete.

NOMINATION OF WOODROW WILSON. The Democrats meanwhile had also been engaged in a spirited contest between the conservative and liberal forces within the party.

The Democratic Convention. As the delegates assembled at Baltimore, it was evident that no candidate for the nomination could control the convention. Champ Clark, Speaker of the House, had both conservative and liberal delegates in his following. The extreme conservatives were kindly disposed toward Governor Judson Harmon of Ohio and Representative Oscar Underwood of Alabama. The liberals had rallied behind Governor Woodrow Wilson of New Jersey, who described himself as a "progressive with the brakes on."

The Influence of Bryan. Speaker Clark would probably have been nominated had it not been for the influence of William Jennings Bryan. Although one of the delegates instructed to vote for Clark, Bryan dramatically denounced the "sinister influences" supporting Clark and on the fourteenth ballot switched to Woodrow Wilson, who was finally nominated on the forty-sixth ballot.

THREE PLATFORMS. The Progressives and Democratic platforms frankly invited the support of those who were willing to enlist in the warfare against political and economic privilege. Even the Republican pronouncement could not be regarded as ultraconservative. Roosevelt's "New Nationalism," which demanded for governmental regulation of economic activity, was not really distasteful to Wilson, though he presented his "New Freedom" in the lofty phrases of economic liberalism. Both candidates were eager to offer some program to meet the social unrest of the times, but Taft seemed anxious to avoid recognition of popular discontent.

DEMOCRATIC VICTORY. The overwhelming nature of the Democratic victory in November was largely due to the disruption of the Republican party. Roosevelt's popular following was amazing, for he had no regular organization and his most ardent supporters were amateurs in politics. He carried six states with 88 electoral votes.

Taft secured only the eight votes of Utah and Vermont; the remaining 435 went to Wilson. The House and Senate were Democratic by wide margins.

AN AGGRESSIVE FOREIGN POLICY

Roosevelt's conspicuous and aggressive activity in the conduct of foreign relations increased the influence and prestige of the United States as a world power.

In the Caribbean. The growing interests of the United States in the Caribbean, tremendously stimulated by the acquisition of the Panama Canal Zone, caused the Roosevelt administration to develop a theory of responsibility for the preservation of order in that area.

INTERPRETING THE MONROE DOCTRINE. Under Roosevelt's direction, the Monroe Doctrine was reinterpreted to justify United States intervention in Latin-American affairs.

The Venezuelan Incident (1902). Great Britain and Germany, endeavoring to collect debts owed to their citizens by the government of Venezuela, established a blockade of Venezuelan ports. Roosevelt feared that the debt question might be made the pretext for a violation of the Monroe Doctrine. His diplomatic pressure behind the scenes, particularly against Germany, probably helped both nations to decide to grant Venezuela's plea for arbitration. Mixed commissions reviewed the claims against the South American republic and Venezuela agreed in 1903 to devote 30 per cent of its customs receipts to pay the valid claims.

The Drago Doctrine. The Venezuelan incident caused Luis Drago, Argentine minister for foreign affairs, to announce the doctrine that no state had a right to make the financial claims of its citizens against another state the pretext for military intervention. The American State Department gave its support to the principles of the Drago Doctrine, and at the Second Hague Conference (1907) the United States delegation secured the adoption of a resolution that no nation should resort to armed force to recover the debts due its citizens "unless the debtor nation refused arbitration, or, having accepted arbitration, failed to submit to the award."

The Roosevelt Corollary. When France, Italy, and Belgium threatened in 1904 to use force in collecting debts owed their citizens by the Dominican Republic, Roosevelt announced that "chronic wrong-doing, or an impotence which results in a general loosening of the ties of civilized society, may in America" compel the United States to exercise "an international police power." Under this corollary of the Monroe Doctrine the administration negotiated a treaty with the Dominican Republic providing for control of the collection of the Dominican customs by the United States. When the Senate refused to ratify the treaty, Roosevelt put the receivership into effect by executive order. This manifestation of "police power" was widely criticized in the United States and aroused grave apprehension throughout Latin America.

BUILDING THE PANAMA CANAL. The results of the Spanish-American War dramatically emphasized the desirability of a canal between the Atlantic and the Pacific under the control of the United States.

Hay-Pauncefote Treaty (1901). By the Clayton-Bulwer Treaty (1850) the United States had agreed that any isthmian canal should be under the joint guarantee of Great Britain and the United States. The abrogation of this agreement was secured by Secretary of State Hay in the Hay-Pauncefote Treaty, which provided that America might build the canal and have full control and policing of it if its use was accorded to all nations on equal terms.

Hay-Herrán Treaty (1903). Meanwhile, Congress had decided to build the canal across Panama, rather than across Nicaragua, and had offered the New Panama Canal Company $40,000,000 for the rights of the old French company which had tried to construct a canal during the eighties. The Hay-Herrán Treaty with Colombia was signed, whereby Colombia granted the United States a ninety-nine-year lease over a zone ten miles wide in the province of Panama in return for $10,000,000 in cash and an annual rental of $250,000 beginning nine years after the agreement was ratified. The Colombian Senate, much to the disgust of President Roosevelt, refused to ratify the treaty, probably hoping to get better terms.

Revolution in Panama. Colombia's rejection of the Hay-Herrán Treaty not only irritated the United States government, but it alarmed those who were interested in the New Panama Canal Company and it aroused patriotic Panamanians who feared the canal would be built in Nicaragua. In the summer of 1903, therefore, it was no surprise to the American government when revolution was fomented in Panama. The revolutionists were successful because the United States, basing its action on a treaty of 1846 with Colombia, maintained "free and uninterrupted transit" across the isthmus.

Actually, this action prevented the Colombian government from moving the necessary troops to quell the revolt.

Hay-Bunau-Varilla Treaty (1903). Two weeks after the revolution the United States concluded a treaty with the Republic of Panama, which Roosevelt had already recognized. The new agreement granted to the United States in perpetuity the use of a canal zone ten miles wide; transferred to its government the properties of the New Panama Canal Company and the Panama Railroad Company; awarded Panama $10,000,000 and an annuity of $250,000 for its concessions. In 1921 the United States quieted Colombian complaints by a treaty in which it agreed to pay the South American republic $25,000,000.

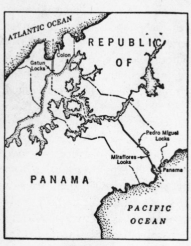

Canal Zone

The Completion of the Canal. Both the Roosevelt and Taft administrations gave constant support to those building the Panama Canal. Construction, after several false starts, went forward rapidly under Col. G. W. Goethals, while Col. W. C. Gorgas conquered sanitation difficulties in the Canal Zone. The first steamer passed through the Canal in August, 1914.

In the Far East. Roosevelt and Taft supported and extended John Hay's vigorous assertion of American interests in the Far East, though they used other methods than the writing of diplomatic notes.

THE RUSSO-JAPANESE WAR. At the outbreak of the Russo-Japanese War (1904), Roosevelt persuaded both powers to recognize the neutrality of Chinese territory outside of Manchuria, and he warned France and Germany that if either power aided the Russians the United States would side with Japan.

THE TREATY OF PORTSMOUTH (1905). Having succeeded in limiting the extent of the war, President Roosevelt intervened to bring it to an end. At his suggestion, representatives of Japan and Russia met at Portsmouth, New Hampshire, and finally signed a treaty terminating hostilities. Roosevelt managed to guide the deliberations of the wrangling delegates and was awarded the Nobel peace prize for his efforts.

RESTRAINING JAPAN. The easy victory of Japan convinced many Americans that the Japanese were a threat to the interests of the United States in the whole Pacific area.

Secret Japanese-American Agreement (1905). By a secret understanding (the Taft-Katsura Memorandum), Japan recognized the sovereignty of the United States in the Philippines, while the United States recognized Japan's control of Korea. The two nations pledged themselves to maintain peaceful conditions in the Far East.

Other Executive Agreements with Japan. Within a year Japanese resentment flared over California's demand that all Japanese immigration be forbidden by Congress and the action of the San Francisco Board of Education in segregating all Oriental students in special schools. Elihu Root, Roosevelt's Secretary of State, found a formula of "Gentlemen's Agreement," in which Japan promised to restrict the emigration of laborers to the United States and the California school officials modified their rulings concerning Japanese pupils. By the Root-Takahira Agreement (1908) both countries agreed to uphold existing territorial arrangements, to respect the political integrity of China, and to maintain the open-door principle.

DOLLAR DIPLOMACY. Roosevelt relied on a vigorous diplomatic policy—"speak softly and carry a big stick"—but Taft was inclined to use economic means to reach diplomatic objectives. Both critics and supporters of the Taft administration called this policy "dollar diplomacy."

The Chinese Consortium. In 1909 Taft's Secretary of State, P. C. Knox, persuaded American financiers to join with British, French, and German bankers in a consortium to construct the Hukuang Railroad in China. Three years later President Taft gave his approval to a more pretentious undertaking—a loan to the Chinese Republic in which American bankers were invited to participate.

The Meaning of Economic Imperialism. The investment of American capital abroad, which so many called "dollar diplomacy," was described by President Taft as merely an effort "directed to the increase of American trade." He sincerely hoped that American dollars would help American diplomats maintain the balance of power in the Orient, thus perpetuating such American policies as the open door and the preservation of the territorial integrity of China. Prior to the First World War, the growth of American foreign investments seemed to follow the pattern of European economic imperialism, but it was fundamentally due to an interest in overseas trade and rarely led to the attempt to impose political control over colonial possessions.

Toward World Peace. Optimistic advocates of international conciliation believed that important progress toward world peace had been made during the first decade of the twentieth century.

ARBITRATION TREATIES. In January, 1905, Roosevelt presented to the Senate identical arbitration treaties with seven European nations. The Senate amended them in a manner which the President deemed undesirable, but two years later Secretary of State Elihu Root, who had succeeded John Hay, had similar treaties ratified, with requirements for Senate advice and consent. In 1911 Secretary of State Knox, negotiated treaties with Great Britain and France providing for arbitration of any matters in dispute between the United States and these nations, but the Senate refused to ratify the treaties.

ALGECIRAS CONFERENCE (1906). The Franco-German conflict over the Moroccan crisis of 1905 was so ominous that Roosevelt exerted diplomatic pressure at both Paris and Berlin to secure agreement to the plan for an international conference. The subsequent meeting at Algeciras revealed the powerful influence of the United States as represented in the person of Henry White. The formula finally accepted by the conference for the international regulation of police, banking, and trade in Morocco did not differ materially from the proposals of Secretary Root.

SECOND HAGUE PEACE CONFERENCE (1907). Roosevelt hoped that the Second Hague Peace Conference would take steps toward disarmament. He was disappointed in the results, however, for the delegates could not agree on specific proposals and adjourned after suggesting that a conference meet in London in 1908 to draw up an international code for naval warfare.

FINANCING THE PEACE MOVEMENT. The so-called "peace movement" reached impressive proportions in the decade prior to the outbreak of the First World War, as American philanthropists and public officials joined forces to arouse public opinion to the dangers of war in the new industrial age.

World Peace Foundation. In 1910 Edwin Ginn, a Boston publisher, endowed the World Peace Foundation with funds for research and publicity in the cause of international conciliation.

Andrew Carnegie's Contributions. In various ways, Andrew Carnegie used his great wealth to promote public understanding of the evils of war and the means by which peace might be achieved. He established in 1911 the Carnegie Endowment for International Peace, and he provided the funds to erect stately public buildings to house the activities of various peace organizations. Among these were the Peace Palace at the Hague, and the Pan-American Union in Washington.

THE LAKE MOHONK CONFERENCES. The most eloquent arguments for a world peace program and for a stable world order under international law were voiced in the annual conferences held at Lake Mohonk, New York, in which President Taft and some of his associates were interested. The high hopes of these enthusiasts were wrecked by the outbreak of war in 1914.

REVIEW QUESTIONS

1. What were the elements of strength in President Theodore Roosevelt's leadership of the movement for political and social reforms?
2. How would the political reforms advocated by the "progressives" have made the government of the United States more responsive to the popular will?
3. Why was Theodore Roosevelt called "the trust-buster"? Did he deserve the nickname?
4. In what respects did Taft's attitude toward conservation of natural resources differ from that of Theodore Roosevelt?
5. How do you explain the growth of "insurgency" within the Republican ranks during Taft's administration?
6. Discuss the wisdom of Theodore Roosevelt's action in forming the Progressive party in 1912.
7. Compare the Republican, Democratic, and Progressive platforms on such issues as (a) the trust problem, (b) the protective tariff, (c) the use of injunctions in labor disputes.
8. Was Theodore Roosevelt justified in his handling of the negotiations with Colombia and Panama which finally enabled the United States to build the Panama Canal?
9. What were the objectives of Roosevelt and Taft in their policies relating to the nations of the Far East?
10. How did Roosevelt justify his "corollary" to the Monroe Doctrine?

CHAPTER IX

WILSONIAN LIBERALISM

Woodrow Wilson had a strong sense of right and wrong which he applied to the study of political science and of international relations. In domestic affairs his administration accomplished a number of reforms relating to the tariff, banking, trusts, agriculture, and labor. In foreign policy, he attempted to modify United States imperialism and to support the development of democracy in other countries.

THE NEW FREEDOM

Wilson was determined to curb any groups or individuals who enjoyed special political or economic privileges and to bring to his countrymen much-needed reforms.

Presidential Leadership. The new President regarded his high office as a means of securing the legislation that would be needed to make government responsive to the will of the people.

THE INAUGURAL ADDRESS. After taking the oath of office, he delivered a stirring inaugural address, summoning "all honest men, all patriotic, all forward-looking men" to join him in service to the nation. In this address, he itemized "things that ought to be altered," including the tariff, banking and currency, the industrial system, and agricultural policies. His seriousness was reflected in his decision not to hold the traditional Inaugural Ball.

POWERFUL COLONEL HOUSE. A mild-mannered and shrewd Texan, Colonel Edward House, became the President's most influential adviser. Wilson admired him for his rare combination of idealism and administrative ability and turned to him constantly for confidential counsel.

A SYMPATHETIC CABINET. The choice of members of his cabinet revealed to Wilson some of the difficulties in his path: (1) his contacts with leaders of his own party were limited; (2) he found it difficult to secure men trained in public office, for his party had long been out of power; (3) there were political debts which had to be paid; (4) the strength of the Democrats in the South tended to give that section undue influence in his administration. With the exceptions of W. J. Bryan (State), W. G. McAdoo (Treasury), and F. K. Lane (Interior), the cabinet appointees were not well known. Most of them, however, worked well under the President's forceful leadership.

Reducing Tariff Schedules. Tariff revision, banking reform, and trust regulation were three cardinal points in Wilson's attack on the "invisible government" which he felt dominated the country.

FIRM PRESIDENTIAL GUIDANCE. Unlike Taft, Wilson constantly exerted pressure upon Congress, while the new tariff act was being framed, in order to secure the sort of schedules which he desired. When it seemed possible that the lobbyists would be able to block some of the reductions in rates, the President appealed directly to the country to aid him in obtaining satisfactory duties.

UNDERWOOD-SIMMONS TARIFF (1913). The completed act contained features which contrasted sharply with the protective principles of Republican tariff laws. Its distinctive characteristics were: (1) an enlarged free list, which contained foodstuffs and other necessities of primary importance in the average citizen's living costs; (2) the reduction of duties on articles which no longer required protection against foreign competition; (3) increased rates on luxuries; (4) use of ad valorem rather than specific duties; (5) imposition of a graduated income tax (authorized by the Sixteenth Amendment) to compensate for any loss in revenue which might result from decrease in customs. Before the effect of the measure either upon domestic and foreign trade or upon governmental finances could be determined, the First World War had ushered in an abnormal era.

Creating a Banking System. Wilson argued forcefully for a banking system capable of supplying currency that would expand and contract in amount according to the needs of business.

FINANCIAL BACKGROUND. The Federal Reserve Act of 1913 was really the culmination of long discussion of the defects of the existing national banks.

Money Panic of 1907. This sharp, but brief, crisis in the New York financial district emphasized the inelasticity of the currency and the rigid regulations concerning bank reserve funds. As temporary relief, Congress passed the Aldrich-Vreeland Act (1908), permitting the Treasury Department to issue emergency currency to be loaned to banks in times of stress.

The "Money Trust." At the time the Aldrich Commission filed its report a special committee of the House, under the chairmanship of Representative Pujo of Louisiana, was investigating the structure of private control of money and credit. Its conclusions, published early in 1913, pointed toward the existence of a "money trust," dominated by a few of the great banking houses in New York City and having its ramifications throughout the transportation, industrial, and commercial establishments of the nation. This reputed concentration of credit resources in the hands of a few gave point to the demand for monetary and banking reform.

THE FEDERAL RESERVE ACT. Rejecting the idea of a central bank, President Wilson participated actively in the discussions which resulted in the framing of the Federal Reserve Act, and in the legislative maneuvering which secured its enactment. The act provided for: (1) the appointment of a Federal Reserve Board to supervise the national banking system; (2) the establishment of Federal Reserve Banks in twelve regions into which the country was divided; (3) the pooling of bank reserves in these regional banks; (4) the issuance by the reserve banks of federal reserve notes, based upon commercial paper and agricultural credits sent in by local banks which had become members of the new system; and (5) the elimination of intersectional transfers of currency and the reduction of collection charges through a great clearing system. Despite numerous defects which became apparent as the act was put into effect, there was abundant evidence that the Federal Reserve System gave the country a more elastic currency, greater flexibility in bank reserves, and more adequate credit facilities than it had ever before enjoyed.

Curbing the Trusts. Having laid down the proposition that "private monopoly is indefensible and intolerable," Wilson urged Congress to undertake the clarification and elaboration of the Sherman Antitrust Law. Somewhat grudgingly, Congress passed two measures.

FEDERAL TRADE COMMISSION. The Bureau of Corporations was replaced by a bipartisan commission of five members which was empowered to promote equitable trade practices between competitive enterprises. The Commission was authorized: (1) to conduct investigations whenever unfair methods of competition in commerce came to its attention; (2) to issue orders against such trade practices as it considered unfair; (3) to apply for judicial injunctions to enforce its orders; and (4) to require annual and special reports from corporations subject to the act. The Commission's findings as to the facts were regarded as final in all judicial proceedings which arose out of its investigations.

CLAYTON ANTITRUST ACT. Whereas the Federal Trade Commission's work was largely preventive, the purpose of the Clayton Act was punitive. Its numerous provisions fell into several categories: (1) the enumeration of unlawful methods of business competition; (2) the prohibition of interlocking directorates in certain banking institutions and concerns engaged in interstate commerce; (3) the listing of various means of securing relief from illegal trade practices; and (4) the labor clause, which exempted labor unions and agricultural associations from the antitrust laws, prohibited the use of injunctions, except in certain instances, in labor disputes, and provided that strikes, boycotts, and peaceful picketing were not violations of the federal laws.

Aiding Agriculture. Three attempts were made by the Wilson administration to meet the needs of the farmers.

SHORT-TERM CREDITS. Provisions in the Federal Reserve Act permitted national banks to loan money on farm mortgages and authorized the rediscount of agricultural paper which was payable within six months. Neither of these provisions actually met the farmer's demand for long-term credits.

SMITH-LEVER ACT (1914). This act granted federal funds to the states for farm extension work, under the joint supervision of the Department of Agriculture and state agricultural colleges.

FEDERAL FARM LOAN ACT (1916). This measure created twelve Federal Land Banks which were empowered to make loans at reasonable rates to co-operative farm loan associations composed solely of farmers wishing to borrow on long-term farm mortgages.

Protecting Labor's Interests. During Wilson's administration the conservative leaders of American labor exercised a political influence which was reflected in several important pieces of legislation. In addition to the features of the Clayton Act designed to protect union labor, the following acts should be noted: (1) the La Follette Seamen's Act (1915), prescribing the minimum wages, food, and accommodation to be accorded seamen employed on ships under American registry; (2) the Keating-Owen Act (1915), forbidding the transit in interstate commerce of products manufactured in establishments using child labor;* and (3) the Adamson Act (1916), establishing the eight-hour day for employees of common carriers engaged in interstate commerce.

IDEALISM AND REALISM IN FOREIGN POLICY

At the beginning of his presidency Woodrow Wilson was little concerned with foreign policy, but it was the irony of his public life that his presidential years were darkened by perplexing international problems.

Controversy Over the Panama Canal. A spirited dispute between the United States and Great Britain alarmed Wilson early in his administration.

THE TOLLS ACT OF 1912. This act had imposed a schedule of tolls upon all foreign vessels using the completed canal, but had provided that vessels of United States registry engaged in the coastwise trade should be exempt from toll payment. Great Britain contended that this was a violation of the "equality of treatment" for the vessels of all nations which the United States had promised in the Hay-Pauncefote Treaty.

REPEAL. Wilson strongly urged repeal of the act on the ground that the British interpretation of the treaty was correct. His attitude was probably determined by: (1) his desire to avoid trouble with the British in the Caribbean area; (2) his feeling that cordial Anglo-American relations were a necessary prelude to Colonel House's mission to promote European peace; and (3) his hope that, in return for repeal of the Tolls Act, Great Britain would support the American policy in Mexico. The act was repealed on June 15, 1914.

The Mexican Situation. President Wilson's determination to "cultivate the friendship and deserve the confidence of our sister republics of Central and South America" was the basis of his well-intentioned, if not highly successful, policy in dealing with Mexico.

THE OVERTHROW OF DIAZ. The despotic regime of Porfirio Diaz (1876–1910) had been brought to a sudden close by the revolt of wealthy liberals and landless peons, under the leadership of Fran-

---

* The Keating-Owen Act was declared unconstitutional by the Supreme Court in 1918.

cisco Madero. From 1910 to 1913 Madero worked in vain to establish his program of reforms—the allotment of land to landless peons, the nationalization of the railroads, the extension of the suffrage, and the grant of provincial autonomy. His efforts were ended by the revolt of one of his military supporters, General Victoriano Huerta.

THE QUARREL WITH HUERTA. Although twenty-five nations accepted Huerta as the *de facto* president of Mexico, Wilson refused to recognize the new regime, charging that it did not represent the will of the people and that it was responsible for the murder of Madero. Huerta retaliated with acts of reprisal on American citizens, culminating in the arrest of a squad of American marines at Tampico in April, 1914. When the United States promptly seized Vera Cruz in order to prevent a shipment of arms from reaching Huerta, war seemed imminent.

THE "ABC" MEDIATION. To avert the outbreak of war, Argentina, Brazil, and Chile (the "ABC" powers) offered their good offices, which were accepted. They proposed the retirement of Huerta and the installation of a reform government. But the several weeks of deliberations were fruitless, since Venustiano Carranza, in revolt against Huerta, refused to sign the protocol to maintain peace and order.

CARRANZA AND VILLA. When Carranza, having seized power, gave promise of establishing an orderly government, President Wilson abandoned "watchful waiting" and accorded the new regime *de facto* recognition. But Carranza failed to restrain the swashbuckling Pancho Villa, who attacked foreigners and finally led a raid against Columbus, New Mexico. The United States, with Carranza's permission, sent a punitive expedition, under General John J. Pershing, into Mexico (1916). It failed to capture Villa and was withdrawn as war with Germany loomed in 1917.

Wilsonian Idealism in Diplomacy. In dealing with Mexico, President Wilson tried to introduce a strongly moral tone into the relations between his country and its neighbors. He insisted: (1) that the United States had no intention of acquiring any further territory in this hemisphere; (2) that peaceful negotiation rather than force should be the chief instrument of American foreign policy; (3) that no foreign government would be recognized if it came into power through violence; and (4) that the United States would maintain scrupulous honesty in its international relations.

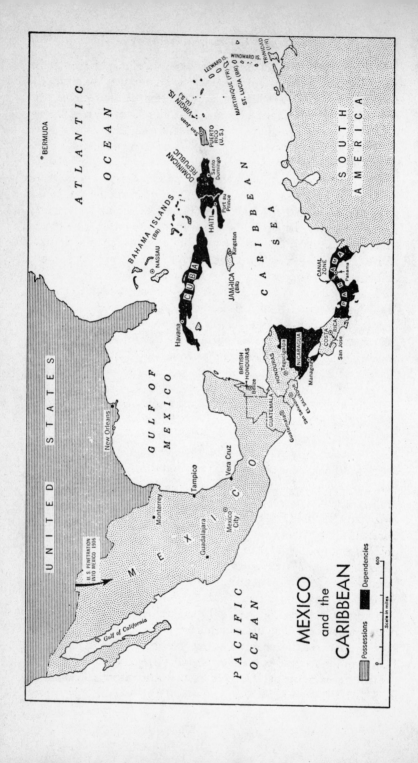

MEXICO
and the
CARIBBEAN

Realism in the Caribbean. Wilson's policy toward the Caribbean countries was less idealistic than his approach to the Mexican situation, but he was motivated more by a desire to promote the political and economic stability of regions close to American shores than to carry out a program of economic imperialism.

THE DOMINICAN REPUBLIC. A revolution in the Dominican Republic in 1916, which threatened the financial convention signed by Theodore Roosevelt in 1907, was the occasion for intervention by the United States and the assumption of political control. For nine years the provisional government, supported by American military forces, gave the natives the benefit of orderly administration despite their protests. In 1924 a new financial convention, superseding that of 1907, was signed and American troops were withdrawn as soon as ratifications had been exchanged.

HAITI. When Haiti's European creditors pronounced the republic bankrupt and threatened drastic action, the United States intervened (1915) and compelled the Haitian government to sign a treaty which established American control of customs, public works, and the constabulary. Native resistance to the subsequent military occupation caused frequent disorders, but American officials went forward with their work of building highways, improving sanitary conditions, and instituting financial reforms. Not until 1934 were the last United States troops withdrawn.

NICARAGUA. From 1912 to 1925 American marines were in Nicaragua to protect the administration of Nicaraguan finances and to maintain political tranquility in the country. During this occupation the Bryan-Chamorro Treaty was negotiated (1916), by which the United States acquired a ninety-nine-year lease to the Corn Islands and permission to establish a naval base on the Gulf of Fonseca. The withdrawal of marines in 1925 was followed by political insurrection, and two years later President Coolidge sanctioned another intervention for the purposes of: (1) protecting the lives and property of American citizens; (2) defending United States canal rights in Nicaragua; (3) enforcing the Central American treaty (1923) which pledged the Central American republics to deny recognition to any government which seized power by force. Having supervised new elections, the marines were withdrawn in 1929, save for a legation guard which left the country in 1933.

THE VIRGIN ISLANDS (1917). The Wilson administration acquired for $25,000,000 the Virgin Islands (Danish West Indies), which the

United States had been endeavoring to purchase from Denmark for more than a decade. The chief motive behind the purchase seems to have been the desire to use the islands as a necessary naval defense for the Panama Canal and the proposed canal through Nicaragua. The territory was placed under an appointed governor and granted limited self-government. In 1927 its inhabitants were made United States citizens.

THE FRUITS OF INTERVENTION. One of the results of the policy of intervention, which went far toward converting the Caribbean into an American lake, was the widespread distrust of the United States in Latin America. Whether American activities were based upon a logical application of the Monroe Doctrine or were merely a manifestation of national self-interest, they were regarded by many publicists in South America as proof of United States desire to establish hegemony of the two Americas. It was not until after the First World War that the United States slowly began to appreciate both the changed status of the Latin-American republics and its new relations to them.

REVIEW QUESTIONS

1. Why did President Wilson give tariff revision so important a place in his program of reform?
2. How did the fundamental principles of the Underwood-Simmons Tariff differ from those of the Payne-Aldrich Tariff?
3. What connection, if any, do you establish between the Federal Reserve Act of 1913 and each of the following:
   a. Aldrich Bill (1912)
   b. Panic of 1907
   c. Pujo Committee Investigation?
4. In what way did the Federal Reserve System provide for greater elasticity in our currency system?
5. Discuss the reasons which impelled Wilson to urge upon Congress a redefinition of the Antitrust laws.
6. How do you account for the difficulties which Wilson encountered in the application of his Mexican policy?
7. What have been the stakes of American diplomacy in the Caribbean in the last half-century?
8. Discuss the relation of the Monroe Doctrine to the present position of the United States in the Caribbean.
9. In what ways did Wilson's Caribbean policy differ from that of Theodore Roosevelt?

Chapter X

IN THE FIRST WORLD WAR

During the early period of the First World War, President Woodrow Wilson attempted to maintain the position of the United States as a disinterested neutral. However, public sympathy with the Allies and opposition to German tactics eventually brought the country into the war. American military and economic powers were swiftly mobilized to support the war effort and contributed greatly to the defeat of Germany. In the ensuing negotiations, Wilson's dream of a "peace without victory" was thwarted by the demands of European nationalists and by the failure of the United States Senate to agree on terms for participation in the League of Nations.

A NEUTRAL IN DIFFICULTY

Inspired by the hope that the United States might eventually be able to mediate in the European conflict which broke out in 1914, Wilson and his advisers tried vainly to maintain American neutrality.

Official Neutrality and Unneutral Opinion. At first President Wilson made no distinction between the war aims of the Triple Entente (Great Britain, France, and Russia) and the Central Powers (Germany and Austria-Hungary). When he issued a proclamation of national neutrality (August 4, 1914), he warned his fellow-countrymen not to be thrown off balance by a "war with which we have nothing to do." From the first, however, American public opinion favored England as the country to which the United States was bound by ties of ancestry, culture, and democracy. It distrusted Germany as an authoritarian nation and, after the invasion of Belgium, as an aggressor.

BRITAIN'S MARITIME POLICY. The first difficulties of the United

States as a neutral were with the British government, which used its control of the seas to try to starve Germany into submission.

The United States Protest. The State Department insisted: (1) that the British method of enforcing the blockade against the Central Powers was not recognized in international law; (2) that the British definition of contraband goods included food and other commodities that had not been listed as articles of war in the Declaration of London (1909); and (3) that British ships were interfering with American shipments to other neutrals.

The British Reply. Great Britain argued: (1) that their definition of contraband could not be restricted by the Declaration of London, which they had never ratified; (2) that their application of the doctrine of "continuous voyage," which had been upheld in American courts during the Civil War, was designed to stop shipments from the United States to neutral countries when it was clear that the ultimate destination was Germany; and (3) that the British government would compensate American nationals for noncontraband goods seized on the high seas.

GERMANY'S MARITIME POLICY. The mild dispute of the United States with Great Britain was quickly overshadowed by the arrogance of Germany's submarine policy, which threatened the lives, as well as the property, of American citizens.

The Menace of the Submarine. Germany declared (February 4, 1915) that the waters surrounding Great Britain and Ireland constituted a "war zone" in which German submarines would destroy all enemy vessels. To avoid "unfortunate mistakes" the German government warned neutral ships to remain outside the zone and advised citizens of neutral countries to refrain from traveling on the Allies' ships. To the spirited protests of the United States against the use of the submarine without observing the rule of visit and search, Germany (1) complained that Americans were allowing the British to violate their rights with impunity; (2) urged them to compel Great Britain to abide by the Declaration of London; and (3) suggested that unrestricted submarine warfare would be abandoned if the United States would cease furnishing the Allies with supplies and munitions.

The Sinking of the Lusitania. The potential threat of the submarine became actual in the sinking (May 7, 1915) of the Cunard liner *Lusitania* off the Irish coast with the loss of 1,153 passengers and crew, 114 of whom were American citizens. Avoiding the clamor of the war party in the United States, President Wilson strove by diplomatic pressure to persuade Germany to abandon unrestricted use of the submarine. The *Lusitania* notes insisted on the maintenance of neutral rights and demanded that Germany stop unrestricted submarine warfare. Secretary of State Bryan resigned in protest against them and was replaced by Robert Lansing, who supported Wilson's policy. In September, 1915, von Bernstorff, the German ambassador, informed the State Department that liners would not be sunk without protection of the lives of noncombatants.

The Sussex *Pledge (May, 1916)*. Despite this assurance, miscellaneous reports of submarine tactics caused misgivings. The French steamer *Sussex* was torpedoed in the English Channel, and several Americans were among the injured. Wilson sent a stern ultimatum to Germany. The official reply reaffirmed Germany's decision not to sink merchant vessels "without warning and without saving human lives." For the next nine months there was little cause for complaint on the score of submarine activities.

Pacifism and Preparedness. The struggle to defend neutral rights was paralleled by the contest between those who desired to avoid every possibility of war and those who wished to prepare effectively for the probability of armed conflict.

ANTIWAR ORGANIZATIONS. The conflict in Europe emphasized the unprepared condition of the United States for any war of considerable proportions, and increased the pressure for adequate armaments and military forces. To counteract this tendency, such peace organizations as the American Union against Militarism, the American League to Limit Armaments, the American Neutrality League, and the Woman's Peace Party labored valiantly. Secretary Bryan and President Wilson were both sympathetic with the aspirations of the antimilitarists in the first years of the administration.

THE PREPAREDNESS CAMPAIGN. General Leonard Wood and former President Theodore Roosevelt campaigned vigorously for a comprehensive program of military preparedness. Their pleas were reinforced by the work of the National Security League, the Navy League, and the American Rights Committee in molding public opinion. As the German submarine warfare developed, and the likelihood of war became more apparent, the preparedness movement gained force. In the spring of 1916 President Wilson abandoned his earlier position and appealed to the electorate to support an increase in the military and naval establishments.

NATIONAL DEFENSE LEGISLATION (1916). The drive for preparedness brought tangible results in the form of congressional legislation. (1) A Shipping Board was created and authorized to build or buy ships which might be transferred to private concerns or operated by government corporations. (2) A Council of National Defense was empowered to formulate plans for the efficient use of the nation's material resources in the event of war. (3). The Naval Appropriation Bill provided for the construction of dreadnaughts, battle cruisers, and other ships at a cost of $500,000,000. (4) The National Defense Act increased the regular army to 223,000 men and the national guard units to 425,000. The Act did not meet Secretary of War Garrison's ideas concerning the regular army, and he resigned. President Wilson appointed Newton D. Baker of Ohio in his place.

The Campaign of 1916. In a rather listless contest the voters, by a very narrow margin, endorsed the policy of neutrality and the progressive legislation which Woodrow Wilson had sponsored. The President was stronger than his party in almost every congressional district.

HUGHES AND THE REPUBLICAN DILEMMA. In an attempt to reunite their party the Republicans nominated Supreme Court Justice Charles Evans Hughes, who had taken no part in the disputes of 1912. Theodore Roosevelt, determined to defeat Wilson, refused the nomination of the Progressive party and urged his followers to vote for Hughes. It soon became apparent, however, that in his effort to please every faction within his party, Hughes was unwilling to take a firm stand on many issues of foreign policy. Cartoonists pictured him as "the Sphinx."

"HE KEPT US OUT OF WAR." The most forceful argument of the Democrats was their repeated assertion that President Wilson had kept the nation out of Europe's quarrels. They insisted that a vote for Hughes would mean American intervention in the war raging across the Atlantic.

WILSON'S SECTIONAL VICTORY. Hughes carried the sixteen northeastern states, except New Hampshire and Ohio, while Wilson won the Solid South and the trans-Mississippi West, except South Dakota and Oregon. It was the old Bryan area that gave him his margin of 277 to 254 in the electoral college.

"Peace Without Victory." Still seeking a negotiated peace in Europe, Wilson hoped that he might become the mediator.

THE MISSION OF COLONEL HOUSE. In January, 1916, the President sent his close friend, Colonel House, to London and Paris to sound out the British and French. Neither nation was ready to discuss a negotiated peace.

THE DEFINITION OF WAR AIMS. In December, 1916, Wilson strongly urged both belligerent groups to state their war aims. The Allies stated their objectives in terms which really meant the complete defeat of the Central Powers. Germany, speaking for the Central Powers, merely indicated a willingness to discuss peace terms at some future time.

WILSON'S PEACE PROPOSALS. Late in January, 1917, Wilson spoke before the Senate, making an eloquent appeal to world-wide opinion. He asked for a settlement of the war issues at once on the following terms: (1) abandonment of secret alliances and the balance of power in Europe; (2) recognition of the equality of rights for all nations; (3) the protection of oppressed minorities; (4) the limitation of land and naval armaments; (5) freedom of the seas for neutral nations. This "peace without victory" proposal found no favor with the belligerents.

Forcing the Issue. The officials of the Imperial German Government had reached the conclusion by 1917 that they could win the war before any military aid from the United States could reach the Allies.

THE SUBMARINE CHALLENGE. With an arrogant disregard for their own *Sussex* pledge (see p. 135) the German war lords announced that after January 31, 1917, the German navy would resume unrestricted submarine warfare.

THE BLUNDER OF THE "ZIMMERMANN NOTE." A few weeks after the German announcement of renewed submarine warfare, British agents intercepted a note, written by German Foreign Secretary Zimmermann, suggesting to Mexico that a German-Mexican alliance might be arranged which would enable Mexico to recover Texas, New Mexico, and Arizona. It was hinted that Japan might also join in an attack on the United States.

THE BREAK WITH BERLIN. The United States answered the submarine threat by immediately breaking off diplomatic relations with Germany and by arming merchant ships. Wilson, however, refused to give up his hopes for peace until he was sure that the Germans would carry out their threats.

Overt Acts of War. During March, 1917, four merchant vessels, flying the American flag, were sunk by a German submarine with a loss of thirty-six lives.

Wilson's War Message. President Wilson called a special session of Congress, which convened on April 2. He asked for a declaration of war against Germany to make the world "safe for democracy."

The Resort to Arms. On Good Friday, April 6, 1917, Congress responded to President Wilson's message and declared that war had been "thrust" upon the nation by the acts of the Imperial German Government.

MOBILIZING THE NATION'S STRENGTH

During the war years the majority of American citizens, and their representatives in Congress, rose above the limitations of partisanship, conferring upon the President the powers which he requested and co-operating in numerous ways to insure victory on the field of battle.

Building the War Machine. Congressional legislation in 1917 dealt with the reorganization of the army and navy, the mobilization of money and material, and the molding of public opinion in support of the war.

SELECTIVE SERVICE. The regular army and the National Guard units were increased by voluntary enlistment to 750,000 men. The Selective Service Act of 1917, based on the principle of universal conscription, compelled all young men between the ages of twenty-one and thirty to register with their local draft boards. Subsequently the age limits were fixed at eighteen to forty-five. More than 24,234,000 persons were enrolled, of whom 2,810,000 were inducted into the federal service. They were trained in thirty-two great cantonments located in various sections of the country.

THE BRIDGE OF SHIPS. The American naval force in European waters numbered 5,000 officers and 70,000 enlisted men. It co-operated with the British and the French in convoying merchantmen and troopships, combatting submarines, and laying down a mine barrage in the North Sea. The merchant marine, likewise, was greatly expanded. By the autumn of 1918 the Shipping Board had a fleet of 2,600 vessels and 10,000,000 tons.

FILLING THE WAR CHEST. Between April, 1917 and October, 1919, governmental appropriations totaled $35,400,000,000. Of this stupendous sum $11,280,000,000 was raised by taxation. Income-tax rates were increased; new levies were imposed on the excess profits of corporations; and a sales tax was placed upon numerous commodities. The bulk of the war expenses, however, was met by borrowing from the public. Four Liberty Loan "drives" and a final Victory Loan brought $21,448,000,000 into the treasury from bond sales.

ORGANIZING MANPOWER AND SUPPLIES. Private business co-operated with the government in numerous ways to insure success in the war. Representatives of organized labor, as well as distinguished industrialists, served upon the boards and commissions created in order to co-ordinate the economic life of the nation in one great war machine. The work of the Council of National Defense was supplemented by a War Industries Board, a War Labor Board, a General Munitions Board, the Federal Food Administration, and the Federal Fuel Administration. The stream of munitions, military supplies, and food to Europe never failed.

NATIONALIZING THE RAILROADS. The extraordinary demands of war proved to be a problem greater than the railroads could solve through voluntary co-operation. Therefore in December, 1917, President Wilson assumed control of the roads and named Secretary McAdoo as director-general to operate them as a unified system. Passenger service was curtailed to facilitate freight in transit; terminals and equipment were improved; wages were raised to spur employees to greater efforts; rates were increased. These methods were costly but successful.

THE PUBLIC MORALE. The government manifested considerable concern to "sell the war" to the country. A Committee on Public Information published an Official Bulletin and furnished governmentally inspired material to the press. Under the terms of the Espionage Act (June, 1917) and the Sedition Act (May, 1918), the government was able to suppress any form of dissent from its policy which it deemed a hindrance to the winning of the war. A number of socialists and pacifists were imprisoned under these laws, which were criticized as violations of the First Amendment. However, the Supreme Court upheld them as valid exercises of federal power to prevent a "clear and present danger," though it reversed some convictions on the ground that intent combined with danger had not been proved. The Department of Justice acted vigorously in ferreting out persons considered obstructionist, while the postal authorities exercised rigorous censorship over material sent through the mails.

The A.E.F. In answer to the pleas of the statesmen and military leaders of the Allies, the United States government pushed forward rapidly its plans for an American Expeditionary Force.

"OVER THERE." General John J. Pershing, who had commanded the punitive expedition into Mexico in 1916 (see p. 129), was given command of the A.E.F. He recommended steps to prepare an army of 3,000,000 men for service overseas. By December, 1917, there were 176,000 American troops in France and one division was holding the quiet sector near Belfort. The training and maintenance of an American army on French soil required the construction of extensive transportation and communication facilities; the establishment of huge depots for the commissary and quartermaster departments; and the erection of cantonments and training schools behind the combat lines. The following table illustrates the acceleration with which American troops were transported overseas during the six months from June to November, 1918:

MONTHS (1918)	STRENGTH OF UNITED STATES ARMY	IN A.E.F.	PERCENTAGE
June	2,112,000	722,000	34
July	2,380,000	996,000	42
August	2,658,000	1,293,000	49
September	3,001,000	1,576,000	52
October	3,433,000	1,843,000	54
November	3,634,000	1,971,000	55

THE WESTERN FRONT. Pershing was resolute in his decision to create an American army, but he postponed his program in order to meet the challenge of the Germans in the spring of 1918.

Allied Counter Offensive. American troops, brigaded with the British and French, participated in the counter-offensives at Montdidier, Cantigny, Belleau Wood, and Vaux.

Marne-Champagne. In July, 1918, more than 85,000 United States soldiers fought in the Marne Valley and in the assaults on the German lines between Soissons and Chateau-Thierry (see p. 141).

Reduction of St. Mihiel Salient. The first distinctly American offensive in September, 1918, reduced the salient at St. Mihiel, which the Germans had held since the first year of the war. Approximately 500,000 United States troops were engaged in four days terrific fighting, which straightened out the Allied lines.

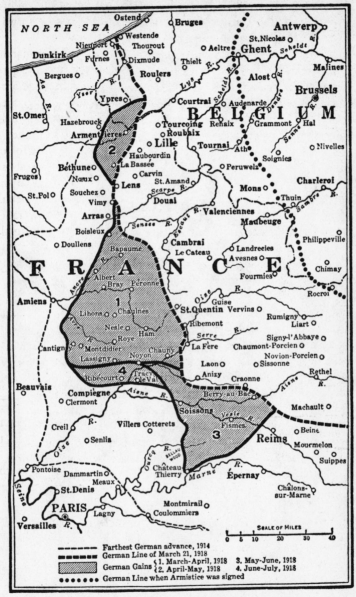

The German Drive and the Allied Response

The Meuse-Argonne. In October, 1918, an American force of 1,200,000 broke the German lines between Metz and Sedan, and hastened Germany's plea for an armistice in November, 1918.

THE ARMISTICE. The Meuse-Argonne offensive was a small part of the general forward movement launched by Marshal Ferdinand Foch, commander-in-chief of the Allied forces. It started the Germans on their last retreat. As it became evident that the Allies were headed for German territory, resistance collapsed and a provisional German government signed the terms of an armistice, dictated by Foch at his headquarters in the forest of Compiègne, on November 11, 1918.

FROM WAR TO PEACE

One of the greatest tragedies of the war was the fact that the mood and manner of the peace conference, and the terms of the Treaty of Versailles, were far removed from the high idealism which President Wilson had voiced during the momentous years of the conflict.

The Background of the Peace. After the entrance of the United States into the war President Wilson became by general consent the spokesman for the cause of the Allies. While his pleas for a "war to make the world safe for democracy" and for a "peace founded upon honor and justice" stirred liberals everywhere, he did not succeed in exorcising the spirit of selfish nationalism.

THE "FOURTEEN POINTS." A powerful statement of Wilsonian war aims was contained in the President's address to Congress on January 8, 1918. His fourteen-point program included political and territorial readjustments dealing with Alsace-Lorraine, Belgium, Italy, Austria-Hungary, Poland, Russia, the Balkan states, and the Turkish Empire, but the important features were: (1) abolition of secret diplomacy, (2) freedom of the seas, (3) removal of international economic barriers, (4) reduction of armaments, (5) impartial adjustment of colonial claims, and (6) establishment of a general association of nations.

NATIONALISTIC AMBITIONS. Many European statesmen, who had accepted the high aspirations of President Wilson, found it difficult to reconcile their nationalistic objectives with his idealistic pronouncements.

French Revenge. The French, led by Clemenceau, were determined to destroy Germany's military power and economic strength. French security, they insisted, meant a permanently crippled Germany.

Britain's Demand for Reparations. In the autumn elections of 1918 British liberalism had succumbed to the leadership of Lloyd George, who demanded that the Kaiser be hanged and the Germans compelled to pay to the last shilling the total costs of the war. Neither in Great Britain nor in France was the official atmosphere congenial for the Wilsonian idealism.

The "Secret Treaties." During the war several of the Allied countries had entered into secret agreements whereby they had divided the spoils which would result from their victory over the Central Powers. These agreements were specific pledges of the precise gains to be realized by Great Britain, France, and Russia, and were promises made to Italy, Japan, Roumania, and Greece in order to win their support for the Allied cause.

The Paris Conference (1919). The conference of more than sixty delegates from twenty-seven nations, which met at Paris on January 18, 1919, completed the Treaty of Versailles on May 7. It was signed by German representatives on June 28, 1919.

ORGANIZATION OF THE CONFERENCE. The representatives of the Central Powers were denied a place at the conference table. So numerous were the delegates accredited to the conference that it was utterly impossible to transact business in plenary sessions. The steering committee was the Council of Ten, consisting of two representatives from each of the five powers—Great Britain, France, the United States, Italy, and Japan. Finally, most important questions were settled by the "Big Four": Wilson, Lloyd George, Clemenceau, and Orlando. The committee of experts filed multitudinous reports for the guidance of the negotiators, though they could not be sure that the memoranda would be used.

WILSON'S DIFFICULTIES. The people of Europe to an astounding degree relied upon the President of the United States to satisfy their nationalistic aspirations and to meet their economic needs. Confronted by the most vexing problems, Wilson was handicapped from the very beginning of the conference. (1) His party had been repudiated at the polls in the congressional elections on the eve of his departure for Paris; (2) his choice of the American delegation— Secretary of State Lansing, Colonel House, Henry White (a career diplomat and the only Republican member), and General Tasker

Bliss—had not increased his influence with the Senate, which was also disquieted by his plans for a League of Nations; (3) his relations with the press at Paris were unfortunate, when he most needed favorable publicity; (4) his failure to thresh out the question of the secret treaties before the conference was a major blunder.

THE FIGHT FOR THE LEAGUE. Wilson's greatest victory at the conference was the writing of the covenant of the League of Nations as an integral part of the Treaty of Versailles. In the course of this victory he was compelled to compromise with the British, French, Italians, and Japanese to secure support. Although Wilson was the chief architect of the League, he received valuable aid from Lord Robert Cecil of England, General Jan Smuts of South Africa, and Leon Bourgeois of France; and he incorporated several suggestions made by Taft, Root, and Hughes. The final draft of the Covenant provided for (1) an Assembly consisting of delegates from all the member states, each of which was entitled to one vote in the periodic meetings at Geneva, Switzerland; (2) a Council of Nine, representing the five great powers and four nations elected by the Assembly; and (3) a secretariat composed of a Secretary-General and assistants to handle routine work of the League. The purposes of the League were to respect and preserve the territorial integrity and political independence of its members, to minimize the possibilities of international strife, to formulate plans for the reduction of armaments, and to provide for the registration of all international agreements. A Permanent Court of International Justice was to be established to facilitate the settlement of serious international disputes.

The Treaty of Versailles. This document of 80,000 words was a punitive settlement imposed by the victors upon a vanquished Germany. It compelled the Central Powers to assume responsibility for the war. By its provisions Germany lost 1,000,000 square miles of colonial possessions and 50,000 square miles of European territory, reduced her army to 100,000 men; surrendered all warships, submarines, airplanes, and other military equipment; and agreed to pay to the Reparations Commission the estimated costs of the war, which were finally fixed at approximately $56,500,000,000 in gold. The furious protests of German statesmen and publicists brought no modification in the treaty provisions, and on June 28, 1919, the German delegation in sullen mood signed the document. Though the burden imposed on Germany was heavy, it was by no means crushing.

The Senate and the Treaty. Having won his fight at Paris to incorporate the League Covenant as an integral part of the treaty, Wilson lost his struggle with the American Senate over ratification.

SENATORIAL HOSTILITY. On July 10, 1919, President Wilson presented the treaty to the Senate, which had previously secured a copy through newspaper channels and had been debating its provisions acrimoniously. The hostility to the document arose chiefly from the League provisions, but there were criticisms of the sections which dismembered the Austro-Hungarian monarchy, which granted rights in the Shantung peninsula to Japan,* and which allotted most of the German colonies under the mandate system to Great Britain and the Dominions. The enemies of the League centered their attack on: (1) the probability that Article X would compel Congress at the dictates of the League Council to defend the territorial integrity and political independence of any member state which was attacked; (2) the fact that the British Commonwealth of Nations had six votes in the Assembly, since all the Dominions were regarded as independent nations; (3) the possibility that the League might interfere in cases arising out of American interpretations of the Monroe Doctrine, or in cases of purely domestic concern; (4) the danger that the League might develop into a supergovernment, impairing the sovereign powers of its members.

WILSON'S APPEAL TO THE COUNTRY. Having failed to persuade the Senate Committee on Foreign Relations (of which Henry Cabot Lodge was chairman) to recommend ratification of the treaty, President Wilson carried his case to the country, speaking to enthusiastic audiences in the Middle and Far West during September, 1919. His tour ended in failure, however, when his health broke, and he was compelled to return to Washington, suffering from a cerebral thrombosis which partially paralyzed his left side. There was no indication that his appeal had aroused the electorate to demand ratification.

THE LODGE RESERVATIONS. On September 10, 1919, the Senate Committee on Foreign Relations reported the treaty with more than forty amendments and four reservations to the League Covenant. After weeks of debate the Senate passed fourteen reservations (the Lodge Reservations) but refused to ratify the treaty either with or

---

* Japan had entered the war on the side of the Allies in 1914 and had thereby strengthened her position in China. Her "special interests" there were recognized by the United States in the Lansing-Ishii Agreement (1917).

without the reservations. Sentiment among the senators seemed to fall into four categories: (1) the fifteen "irreconcilables" (led by Hiram Johnson, William Borah, and Robert La Follette); (2) the supporters of the Lodge Reservations; (3) the "mild reservationists," who were willing to accept the treaty with minor changes; and (4) the Wilsonians, who demanded that the treaty be ratified without change.

THE REJECTION OF THE TREATY. In the spring of 1920 the Senate returned to a consideration of the treaty and the Lodge Reservations. (At this time a fifteenth reservation was adopted, expressing sympathy with Irish self-government.) The final test came on March 19, when the treaty with reservations received fifty-seven ayes and thirty-nine nays, less than the two-thirds necessary for ratification. In May President Wilson vetoed the joint resolution declaring the war with Germany at an end, but President Harding signed a similar resolution on July 2, 1921. Subsequently, treaties were negotiated with Germany, Austria, and Hungary, and were promptly ratified by the Senate.

REVIEW QUESTIONS

1. Why did the United States government protest more vigorously against the German violations than the British infringements of neutral rights?
2. Was Germany justified in demanding that the United States make its neutrality real by refusing to sell munitions and supplies to the Allies?
3. Do you regard the resumption of submarine warfare in January, 1917, as the sole reason for the entrance of the United States into the First World War? Why?
4. How do you explain the victory of President Wilson in the presidential election of 1916?
5. In what ways were the "secret treaties" and the "Fourteen Points" irreconcilable?
6. Why was President Wilson so determined to write the Covenant of the League of Nations into the Treaty of Versailles?
7. Discuss the opposition to the treaty which developed in the United States Senate.
8. Who was to blame for the failure of the Senate to ratify the treaty? Discuss fully.
9. Why did the economic provisions of the treaty prove to be so difficult to enforce?

CHAPTER XI

THE PROMISE OF NATIONAL PROSPERITY

After the end of the First World War, the people of the United States attempted to withdraw from world commitments—to return to peacetime interests and to "normalcy." However, serious social and economic problems remained unsolved: how to achieve an economic balance between the demands of industry and of agriculture; how to cope with large-scale immigration; how to combat radicalism without destroying civil liberties; and how to control the prohibition experiment. The general prosperity that characterized the 1920's proved to be insecurely founded, and the decade ended with the stock-market crash, prelude to the most serious economic depression in American history.

WAR'S AFTERMATH

The period immediately following the cessation of hostilities in Europe was marked by governmental indecision, industrial strife, and social unrest.

Swift Military Demobilization. The return to civilian status of 4,000,000 soldiers and sailors and more than 11,000,000 war workers was speedily accomplished as industry was able to absorb an increasing labor force during the first half of the year 1919.

REORGANIZING THE ARMY. An Army Act of 1920 placed the peacetime strength of the regular army at 300,000 men and provided for closer contact between the representatives of the federal government and the National Guard units in the various states.

CARING FOR THE VETERANS. Congress promptly passed legislation to care for the veterans of the war who needed government assistance.

The Veterans' Bureau. The Bureau of War Risk Insurance, reorganized in 1921 as the Veterans' Bureau, was authorized to handle insurance claims and payments, to provide adequate hospitalization for wounded men, and to establish vocational training for those who were physically handicapped.

The Bonus. In 1920 the American Legion, formed by World War Veterans the previous year, championed a demand for "adjusted compensation," or bonus. President Harding vetoed a bonus bill in 1922; but Congress passed an act in 1924 (over President Coolidge's veto), which authorized the Treasury to issue twenty-year paid-up certificates against which the veterans might borrow money from the government at 6 per cent interest. Seven years later Congress refused to yield to the demand for immediate cash redemption of the certificates but increased the loan value of the certificates and reduced the interest rates. In 1936 the veterans' certificates paid off in 3 per cent bonds, which could be redeemed for cash on demand.

SCRAPPING THE WAR MACHINE. The government followed no consistent program in liquidating the vast and complicated administrative organization of the war years; in some instances boards and commissions merely ceased to function, but in most cases executive orders transferred power to the regular governmental departments.

Surplus Materials. Governmental losses were heavy in disposing of surplus materials and in canceling contracts for goods and services no longer needed. Construction projects in France and mobile supplies were sold to European buyers at approximately half their cost. The Board of War Claims and the Liquidation Commission (1919) managed to salvage about $7,000,000,000 through the adjustment of war contracts.

Decline and Recovery of the Merchant Marine. The greatest loss, however, was suffered by the governmental agencies which tried to sell the excess ship tonnage built during the war. The Merchant Marine Act of 1920 enabled the Shipping Board to sell about 40 per cent of its fleet to private shippers at bargain prices. However, American shipping still lagged behind that of other nations. The Jones-White Act of 1928 provided an indirect subsidy in the form of construction loans and mail contracts for private shipowners. This act stimulated the sale of old ships and the building of a more modern merchant fleet. By 1930 the percentage of United States foreign trade carried in American bottoms had tripled as compared with prewar years.

Denationalizing the Railroads. The operation of the railroads by the government as a war measure stimulated the demand in certain quarters for government ownership and operation, but President Wilson recommended the return of the roads to private operation, warning against the re-establishment of "the old conditions unmodified."

THE PLUMB PLAN. A plan formulated by Glenn E. Plumb of Chicago had the support of the Railroad Brotherhoods and the American Federation of Labor. It provided for: (1) the purchase of the railroads by the government; (2) the operation of the lines by a National Railway Operating Corporation composed of all railroad officials and employees; (3) the direction of the Operating Corporation by a board of fifteen, five chosen by the officials, five by the workers, and five by the government; and (4) the establishment by the board of directors of a wage scale and a schedule of rates, subject to review by the Interstate Commerce Commission. Although the Plumb plan was widely debated, hostility in Congress prevented its serious consideration.

THE ESCH-CUMMINS ACT. Congressional discussion of numerous proposals for the revamping of the transportation system finally resulted in the passage of the Esch-Cummins Bill, or Railroad Transportation Act, in February, 1920. Its salient features were: (1) increased regulation of the railroads by the Interstate Commerce Commission, which was granted control of security issues, traffic regulations, and consolidation of lines for the purpose of eliminating unnecessary competition; (2) the guarantee by the government of a fair return ($5\frac{1}{2}$ per cent) to the owners for a period of two years; (3) the creation of a revolving fund (supplied from one half of net earnings over 6 per cent) to facilitate railroad loans for improvements; and (4) the compulsory arbitration of labor disputes by a Railway Labor Board composed of three from the owners, three from the workers, and three from the public.

Industrial Disturbances. The period immediately following the war was marked by excessive profiteering in commodity prices, bitter strife between employers and employees over wage scales, and costly strikes and lockouts in numerous industries.

HIGH PRICES AND PROFITEERING. The upward trend of prices, which began with the extraordinary demand for commodities as a result of the European war, and which was accentuated by the inflationary financial policy of the war years, caused an investigation by the

Federal Trade Commission in 1919. The evidence of unscrupulous profiteering by manufacturers and middlemen resulted in a series of ineffective prosecutions by the Department of Justice against illegal trade practices. Much more significant was the spontaneous but widespread "buyers strike" in the summer of 1920 which sent prices rapidly downward from the peak.

INDUSTRIAL CONFERENCE. In 1919 the government was much more concerned with foreign affairs than with domestic problems, but it could not continue to ignore the devastating effect of the warfare between capital and labor. President Wilson summoned representatives of employers, employees, and the public to meet at Washington in October, 1919. These deliberations ended in failure as did a later attempt by industrialists and government officials to create regional tribunals to settle labor disputes.

STEEL STRIKE (1919). One of the most serious of the numerous strikes was that of 370,000 steel workers, growing out of the efforts of the A.F. of L. to unionize the steel industry. The report filed by an investigating committee of the Interchurch World Movement indicated that the workers' demands (for wage increases, union recognition, and an end to the twelve-hour day) were justified; but the strike was associated with bolshevism and anarchism in the minds of many, and the employers broke it with nonunion labor.

COAL STRIKE (1919). The strongly unionized miners in the bituminous coal fields went out on strike (November 1, 1919) for higher wages. The government branded the strike as "not only unjustifiable, but unlawful," and secured an injunction restraining the officials of the United Mine Workers from directing the strikers' activities. When a second injunction demanded the speedy recall of the general strike order, the United Mine Workers agreed to confer with representatives of the government and the operators. A special commission formulated a new wage agreement which was made effective in April, 1920.

THE "RETURN TO NORMALCY" — *Harding*

The Progressive era came to an end with the election of 1920. Millions of voters, desiring to escape from the challenge of Wilsonian idealism and the responsibilities of world leadership, believed they were taking the road back to normal conditions by returning the Republican party to power.

Republican Triumph. For the first time since the Progressive party was formed by Theodore Roosevelt in 1912, the Republican party was united.

HARDING AND COOLIDGE. In order to prevent a deadlock between supporters of General Leonard Wood and Governor Frank Lowden of Illinois, the Republican convention nominated a "dark horse," Senator Warren G. Harding of Ohio. For Vice-President the delegates named Governor Calvin Coolidge of Massachusetts.

COX AND ROOSEVELT. The Democrats, dispirited and disorganized, finally chose Governor James M. Cox of Ohio and young Franklin D. Roosevelt of New York, who had served as Assistant Secretary of the Navy under Wilson.

A COLOSSAL LANDSLIDE. Though President Wilson had hoped that the election would be a "solemn referendum" on the League of Nations, it really was a mass protest which arose out of the animosities of the war years and the disappointments of the period of reconstruction. Harding received slightly more than sixteen million votes, while Cox had approximately nine million. As one Democrat remarked: "It was not a landslide, it was an earthquake."

Harding's Tragedy. A handsome man of amiable disposition, Warren Harding placed great confidence in his personal friends and political associates. Some of them betrayed that trust. *Dumb like Grant.*

THE CABINET IN CONTROL. President Harding was eager to cooperate with Republican party leaders in formulating policies. His choice of "best minds" for the cabinet included Charles E. Hughes (State), Andrew W. Mellon (Treasury), and Herbert Hoover (Commerce). Less distinguished, but probably more influential in the administration were Harry M. Daugherty (Attorney General), Albert B. Fall (Interior), and Will H. Hays (Postmaster General).

MELLON'S FINANCIAL PROGRAM. Hailed as the "greatest secretary of the treasury since Alexander Hamilton," Andrew Mellon set the financial policies of the Harding administration.

Budgetary Reform. In order to reduce government expenditures, Secretary Mellon advocated the adoption of a budget system. Under the Budget and Accounting Act (1921), General Charles G. Dawes became supervisor of the government's economy campaign.

Tax Reductions. President Harding and Secretary Mellon won the acclaim of industrialists by their efforts to reduce taxes on business and to lighten tax rates in the higher income brackets. Though taxes were reduced, government revenues continued to be large and the national debt was gradually reduced.

CONGRESSIONAL DISSENT. Mellon's tax program was not entirely successful in Congress, where a combination of Democrats and insurgent Republicans compelled the administration to accept higher rates on large incomes than the Treasury proposed. This political dissent centered in the so-called "farm bloc," representing constituencies of the "corn belt," who were insistent that agriculture receive governmental favors equivalent to those conferred upon industry.

SCANDAL IN ADMINISTRATIVE CIRCLES. The last months of President Harding's life were darkened by his awareness that a few of his close advisers had betrayed him and their public trust. Shortly before his death he realized that evidence of gross political corruption would soon be revealed. He died suddenly in San Francisco on August 2, 1923, as he was returning from a visit to Alaska.

"Keeping Cool With Coolidge." Harding's unexpected death made Vice-President Coolidge President of the United States. A man of few words, he quickly won the confidence of his fellow-countrymen, who admired his courage and personal integrity.

COMBATTING PUBLIC SCANDALS. President Coolidge insisted that his associates should assist in the investigation of corrupt political acts committed during the Harding administration.

Fraud in the Veterans' Bureau. Charles R. Forbes, Director of the Veterans' Bureau, was convicted of graft and of accepting bribes.

Misappropriation of Government Funds. The Alien Property Custodian was sentenced for conspiracy to defraud the government.

The Illegal Oil Leases. Secretary of the Interior Albert B. Fall leased the Elk Hills government reserves in California and the Teapot Dome field in Wyoming to private oil companies. In both cases he was convicted of receiving bribes for making the leases.

Charges against Daugherty. Attorney General Harry M. Daugherty was forced to resign after evidence was produced that he had conspired with liquor dealers to evade the prohibition laws.

CONTINUING MELLON'S FINANCIAL POLICIES. Coolidge, like Harding, enthusiastically supported the financial policies of Secretary Mellon. Despite repeated assurances that the White House was directing an energetic economy campaign, the federal budget did not shrink appreciably during the Coolidge administration. Instead, the increasing prosperity of the country enabled the Treasury at the same time to reduce tax rates, to collect more than enough revenue to meet current expenses, and to apply the surplus to the steady reduction of the national debt.

ELECTION OF 1924. Within ten months of Coolidge's induction into office, the presidential campaign of 1924 was in full swing.

Republican Convention. So successful had the new President been in removing the stigma of corruption from his party and in winning the favor of the business interests of the country, that he was the unanimous choice of the delegates to the Republican national convention. The platform was an appeal to the conservative business interests, already feeling the quickening influence of more prosperous times.

Democratic Confusion. Trouble developed in the Democratic ranks over the platform. After prolonged and acrimonious debate the delegates rejected (1) a plan demanding American membership in the League of Nations and (2) a resolution denouncing by name the Ku Klux Klan, an organization designed to maintain the political supremacy of native-born, white, Protestant citizens. (The convention adopted a plank advocating a referendum on the question of League membership.) The contest for the nomination broke all records. The followers of Governor Alfred E. Smith of New York and William G. McAdoo (who had been Wilson's Secretary of the Treasury) prevented a choice until the 103rd ballot, when the delegates stampeded to John W. Davis, a native of West Virginia who had become a prominent New York lawyer.

La Follette's Candidacy. The dissatisfaction of the Western farmers and organized labor with the two major parties resulted in the formation of a third party, which nominated Robert M. La Follette of Wisconsin. The new group had the endorsement of the Conference for Progressive Political Action, sponsored by the Railroad Brotherhoods, the American Federation of Labor, and the Socialist party. The platform, drafted by Senator La Follette, was largely an expression of agrarian discontent and labor unrest.

The Campaign. La Follette provided the action in a rather listless campaign. Davis tried unsuccessfully to raise the cry of corruption against the Republicans. The Republican strategy was to frighten the voters with the charge that La Follette was a dangerous radical and to proclaim that the best way to defeat him was to vote for Coolidge. The result revealed the drift away from the Democrats.

Coolidge received 15,725,000 votes against 8,386,000 for Davis and 4,822,000 for La Follette. Davis secured only the Solid South and Oklahoma, while La Follette won his own state, Wisconsin.

THE MOOD OF CHANGING TIMES

The decade of the 1920's—frequently called "the jazz age"—was a period marked by an exciting acceleration in the tempo of American life. Bored by reform movements and disillusioned by the failure of the war to bring genuine peace, the people used their increasing leisure time to experiment with new amusements and to seek relief from serious problems.

Importance of Recreation. One of the significant results of the industrial revolution had been the larger amount of leisure time enjoyed by all—employers and employees alike. As a result, in the United States, the search for recreation became almost as intensive as the search for a job.

POPULAR DIVERSIONS. Most Americans became spectators rather than participants in sports and amusements.

Motion Pictures. By 1914 the movies were setting the styles in manners and fashions. The nation regarded movie stars—Francis X. Bushman, Douglas Fairbanks, Mary Pickford, Charlie Chaplin, the Gish sisters, and many others—as heroes and heroines. "Talking pictures," which became possible in 1927, made movies the most popular form of entertainment for many years.

Commercial Radio. During the 1920's the use of the radio for broadcasting news, music, dramatic sketches, and public events was made possible by a combination of electronic skill and financial support from advertising agencies. The first commercial station—KDKA in Pittsburgh—broadcast the Harding-Cox election returns on November 2, 1920. By 1927 there were two coast-to-coast radio chains—NBC and CBS—and the government had established the Federal Communications Commission to regulate seven hundred stations then in operation.

Radio Programs. A few influential leaders saw the possibility of radio broadcasting as an instrument of mass education, but most programs were designed merely for entertainment or to advertise new and old products. With tens of millions of listeners tuned into the same programs, a nation-wide appeal became reality. Increasingly the people of the United States listened to the same news, heard the same jokes and dramatic sketches, bought the same products, and ate the same advertised brands of processed foods. The result was a greater uniformity in manners and customs than had ever been true in the nation's history.

Fads in Fun. The radio seemed to stimulate an almost frenzied desire to find novelty and excitement in entertainment. Jazz music brought unconventional rhythms in social dancing. Marathon dancing, miniature golf, flag-pole sitting, crossword puzzles, and mah-jongg became the rage—for a brief period.

SPECTATORS' SPORTS. Athletic games, whether played by amateurs or professionals, were organized along lines similar to those of business enterprise.

Professionalism. Though organized sport is not synonymous with professionalism, the greatest crowds flocked to see professional athletes. Baseball, well managed in the two major leagues, was highly profitable. Promoters found profits also in wrestling, boxing, tennis, basketball, and football, all of which catered to the spectators' desire for excitement.

The Growth of Team Play. Supervised team play on municipal playgrounds had become a feature of city life by the 1920's. Boys and girls from various national backgrounds here learned to play together in competitive sports. This proved to be a truly democratic force, often counteracting tendencies toward class distinction.

CONSPICUOUS LEISURE. During the decade after the First World War, the sport of golf transformed the exclusive country club into a national institution. Every urban community strove to build and maintain a country club and hundreds of thousands of business and professional men and women learned to play golf, as an important part of the clubs' social programs. By 1929 there were more than four thousand golf courses in the United States, exclusive of the municipal links.

THE LURE OF THE GREAT OUT-OF-DOORS. Americans were slowly learning that it was worth while to enjoy the beauties and natural features of the countryside in which they lived. The federal and state governments had provided the opportunity in national and state parks. By 1930 the domain of the national parks included twenty-three units, larger in total area than the kingdom of Belgium. More than three million travelers visited these parks in 1929.

A Nation On Wheels. The coming of the automobile into general use gave the people of the United States greater mobility at a time when they were enjoying more leisure. These two factors revolutionized American social life.

THE EUROPEAN "HORSELESS CARRIAGE." The first automobiles, built in Europe for well-to-do Americans, looked very much like a carriage without the horse. At first, Americans lagged behind European manufacturers in making improvements, even using steam-driven automobiles after Europeans had demonstrated the advantages of gasoline engines.

HENRY FORD AND THE "MODEL T." Henry Ford, a Detroit mechanic and inventor, realized that there was a potential market for a low-priced car, easily repaired, that would be durable even on rough roads.

The Assembly Line. Early in the twentieth century, Ford invented a simple gasoline engine and in 1908 installed it in the "Model T." Within five years he was producing over five hundred cars a day. Production mounted rapidly to keep up with sales. This was possible because Henry Ford proved that the assembly-line system of manufacturing cars was practical. By using a continuous conveyor belt to bring materials to the workmen, he reduced costs to a minimum.

Mass Production. By amazingly efficient production methods, Ford managed to decrease the price of his "tin Lizzies" almost every year. In 1924 they were selling for less than $300 each. It was the Ford Motor Company's boast that the "Model T" had reached every quarter of the globe.

THE AUTOMOTIVE INDUSTRY. By 1930 more than 24 million cars were on the roads, and Ford, General Motors, and other manufacturers were producing annually about $3,500,000,000 worth of automobiles. Some Americans were talking about "two cars in every garage."

THE AUTOMOBILE AS A SOCIAL FORCE. The impact of the automobile on American society was tremendous. It probably freed the nation from provincialism, while it standardized manners and customs. It brought farm and city into a closer relation. It stimulated the rubber and steel industries, revolutionized the transport of people and goods, and created the new industry of "tourism," in which millions of Americans on vacation participated. It promoted construction of better roads. Most important, it was a strong force in the rapid democratization of American society.

The Opening of the Air Age. In 1903 the Wright Brothers— Orville and Wilbur—had stayed aloft twelve seconds in a heavier-than-air machine on a trial flight at Kitty Hawk, North Carolina. During the First World War the infant airplane industry produced a few thousand military planes.

CARRYING THE MAILS. The cancellation of government contracts at the close of the war was a severe setback to aviation. The Post Office Department helped a little by opening a daily airmail route between New York and Washington in 1918, but it was seven years before Congress granted subsidies to regular airlines for carrying the mails.

THE AIR COMMERCE ACT, 1926. This law gave the Commerce Department control over commercial aviation. Within a year eighteen lines had established passenger routes that covered 3,200 miles.

THE "LONE EAGLE." It was an airmail pilot, Charles A. Lindbergh of Minnesota, who gave his fellow-countrymen a lively interest in the adventures of aviation.

The Trans-Atlantic Flight. On May 20–21, 1927, Lindbergh piloted his plane, *The Spirit of St. Louis,* from Long Island to Le Bourget Airfield near Paris in 33½ hours.

The Hero's Welcome. Nicknamed the "Lone Eagle," because of this feat, Lindbergh quickly became a symbol of the best in the decade of the 1920's. His enthusiastic reception in New York City cost the city $16,000 merely to clean up the confetti that was showered upon him!

Possibilities of Aviation. The thrilling Lindbergh flight awakened many Americans to the business opportunities of aviation. Early in 1929 the aircraft industry reported 48 airways with a combined length of 20,000 miles, serving 355 cities that possessed municipal airports.

PERSISTENT SOCIAL AND ECONOMIC PROBLEMS

Beneath the noisy and carefree mood of the postwar decade there were many difficult economic and social problems which Americans were reluctant to face.

Economic Nationalism. In spite of the growing realization of the interdependence of industry and commerce throughout the world, there was a significant increase in tariff barriers and trade discriminations after the First World War.

THE FORDNEY-McCUMBER TARIFF (1922). This bill represented a return to protectionist principles. An elaboration of the emergency act of 1921, which had superseded the Underwood Tariff, it (1) reduced the commodities on the free list; (2) increased the rates on agricultural products; (3) created a Tariff Commission to investigate and compare costs of production here and abroad; and (4) authorized the President to revise rates (up to 50 per cent) whenever it seemed advisable on the basis of the Commission's reports. In general, the act restored the levels of the Payne-Aldrich Tariff of 1909.

THE SMOOT-HAWLEY TARIFF (1930). This bill, which President Hoover rather reluctantly signed on June 14, 1930, contained rates which in one quarter of the schedules were higher than the Fordney-McCumber Tariff. The Tariff Commission was made more effective and the principle of flexible rates was retained.

DEMAND FOR TARIFF REVISION. The act of 1930 was widely criticized. Many economists denounced it as an outrageous evidence of economic nationalism which would cause unjustifiable increases in the cost of living; importers, exporters, and international bankers feared its effect upon foreign trade and American investments abroad; the pacifists regretted its unfortunate effect upon international relations.

Agricultural Surpluses and the Farmer. The perennial problem of the relation of agriculture to the new industrial order became acute after the First World War, for the farmer did not share with the manufacturer, merchant, and banker the prosperity of the third decade of the twentieth century.

THE GOLDEN HARVEST. The First World War brought unprecedented good times to American farmers, who were tempted by the phenomenal rise in the prices of their staples to buy more acres and to strive for an increase in the productivity of the acreage already under cultivation. The mechanization of agriculture, which went forward rapidly in response to the needs of the warring nations, brought increasing returns to progressive farmers.

THE AGRARIAN REVERSAL. The farmer's prosperous years were few. Peace brought a quick descent to the prewar price level. Between 1919 and 1921 the value of farm products was cut in half, though production slightly increased. The farmer's plight, to which abandoned farms and foreclosed mortgages bore mute witness, was the result of: (1) the excessive expansion of agricultural lands, many of them submarginal; (2) the increased productivity per acre due to improved machines and methods; and (3) the decline of commodity prices in the great world markets where the agrarian surplus of the United States competed with the surplus of other nations.

LEGISLATIVE RELIEF. Like the Grangers and the Populists of other days, the farmers turned to Congress for relief from their economic hardships.

The Farm Bloc. The pressure exerted by the National Grange, the Farmers' Union, and the Farm Bureau Federation caused the formation in Congress of a bipartisan "farm bloc" which worked

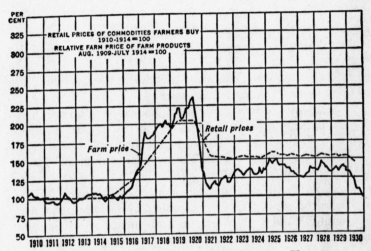

The Effect of the War and of the Postwar Years
on the Farmer's Budget

for agrarian legislation. As a result Congress enacted a Futures Trading Act (1921) to curb speculation in grain prices; a Filled Milk Act (1922) to protect dairymen against dishonest competition; an Intermediate Credit Act (1923) to extend agricultural credit on easier terms; and a Co-operative Act (1924) to exempt agricultural co-operatives from the antitrust laws.

The McNary-Haugen Bill. The basic problem of agricultural surpluses was attacked in the McNary-Haugen Bill which passed Congress in February, 1927, only to be vetoed by President Coolidge. Its sponsors modified some of its provisions and secured its passage in May, 1928, but again Coolidge vetoed the bill. The central feature of the scheme was the attempt to equalize the price of American farm surpluses in the world market with the price in the protected domestic market by the imposition of an "equalization fee" assessed against the farmers producing each staple. It was asserted that the fee would operate automatically to curb excessive production of any staple. A federal board was to handle the marketing of all surplus staples and to collect the equalization fee.

Assisting the Railroads. Like the farmers, the railroad owners and operators, still hostile to government regulation, nevertheless turned to the federal government for relief.

NEW FORMS OF COMPETITION. After 1920 the railroads were alarmed over the competition offered by: (1) the barge canals and improved internal waterways; (2) the motor-transport companies; (3) the expanding pipeline facilities; and (4) the airways. From the railroad executives came insistent demands that Congress place their competitors under governmental supervision.

CONSOLIDATION. The solution of the railroad problem which was implicit in the Railroad Transportation Act of 1920 was the unification of independent lines into great systems based upon a careful analysis of the country's needs. The Interstate Commerce Commission and the railroad executives alike studied the difficulties and possibilities of consolidation, but action was slow. Between 1920 and 1929 hundreds of short lines were acquired by the larger rail systems. Not until 1931 did the Northeastern roads submit a plan for unification which the Interstate Commerce Commission approved with certain changes in details. There were to be four great networks in the Northeast: (1) The New York Central, with 12,920 miles; (2) the Pennsylvania, with 16,548 miles; (3) the Baltimore and Ohio, with 11,156 miles; and (4) the unified Van Sweringen holdings, with 12,554 miles.

CO-ORDINATION BILL (1933). The Reconstruction Finance Corporation helped many railroads by its generous loans during the depression. In June, 1933, Congress passed an act providing for a scheme of railroad co-ordination which would effect economies in the transportation system. Joseph B. Eastman was named Federal Co-ordinator of Railroads.

The Power Issue. During the postwar decade popular demand for governmental regulation of public utilities, especially those producing and distributing electric power, brought action from state and federal authorities.

STATE REGULATION. The public-utility companies, which had widely extended their activities through mergers and holding companies, were gradually brought under some sort of state supervision. By 1930 nearly every state had created a public-service commission, but the commissions were handicapped by the modest character of their powers and by the fact that the great utilities organizations were engaged in enterprises which crossed state lines.

FEDERAL WATER-POWER COMMISSION. Congress created this agency in 1920 and empowered it to license hydroelectric plants on the navigable rivers or on public lands and Indian reservations. Over its licensees the Commission had regulatory powers affecting rates whenever electricity was sold across state lines. After ten years, only 5 per cent of the nation's hydroelectric power was produced under the Commission's supervision.

MUSCLE SHOALS. The champions of government ownership and operation of electric power facilities centered their campaign upon Muscle Shoals, the gigantic project on the Tennessee River which had been started under congressional appropriation as a nitrate-fixation plant in 1917. In 1928 Congress passed a bill, sponsored by Senator Norris of Nebraska, providing for the creation of a government-owned corporation to work the nitrate plants and to sell the surplus power generated at the hydroelectric station. President Coolidge vetoed the bill. Two years later a similar measure, author-izing the government to enlarge and operate the power station, was vetoed by President Hoover, who denounced the entrance of the federal government into the public-utilities field.

Closing the Gates to the Immigrant. One of the direct consequences of the First World War was the reversal by the United States of its traditional immigration policy.

THE DEMAND FOR RESTRICTION. Prior to 1914 the United States permitted unrestricted European immigration, barring only such aliens as seemed undesirable from considerations of public health, safety, and morals. America was proud to be an asylum for the oppressed of the Old World; and the nation needed cheap labor to exploit its abundant resources, build its railroads, and expand its industries. Yet there was a growing demand for a restrictive and selective immigration policy.

ACT OF 1921. When it became apparent at the close of the First World War that "the world was preparing to move to the United States," Congress rather hastily adopted a policy of restriction. The

over

legislation of 1921 provided that no European country could send to the United States in any year more than 3 per cent of its nationals resident here at the time of the census of 1910.

QUOTA OF 1924. This legislation further restricted the number of immigrants and drastically reduced the quotas from the nations of southern and eastern Europe. It permitted each country to send 2 per cent of the number of its nationals who had resided in the United States at the time of the census of 1890. The changing of the census base automatically increased the proportion of immigrants from northern and western Europe.

NATIONAL-ORIGINS PRINCIPLE. The quota of 1924 was to remain in effect three years. Then each country was to be accorded "that proportion of 150,000 which the number of persons of a given national origin residing in the United States in 1920 bears to the country's total population in 1920." So difficult did this calculation prove that the new quotas were not made effective until 1929.

NONQUOTA GROUPS. The quota system did not apply to Canada or to the independent nations of Latin America. So wide was the latitude for administrative discretion under the law, however, that the officials of the State and Labor departments were able to restrict selectively even nonquota groups by requiring property and other qualifications. Mexican immigration was greatly reduced as a result of this administrative action.

AMENDMENT OF 1965. This law, which went into effect in 1968, replaced the national-origins quota system with a system of numerical limitations for Eastern and Western hemispheres.

Activity in the Labor Movement. The armies of labor emerged from the First World War in truculent mood, but most of them quickly succumbed to the pleasant features of the higher standard of living which the prosperous decade of the twenties made possible.

TRADE-UNIONISM. Prior to 1920 organized labor had grown steadily, but in the postwar decade it declined both in activity and in prestige. The American Federation of Labor, for example, reported 4,078,740 members in 1920; 2,961,096 in 1930; and 2,532,261 in 1932. Several circumstances explain this decline in conservative trade-unionism: (1) the Federation clung to craft distinctions which were rapidly becoming meaningless; (2) it failed to face the problem of "technological unemployment"; (3) it had nothing to offer the unskilled worker; (4) its affiliated unions ignored the entrance of the Negro into important trades and industries; (5) its organizers found it difficult to break the open-shop policy of employers who could rely upon the injunction to win labor disputes; (6) the company programs for health protection, sickness-insurance, recreational facilities, and profit sharing made the union benefits less desirable to thousands of workers. The decline of organized labor was sharply accentuated after 1929 by the industrial depression.

LEFT-WING RADICALISM. The radical wing of American labor was temporarily curbed by the activities of state and national governments during the "Red Scare" of 1919 (see below). The I.W.W. never recovered from this onslaught, and by 1924 it had virtually disappeared. Radical workers were responsible for the organization of the Communist party, the American section of the Third International, in 1928. This party never polled more than 60,000 votes for its presidential candidate. In labor circles the Communists at first strove to capture conservative unions by a policy of "boring from within," but in 1929 they began a concerted movement to form new industrial unions committed to the accentuation of the class struggle.

Combating the Radicals.
Events in Europe as well as in this country convinced many Americans that the Communists and their sympathizers were using the postwar bitterness to secure greater political power.

THE "RED SCARE." The apparent success of the Communist revolution in Russia put law enforcement agencies, both state and federal, on their guard against radical uprisings. Aliens whose views were regarded as dangerous were deported. A bomb explosion in Wall Street, which killed more than thirty people, sent a wave of fear over the country. Attorney General A. Mitchell Palmer asserted that the Reds were ready to "destroy the government at one fell swoop."

The Boston Police Strike. A dispute in Boston between the police force and the city government led to a strike of all uniformed police. To prevent the collapse of law enforcement, Calvin Coolidge, then governor of Massachusetts, sent National Guard units to the city. He won widespread approval by his statement that there is "no right to strike against the public safety by anybody, anywhere, anytime."

The Sacco-Vanzetti Case. Fear of radicalism was evident in the handling of the case against Nicola Sacco and Bartolomeo Vanzetti, known anarchists. Despite inconclusive evidence, the men were convicted of murdering a factory paymaster in Braintree, Massachusetts, in 1921. For six years appeals dragged through the courts, since many people in all parts of the world believed that they had been improperly sentenced to death. They were executed in 1927, but the case probably caused Americans to reappraise their fears of radical agitators.

THE DECLINE OF REFORM. Even the moderate reforms of the Progressive era came under suspicion during the wave of fear that radicalism might destroy American traditions. As a result some who had been reformers in their youthful years now gained prominence as defenders of the existing economic and social order.

A Flash of Intolerance. Fear often creates intolerance. It did so in the United States during the early 1920's, when individuals and organized groups denounced anyone who disagreed with them on political, economic, or religious matters.

The Ku Klux Klan. The most notorious manifestation of organized intolerance was the modern Ku Klux Klan. Organized in 1915, it grew rapidly after 1920, aiming its attacks at the Negroes, the Jews, the immigrants, and especially the Roman Catholics. Its officers —called "wizards," "goblins," and "kleagles"—often condoned brutality and terror and preached an intolerance quite contrary to the democratic principles they professed to be protecting.

THE DEFENSE OF TRADITIONAL RELIGION. Conservative fear of radicalism had a counterpart in the field of religion, as many feared that the changing mood of the nation would weaken traditional religious beliefs.

New Viewpoints in Protestantism. The liberals or "modernists" among Protestant clergy and laymen feared that a literal acceptance of every Biblical idea and a denial of the discoveries of science would separate the Christian churches from any contact with modern culture. They were at times inclined to test traditional religious beliefs by the standards of the twentieth century.

The Fundamentalists. The conservatives or "reactionaries" in the theological dispute feared that the liberal interpretation of the Scriptures would destroy the power of Protestantism to maintain its evangelical influence in human affairs.

The Scopes Trial. Among conservative Protestant laymen none spoke more forcefully than William Jennings Bryan. He had urged state legislatures to bar the teaching of the theory of evolution in the public schools. When young John T. Scopes was indicted under a Tennessee law for teaching evolutionary theory in his high-school biology class, Bryan volunteered to argue the case against him. Scopes' counsel was Clarence Darrow, the most famous criminal lawyer of his day. The arguments of these distinguished counsellors focused the attention of the world on the trial in 1925. Scopes was found guilty of violating the law. Bryan's strenuous efforts for the conservative point of view, however, probably shortened his life, and the Fundamentalist cause steadily declined thereafter.

The Prohibition Experiment. Probably no public question of the postwar period had been so widely debated over the years as the prohibition of the manufacture and sale of intoxicating beverages.

PROHIBITION MOVEMENT. National prohibition was the culmination of a long campaign against the liquor traffic. From its inception early in the nineteenth century, the movement rested upon the conviction of an increasing portion of the American people that intoxicants: (1) had injurious effects upon the human body and mind; (2) contributed to poverty, vice, and crime; (3) were responsible for heavy taxes to support workhouses, asylums, and jails; (4) debauched the electorate and perpetuated evil influences in politics; (5) reduced the efficiency of workers and increased the problems of employers; (6) constituted a menace to life and property in an industrialized society. Three organizations were particularly effective in the prohibition movement: (1) the Prohibition party, formed in 1869, which placed the destruction of the liquor traffic above every other issue; (2) The Woman's Christian Temperance Union, which began an educational campaign in 1874; and (3) the Anti-Saloon League, organized in 1893, which mobilized the sentiment of evangelical Protestantism with great political astuteness.

THE EIGHTEENTH AMENDMENT. So successful were the tactics of the Anti-Saloon League that by the autumn of 1917 the legislatures of more than half the states had banned the liquor traffic, and fully two-thirds of the people of the country were living in territory which was "dry" either by state or local legislation. It is not surprising that after the Eighteenth Amendment was passed by Congress (December, 1917) the list of ratifications by state legislatures was soon long enough to insure its incorporation in the Constitution (January, 1919).

THE VOLSTEAD ACT. In September, 1919, Congress defined as intoxicating all beverages containing more than one half of 1 per cent of alcohol and provided the machinery to make prohibition effective. The obstacles in the way of successful enforcement of the Volstead Act were many: (1) the fact that some communities, especially the larger cities, were opposed to national prohibition; (2) the lack of co-operation between federal and local authorities; (3) the interference of politicians with the work of the prohibition unit in the Treasury Department; (4) the corruption of enforcement agents who accepted bribes from "bootleggers," earning large profits in an illicit business; (5) the failure of the Treasury and Justice departments to centralize control of the enforcement service. The difficulties of making the Volstead Act effective caused the enemies of prohibition to denounce the Eighteenth Amendment as a failure, the chief fruits of which had been an increasing disrespect for all laws and the rise of the bootlegger, the hijacker, the racketeer, and the gangster.

THE WICKERSHAM REPORT. In 1929 President Hoover appointed a commission, headed by George W. Wickersham, to study the problem of law enforcement in general and its relation to the prohibition experiment in particular. The report submitted in January, 1931, was a confession of the breakdown of federal enforcement of the liquor laws, but the Commission advised further trial of the Volstead Act and the Eighteenth Amendment.

THE COLLAPSE OF BOOM TIMES

The industrial expansion of the 1920's with its high profits and increasing production of goods, culminated in an orgy of speculation that collapsed with disastrous results in 1929.

The Rising Standard of Living. Between 1919 and 1929 the people of the United States experienced a change in their standard of living more remarkable than any change that had taken place in any previous decade.

THE BUSINESS SCENE. The apparent prosperity of the nation was marked not only by an increase in the national wealth but also by significant changes in the production and distribution of wealth. Business statistics during the 1920's emphasized: (1) the growing power and resources of corporations and the wider distribution of ownership shares in corporate enterprises; (2) the decline in manufacturing costs which resulted from standardized methods and uniform products; (3) the extension of consumers' credits through installment buying; (4) the multiplication of chain stores; (5) the upward trend of most industrial wages; and (6) the increase in real income per person each year.

THE POLITICAL SCENE. The Coolidge administration received widespread popular approval as a result of the prosperous years between 1923 and 1928.

The Campaign of 1928. President Coolidge's cryptic statement that he did not "choose to run in 1928" opened the door to the nomination of his Secretary of Commerce, Herbert Hoover. The Republicans named him on the first ballot of the national nominating convention. Likewise on the first ballot, the Democratic convention nominated Governor Alfred E. Smith of New York.

HOOVER'S ELECTION. Governor Smith's energetic campaign was doomed from the outset. He was handicapped in the South and Middle West by his antiprohibition views, his Catholic religious faith, and his affiliation with Tammany Hall. Most important of all, the country was prosperous and in no mood to break the spell which seemed to have been induced by Republican rule. The Democrats carried only eight states and lost such strongholds in the Solid South as Texas, Florida, North Carolina, and Virginia.

Business Confidence. President-elect Hoover was hailed by his friends as an engineer-businessman who would run the complicated machinery of government with skill and efficiency. Hoover himself declared that the economy of the nation was sound, as he took the oath of office.

The Speculative Mania.

The vast expansion and consolidation of business enterprise from 1919 to 1929 had concealed from many economists the highly speculative nature of these years of industrial prosperity. Stock-market quotations rather than profit-and-loss statements became the index of a firm's net worth. Hundreds of thousands of Americans, for the first time, were buying securities on the stock exchange, and many were buying their shares on credit.

SIGNS OF DANGER. Several disquieting features of these boom years were becoming alarming at the beginning of the Hoover administration. (1) Agricultural income was lagging far behind industrial income. (2) Wages of factory workers were increasing, but not as rapidly as the prices of manufactured goods. (3) The nation's mills, factories, and farms were producing more goods than American and foreign consumers could buy. (The high tariff curtailed the foreign market.) (4) Consumers were buying more goods on credit and thus were increasing the total outstanding private debts. (5) Too large a proportion of the total national income each year was being invested in highly speculative industrial, mining, and transportation enterprises.

THE STOCK-MARKET CRASH. Late in October, 1929, panic developed in the great securities markets. Prices of stocks and bonds dropped with startling rapidity to low levels. At no previous period in their history had so many Americans been directly interested in corporate securities. The collapse of the financial markets, therefore, was but the prelude to economic disaster.

REVIEW QUESTIONS

1. What did President Harding's phrase "return to normalcy" imply?
2. Explain the economic factors which were responsible for the formation of the congressional "farm bloc."
3. What was the purpose of the government's immigration policy after the First World War? How was that purpose carried into effect?
4. How do you account for the rapid rise of the movement to repeal the Eighteenth Amendment?
5. Describe the changes which were made in United States tariff laws during the Harding and Coolidge administrations.
6. Discuss the social and economic effects of the rapid rise of the automobile industry.
7. What was the significance of Charles A. Lindbergh's trans-Atlantic flight?
8. How do you account for the "Red Scare" following the First World War?

CHAPTER XII

ECONOMIC CRISIS AND THE NEW DEAL

It gradually become apparent that strong measures would be necessary to combat the depression. The New Deal, under President Franklin D. Roosevelt, attempted by experimental legislation to cope with the emergency situation. It also enacted long-range reforms to promote the economic security and social welfare of the whole people. In many ways this program represented a continuation of the reform movement begun in the previous century.

THE LENGTHENING SHADOW

The stock-market crash of October, 1929, marked the beginning of the worst economic depression in American history. In many ways it gave a new direction to the policies of the federal government.

The Coming of Depression. The reversal of the economic trend was at first regarded as merely temporary, but the nation slowly realized that it would be many years before the damage caused by excessive speculation could be repaired.

UNEMPLOYMENT. Some factories put up "no work" signs, while others closed their doors. By the end of 1931, almost ten million wage earners were unemployed. During 1932 between four and five million more were looking for jobs—any jobs.

BUSINESS FAILURES. Between 1929 and 1932 there were 85,000 business failures involving four and a half billion dollars. Much of the nation's industrial plant stood idle, with machines rusting and in disrepair.

DECLINING INCOMES. The scope of the nation's suffering was revealed in the statistics of national income. The total had stood at 81 billion dollars in 1929; in 1931 it fell to 53 billion and a year later to

41 billion. Savings in nine million accounts were literally wiped out to meet current family expenses.

THE NADIR OF NATIONAL MORALE. Perhaps the most serious injury suffered by the American people was spiritual rather than material. In the descent "from riches to rags" many of them lost self-confidence and felt that all the old guideposts had been destroyed.

The Apple-Vendors. In 1930 the International Apple Shippers' Association devised a scheme to market surplus apples and help the jobless. Soon thousands of apple-sellers had taken their stands on the sidewalks of New York, Chicago, and other large cities. The scheme brought a pittance to a few, but it was a symbol of the reluctance of the people to turn to government for direct relief.

Homes for the Homeless. In New York City homeless men slept in subway stations. Elsewhere they found abandoned factories, idle freight cars, or built shacks of flattened tin cans, cardboard, tar paper, and waste lumber.

Soup Kitchens and Bread Lines. A few died from starvation, but in every community voluntary charitable agencies tried to care for the hungry and the destitute. Churches, community centers, welfare societies, the Red Cross, and the Salvation Army joined forces in an attempt to help the people to help one another.

The "Bonus Army." In the spring of 1932, thousands of unemployed ex-servicemen began to converge on Washington. Their aim was to urge Congress to pass a bill which would enable them to collect immediately the bonus voted in 1924 for all veterans of the First World War (see p. 148). When it seemed probable that the "bonus army" would resort to force, President Hoover ordered United States troops to drive the men from the capital.

A Change in Political Command. It was President Hoover's misfortune that his years in the White House coincided with the most difficult phase of the Great Depression.

HOOVER'S PHILOSOPHY. The President in 1929 took the traditional American view that the surest and quickest way out of a depression was to rely chiefly on individual initiative. He clung to the hope that self-help and voluntary charity, with a minimum of governmental intervention, would restore more prosperous times.

LIMITED GOVERMENTAL ASSISTANCE. The federal government was not entirely inactive. The Hoover administration tried several remedies which it believed would encourage farmers, businessmen, and workers.

Agricultural Marketing Act (1929). Through this measure, the federal government tried to prevent farm prices, already low, from falling to disastrous levels. It also wanted to discourage the raising of surplus crops. The act created a Federal Farm Board to encourage the marketing of farm products through co-operatives. The Board was empowered to make low-interest loans to the co-operatives for the buying and selling of surpluses.

Policy of the Federal Reserve Board. In order to stimulate business activity, the Federal Reserve Banks were authorized to make loans to industry at relatively low rates for plant improvement or expansion.

Public Works Program. Wherever possible, the Hoover administration speeded up construction of public buildings and spent larger sums on government contracts that would increase employment of workers in the building and associated trades.

Reconstruction Finance Corporation (RFC). President Hoover finally accepted in 1932 a plan to "pump" government funds into the channels of private business enterprise. Congress created the Reconstruction Finance Corporation and empowered it to use two billion dollars in making loans to banks, insurance companies, building and loan associations, railroads, and farm credit organizations.

Norris-LaGuardia Act. This act, passed in March, 1932, narrowly restricted the use of injunctions in labor disputes and made "yellow-dog" contracts unenforceable in federal courts.

Direct Unemployment Relief. In July, 1932, Congress and President Hoover yielded to the pressure for emergency relief funds. Slightly more than two billion dollars was granted to states and municipalities for construction of public buildings and for emergency unemployment relief.

VICTORY OF FRANKLIN D. ROOSEVELT. The landslide victory of the Democrats in the presidential election of 1932 was not so much a vote of confidence in the Democratic party and its leaders as a measure of the resentment, inspired in large part by the economic depression, against the Hoover administration.

The Republican Convention. President Hoover controlled the proceedings of the Republican convention. The platform, which was drafted in the White House, was adopted after a spirited battle over the prohibition plank. (As finally adopted, the plank called for a referendum on the question.) Hoover's nomination on the first ballot was quickly made unanimous, and in accordance with the

President's wishes, Charles Curtis was renominated for Vice-President.

The Democratic Convention. The preconvention campaign of Governor Franklin D. Roosevelt of New York had made such headway that the only question in the minds of the delegates was whether a combination could be effected to prevent him from securing the necessary two-thirds vote. When the "stop Roosevelt" movement, led by Alfred E. Smith, collapsed, the New York governor was nominated on the fourth ballot. The platform, which was unusually brief and specific, committed the party to repeal of the Eighteenth Amendment and "continuous responsibility of government for human welfare."

Roosevelt's Election. Both President Hoover and Governor Roosevelt carried out extensive programs of speech-making. The President defended his party's protective tariff, farm relief, and economic recovery policies and denounced the proposals of the opposition as demagogic appeals. Roosevelt stressed the "new deal" for the "forgotten man" without clearly indicating the specific measures of his program. He accused the Republicans of seeking prosperity by conferring favors on the "special interests" and stressed the government's responsibility to promote the well-being of the great masses of its citizens. The result at the polls was an unprecedented majority for the Democrats. President Hoover carried only six states with 59 electoral votes.

THE NEW DEAL IN ACTION

Between Roosevelt's election and his inauguration, economic conditions had steadily worsened.* His inaugural address, however, sounded a high note of confidence: "The only thing we have to fear is fear itself."

Teamwork of Politicians and Economists. Franklin Roosevelt had no panacea for the depression. He was eager to persuade his associates that he was not afraid of experimentation if they would show him what experiments to try.

CAPTAIN OF THE TEAM. The President himself was an experienced and able politician who had great respect for economic theorists.

---

* Roosevelt was inaugurated on March 4. The Twentieth Amendment, which provided for the inauguration of succeeding Presidents on January 20, went into effect the following October.

He had served as a member of the New York State Senate, as Assistant Secretary of the Navy under President Wilson, and as candidate for the vice-presidency on the Democratic ticket in 1920 (see p. 151). Though stricken with polio in 1921, he had been convinced by his wife and devoted friends that his public career was not ended. After two terms in the governorship of New York, he won the presidency, aided by such astute politicians as James A. Farley and Louis M. Howe.

IMPROVISING A TEAM. F.D.R., as the President soon came to be known, chose his administrative assistants with considerable skill.

The Cabinet. Tennessee Senator Cordell Hull, a powerful congressional leader, became Secretary of State; William H. Woodin, conservative industrialist, served as Secretary of the Treasury, until his untimely death and was succeeded by Roosevelt's neighbor and close friend, Henry Morgenthau, Jr., of New York; Harold Ickes of Illinois, a former Progressive supporter of Theodore Roosevelt, brought reforming zeal into the Interior Department; Frances Perkins, who had been helpful to the President in framing social legislation for New York state became Secretary of Labor, the first woman to sit in a President's cabinet.

The "Brain Trust." Roosevelt consulted a group of unofficial advisers, whom the newspaper reporters soon nicknamed the "Brain Trust." Its membership shifted frequently, but in the early days of his administration it included college professors like Raymond Moley, Adolph A. Berle, Jr., and Rexford Tugwell; labor leaders like Sidney Hillman and William Green; and the financier Bernard M. Baruch.

CALLING NEW SIGNALS. Much of Roosevelt's approach to the difficult problems of the depression was pure experimentation, but the experiments which he tested indicated that the nation was moving away from traditional principles of economic individualism toward a planned economy. Administration leaders maintained that by such planning it was possible to establish an enduring balance in the economic system among conflicting interests and classes.

The "Hundred Days." Congress, called into special session on March 9, 1933, enacted a series of measures which President Roosevelt deemed essential. It was a remarkable period—the Hundred Days—of co-operation between the legislative and executive branches of the government.

THE RECOVERY PROGRAM. Any attempt to remedy the fundamental

economic and social weaknesses had to wait until emergency measures could meet the immediate needs of a discouraged people, many of whom were destitute.

Emergency Banking Act. Runs on banks had forced most of them to suspend operations. Fearful that the banking system was on the verge of collapse, President Roosevelt declared a bank holiday (March 5–9, 1933) which closed all national banks and other banking institutions affiliated with them. Congress quickly passed the Emergency Banking Law, giving the President power to reorganize insolvent national banks.

Federal Emergency Relief Administration (FERA). This agency was created to assist the states in caring for the unemployed. It was authorized to match funds with state and local governments in distributing aid to the jobless.

Civilian Conservation Corps (CCC). A dramatic recovery measure was the creation of the Civilian Conservation Corps, providing work for unemployed young men. They were used in national parks and forests and in reclamation projects in wilderness areas throughout the nation.

Home Owners' Loan Corporation (HOLC). The act creating this corporation provided for the issuance of three billion dollars in bonds, principal and interest guaranteed by the government, to be used to refinance mortgages of home-owners who were about to lose their properties through foreclosures.

The National Recovery Administration (NRA). It was the function of this organization to help representatives of government, employers, and employees to prepare codes in each industry which would eliminate unfair competitive practices, abolish child labor and sweatshops, establish minimum wages and maximum hours, create additional jobs for the unemployed, and insure labor the right of collective bargaining. Hundreds of these codes were drafted and administered by the NRA under the chairmanship of Hugh Johnson, but few proved to be effective.

Agricultural Adjustment Act. Passed in May, 1933, this act remained in operation until it was declared unconstitutional by the Supreme Court in January, 1936. It created an Agricultural Adjustment Administration (AAA) authorized: (1) to control production of wheat, cotton, corn, rice, tobacco, hogs, and certain other commodities by paying cash subsidies to farmers who voluntarily restricted acreage planted to such crops or reduced the numbers of their livestock; (2) to impose taxes upon the processors of agricultural commodities—like the flour miller or meat packer—in order to secure the funds to pay these subsidies; and (3) to pay farmers to sow grasses on untilled land that would provide cover for top soil and prevent dust storms.

LONG-RANGE REFORMS. While Congress was enacting the various laws that constituted a recovery program, it was also considering legislation to deal with serious problems only indirectly related to the economic depression.

Tennessee Valley Authority Act (TVA). This law marked the triumph of Republican Senator George Norris of Nebraska, who had long sought to place the power resources of the Tennessee River at the disposal of the people. It created an independent public corporation to develop the economic and social well-being of an area embracing parts of seven states and including the power project at Muscle Shoals (see p. 161). Through construction of dams, power plants, and transmission lines, many farms and villages in the Tennessee Valley were supplied with electric current at low rates. Important by-products of the Authority's work were the production of nitrogen fertilizers, plans for flood control, and the improvement of navigation on inland rivers. (TVA power aided atomic research at Oak Ridge after 1945.)

Securities Exchanges. To protect the investing public against fraudulent practices, the Federal Securities Act of 1933 provided for federal registration and supervision of new issues, penalized issuing firms and dealers for sending out misleading information, and defined in somewhat general terms the responsibility of the seller in connection with fraudulent issues. This act was supplemented in 1934 by an act putting the regulation of exchanges under a Securities and Exchange Commission of five members.

Control of Banking. A third great reform law was the Glass-Steagall Banking Act, passed in June, 1933. It created a Federal Deposit Insurance Corporation (FDIC) sponsored by the banks and the government to insure bank deposits up to $5000 each and to insure larger accounts on a partial basis. It provided that no commercial bank in the Federal Reserve System could loan to any subsidiary or affiliate more than 10 per cent of its capital and surplus and that member banks could not make loans to their own officers. National control of the banking system was further strengthened by the Banking Act of 1935, which provided (1) that all state banks

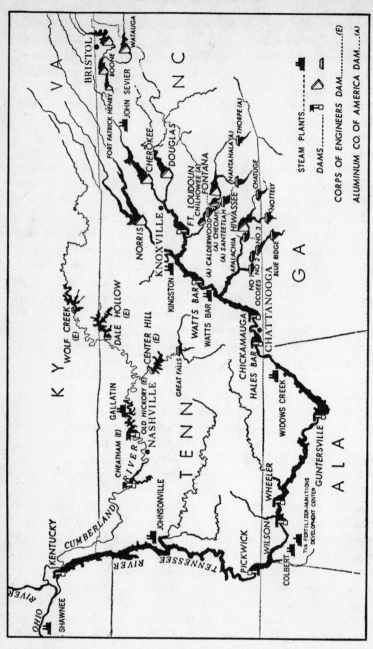

Tennessee Valley Authority—1959

with deposits of $1,000,000 or more must join the Federal Reserve System by 1942 to have their deposits insured by the government; and (2) that control of open-market transactions in federal bonds and other securities was to be vested in a special board consisting of five members representing the regional Federal Reserve Banks and seven members nominated by the President.

Inconclusive Signs of Recovery. By the spring of 1934 President Roosevelt was cheerfully declaring that legislation on the statute books would "cure" the depression ills. There were some superficial indications that the spirit of the nation had improved but no clear proof of recovery.

THE END OF THE "DRY" ERA. On December 5, 1933, the Secretary of State announced that the legislatures of three-fourths of the states had ratified the Twenty-first Amendment, which repealed the Eighteenth or Prohibition Amendment. Thereupon, control of the liquor traffic reverted to the states. All but eight promptly permitted the manufacture and sale of intoxicants, under various types of regulation. Revenue from liquor taxes soon was helping to pay increasing national and state expenditures.

ENCOURAGING AN INFLATIONARY TREND. The New Dealers, including the President, favored a monetary policy which would induce a general rise in the price level and minimize the fluctuations in prices characteristic of former periods of prosperity and depression.

The Gold Policy. Congress, eager for an inflationary plan to raise prices, granted the President discretionary power. He was authorized: (1) to issue legal-tender notes similar to the "greenbacks" of the Civil War years, (2) to establish free and unlimited coinage of silver at a fixed ratio with gold, (3) to reduce the gold content of the dollar by any amount up to 50 per cent. President Roosevelt chose dollar devaluation. After months of forcing up the price of gold through government purchases above the market price, Congress granted permission to stabilize the dollar within certain limits. This was done on January 31, 1934, by an executive order which fixed the gold content of the dollar at 59.06 per cent of its former value, transferred title to all gold in the Federal Reserve Banks to the government, and created a two-billion dollar stabilization fund to maintain the dollar at a desired level in international exchange.

Gold Clause Act. That the Roosevelt administration intended to retain its complete control over a managed currency was evident in the terms of the Gold Clause Act (1935), which denied to any person the right to sue the federal government in connection with gold-clause contracts or claims arising out of changes in the metallic content of the dollar.

STIMULATING PURCHASING POWER. The Civil Works Administration (CWA), like its predecessor FERA, was a form of unemployment relief, but it was not operated through the states. Under Administrator Harry Hopkins it put some four million people to work by February, 1934, thus increasing purchasing power and indirectly aiding private enterprise.

CRITICISM OF THE NEW DEAL. The very fact that many businessmen and political leaders began to resist what they considered the "radical" policies of the New Dealers indicated that confidence in the national economy had been restored. Complaints increased, however, that the Roosevelt administration was undermining the capitalistic system with its bold experimentation. Conservatives charged that the government was destroying private enterprise through interference in every phase of business activity.

POLITICAL ENDORSEMENT OF RECOVERY MEASURES. Whatever the effects of the New Deal legislation, they were approved by the voters in the congressional elections of 1934. The Roosevelt administration not only maintained its dominant position but also increased its strength in both houses of Congress. The number of Democrats in the House rose from 309 to 322, while in the Senate the Republican opposition was reduced to twenty-five members. Although the administration leaders experienced difficulty in maintaining unity of action among the Democrats, they met with no serious reversals in guiding the presidential program of legislation through the Seventy-fourth Congress.

THE SECOND NEW DEAL

Soon after the congressional election returns were known, the President's advisers indicated that the administration was ready to sponsor a comprehensive program to assist the underprivileged throughout the nation. In his 1935 message to Congress, Roosevelt stated the objectives of what is now known as the "Second New Deal."

Social Security. One of the most important reasons for Roosevelt's strong support of attempt to give the nation's workers a greater sense of security was the appeal being made by several extremist programs. These included Huey Long's share-the-wealth movement in Louisiana, Dr. Townsend's $200 a month pension scheme, and the demand by Father Charles E. Coughlin, a Michigan priest who made effective propaganda use of the radio, for radical inflation of the currency.

THE SOCIAL SECURITY ACT (1935). This law provided: (1) a federal program of old-age benefits, based on the workers' earnings before the age of sixty-five, to be paid out of funds derived from an income tax on employees and a payroll tax on employers; (2) a program of unemployment compensation administered by the states with federal grants approved by the Social Security Board; and (3) federal aid to the states for maternal and child-health services, for medical work among crippled children, and for welfare services among the aged and the blind.

WAGES AND HOURS ACT. The Fair Labor Standards Act, which became effective in the autumn of 1938, was an attempt to reach a standard of minimum wages and maximum hours in the country's chief industries. Committees for each industry, representing employers and employees, were to recommend the highest minimum wage up to forty cents an hour which seemed compatible with economic conditions in the industry. Maximum hours per week were to be reduced gradually to forty. The statute was enforced by the Wage and Hour Division in the Department of Labor.

Defense of Organized Labor. The New Dealers gained some of their most substantial victories in the field of labor legislation. Changes within the labor movement itself had great influence on the principles written into this legislation.

INDUSTRIAL VERSUS CRAFT UNIONS. The activity of labor organizers, stimulated by the collective bargaining provisions of the National Industrial Recovery Act, raised anew the problem of the unskilled industrial worker. Within the AFL certain groups (notably the United Mine Workers, United Textile Workers, Amalgamated Clothing Workers, and the International Typographical Union) sponsored industrial unionism.

Attitude of the AFL. At the national convention of the AFL in 1935 President William Green and his associates blocked an attempt made by John L. Lewis to commit the Federation to industrial unionism. A majority of the delegates favored the traditional organization based upon representation of the skilled crafts.

The Formation of the CIO. Under the leadership of Lewis and his mine workers, the Committee for Industrial Organization (CIO) defied the executive committee of the AFL and proceeded to organize the automotive and steel industries.

Success of the CIO. Rejected by the conservative AFL, the CIO formed a separate federation calling itself the Committee for Industrial Organization. By the spring of 1937 the CIO had secured partial recognition from the General Motors Corporation and several subsidiaries of United States Steel.

Violent Industrial Strife. The vigorous efforts of the CIO to organize the steel and automobile industries brought strikes marked by violence and bloodshed.

The "Sit-Down" Strike. In the automobile industry, striking workers used a new weapon, the "sit-down." They refused to leave plants against which their unions had called a work stoppage.

Resort to Force. When employers used forceful eviction to drive out striking workers or pickets, the labor organizers seemed to condone meeting force with force. A riot at a steel plant in South Chicago on Memorial Day, 1937, brought a pitched battle in which ten men were killed.

Recognition of Collective Bargaining. In spite of outbursts of violence, organized labor made great gains in winning public support and the recognition of its rights by employers generally. The Roosevelt administration was friendly toward labor's aspirations for a higher status in American life.

The NIRA and Organized Labor. Section 7 (a) of the National Industrial Recovery Act provided: (1) that laborers under the various codes should have the right of collective bargaining; (2) that they should choose their own representatives for such bargaining in free elections; and (3) that employers should recognize such representatives. This "charter of liberties" stimulated the growth of trade unions, greatly increasing their membership. However, there were many disputes over the way in which its provisions should be put into effect.

Labor Disputes Joint Resolution. The task of settling these industrial disputes proved too difficult for the National Labor Board set up under NRA, and Congress passed (June, 1934) the Labor Disputes Joint Resolution which authorized the creation of special labor investigating boards to report on the causes of friction. These boards were finally co-ordinated under a National Labor Relations Board with power of final review in all disputed cases.

National Labor Relations Act. After the National Industrial Recovery Act was declared unconstitutional, Senator Wagner of New York sponsored a plan to protect effectively labor's right to organize. The National Labor Relations Act of July, 1935, created a National Labor Relations Board (NLRB) of three members empowered to determine suitable units for collective bargaining, to conduct elections for the choice of labor's representatives, and to prevent interference with such elections. The Board was empowered to investigate complaints of unfair labor practices and to issue restraining orders, which it could petition federal courts to enforce. The Board's work was made difficult by the hostility of employers, who felt that the act was class legislation, and by the quarrel within the ranks of labor between the American Federation of Labor and the Committee for Industrial Organization.

The Continuing Menace of Unemployment.

On the basis of experience secured from the CWA, Roosevelt put a more comprehensive plan into operation early in 1935 to overcome persistent unemployment in both urban and rural areas.

THE WORKS PROGRESS ADMINISTRATION (WPA). This organization was instructed to find projects that could be carried out on public property at federal expense. By December, 1935, almost three million workers were receiving federal assistance through employment on government projects. By the terminal date in 1943, WPA had spent approximately eleven billion dollars and had helped 8,500,000 persons to find temporary jobs. Its activities included conservation, construction, educational, and cultural programs.

NATIONAL YOUTH ADMINISTRATION (NYA). This agency arranged part-time jobs for thousands of high-school and college students, so that they could work on worthwhile projects and still continue their education.

RURAL REHABILITATION. The problem of tenant farmers and agricultural laborers, trying to make a living on inferior and submarginal lands, became an important concern of the Roosevelt administration.

The Resettlement Administration (RA). This organization, formed in 1935, took large areas of substandard land out of cultivation, made loans to needy families at low interest rates, and resettled families on new farmsteads. In four years more than 785,000 farm families received rehabilitation loans.

The Farm Security Administration (FSA). The work of the RA was continued by the FSA. In addition FSA experimented with the resettlement of rural groups in co-operative communities and carried out a program of aid to migrant workers.

THE CONSTITUTIONAL CHALLENGE

The executive and legislative branches of the government seemed to be in substantial agreement concerning the need for the laws which comprised the recovery and reform programs of the New Deal. It remained for the Supreme Court to pass upon the constitutionality of the legislation.

Conservatives Domination of the Court. Decisions of the Supreme Court for more than half a century had indicated that the justices generally were opposed to increasing the role of government in the nation's economic affairs and reluctant to approve social reforms that imposed severe restrictions on individual initiative and action. The Court soon showed its hostility toward much of the New Deal reform legislation.

THE UNCONSTITUTIONALITY OF NRA. In the so-called "sick chicken" case, the Supreme Court in 1935 held that a Brooklyn, New York, poultry dealer could not be prosecuted for violating the NRA codes governing quality of the chickens he sold and the level of the wages he paid his employees. The justices agreed unanimously that the retail poultry business was not interstate commerce and that Congress had no jurisdiction over it. Roosevelt angrily retorted that this was a "horse-and-buggy" definition of interstate commerce.

JUDICIAL ATTACK ON THE AAA. In this decision the Supreme Court ruled by a 6–3 vote that the processing taxes imposed under the Agricultural Adjustment Act were not levied for the "general welfare," but were designed to regulate farm production. The Court held that it was beyond the power of the federal government to levy such a tax and that the Agricultural Adjustment Act was therefore unconstitutional.

Roosevelt's War on the Supreme Court. In spite of his anger and his fear that the courts would invalidate all New Deal legislation, President Roosevelt postponed action until the results of the presidential election of 1936 were known.

POPULAR APPROVAL OF THE ROOSEVELT ADMINISTRATION. In a campaign marked by vigorous defense and bitter denunciation of the

New Deal, F.D.R. was re-elected by a majority of ten million votes. He carried every state except Maine and Vermont.

The Issues. The voters did not weigh such issues as the philosophy underlying direct federal benefits, the centralization of power in the national government, the delegation of unusual authority to the President, and the relation of a heavily unbalanced budget to the economy of the nation. Democrats were content to defend their record, which, they insisted, was responsible for the return of prosperity; the Republicans denounced the administration for reckless experimentation, extravagant spending, use of the spoils system, and failure to suppress communism.

Campaign Strategy. The conduct of the campaign by the Republicans was hesitant and inept, sharply contrasting with the assurance and skill of the politicians who managed the Democratic machine. President Roosevelt carried the brunt of the battle for his party, while Governor Landon of Kansas, nominated by the Republicans, proved to be a poor campaigner both in his direct appeals and in his radio speeches.

The Democratic Victory. The popular vote for President Roosevelt cut across party lines. The overwhelming character of his victory was bound to be embarrassing, for many were drawn into the Democratic ranks who had little interest in the administration's long-range objectives. Roosevelt, however, chose to interpret his re-election as a blanket endorsement of his policies. He quickly made plans to get around the opposition of the Supreme Court.

THE "NINE OLD MEN." Because six of the Supreme Court justices were over seventy years of age, the President struck at them as men too old to remain in office. He also charged that the Court was violating the Constitution by acting as a "policy-making body." But he avoided a careful analysis of the basis of its judicial opinions.

"Packing" the Court. On February 5, 1937, Roosevelt proposed to Congress a plan to appoint additional judges in the various federal courts, "where there are incumbent judges of retirement age who do not choose to resign." In the case of the Supreme Court the retirement age was to be seventy years, and the President was to appoint not more than six additional members to supplement non-retiring justices.

Failure in Congress. The storm over the "Court Packing Bill" so impressed the members of the Senate that the administration could not persuade conservative Democrats to support the measure. This marked the first clear division between the two wings of the party. After the death of Senator Joseph T. Robinson of Arkansas, who had directed parliamentary tactics, Roosevelt reluctantly abandoned the contest.

Victory in the Court. In the end, however, the President won. Several major New Deal laws were sustained by the Court in the spring of 1937. Among them were the Social Security Act, the National Labor Relations Act, and a farm mortgage moratorium act. Also in 1937 the Court reversed earlier decisions by upholding a state minimum-wage law. After 1937 resignation and death brought such a change in the membership of the Court that a reversal in interpretation of the powers of Congress over economic and social matters was even more apparent. By 1941 Roosevelt had named seven of the nine justices. With the retirement in that year of Chief Justice Charles Evans Hughes, the President elevated Justice Harlan Stone to the vacant position. Among the legislation sustained by the Court's new members were the Fair Labor Standards Act and a second Agricultural Adjustment Act that provided for soil conservation payments, the allotment of acreage for staple crops, and "parity" loans on surplus crops (based on 1909–1914 prices).

THE BALANCE SHEET

Franklin D. Roosevelt's years in the presidency constituted one of the most controversial periods in our history. As the nation's leader he was greatly loved and bitterly hated. His ardent admirers thought he could do no wrong, while his foes believed that he was destroying the traditional American way of life.

Counting the Financial Cost. The elaborate spending program and the extensive loans to private enterprise that characterized the New Deal efforts to promote recovery placed an extraordinary burden on the Treasury Department.

TAXATION. The Roosevelt administration was slow to revise the nation's tax system, but it tried to increase the annual tax revenues.

Revenue Act of 1935. Congress reluctantly yielded to presidential insistence in 1935 and passed a federal revenue act which increased the rates on individual incomes over $50,000, on gifts, on estates, on corporate earnings, and on excess profits.

Revenue Act of 1936. Not satisfied that the larger corporations were being adequately assessed, the President urged Congress to modify the tax law so as to place a high levy against undistributed corporate profits and against all gains realized through the transfer of capital assets. Opposition to these two features was so widespread that in 1938 the rates in both instances were drastically revised in favor of the taxpayer.

DEFICIT FINANCING. Taxation did not provide sufficient revenue to pay for the experiments of the New Deal.

Unbalanced Budgets. In five years after 1933 the accumulating annual deficits reached a sum slightly in excess of ten billion dollars.

The Public Debt. On June 30, 1933, the gross debt of the United States had stood at $22,500,000,000. Six years later it had increased to $40,439,000,000. The government claimed that it had some four billion dollars in recoverable enterprises to offset this. Deficit financing, however, had almost doubled the national debt in six years. This rapid increase was slight in comparison with the crushing burden of debt piled up during the Second World War.

The Continuity of Reform. In many ways Franklin Roosevelt's program was a continuation of reforms which had been interrupted by the outbreak of the First World War.

REPUBLICAN AND DEMOCRATIC PRECEDENTS. The New Deal regulation of business emphasized some of the principles laid down in the Interstate Commerce Act of 1887 and the Sherman Antitrust Act of 1890, the latter signed by a Republican President; and much of Roosevelt's farm relief program was foreshadowed by proposals to aid agriculture during Woodrow Wilson's administration.

BORROWINGS FROM THE POPULISTS AND THE PROGRESSIVES. Roosevelt's attack on the captains of industry as "economic royalists" was reminiscent of the campaigns against the "money power" carried on by both the Populists and the Progressives. A number of New Deal reforms had been demanded first by those groups.

New Directions in Public Policy. The New Deal, however, revealed the federal government to most citizens in an entirely new role. It was not merely a restrictive and coercive force but an instrument to enable democracy to solve its problems with speed and decision. Primarily, it was a vital agency in providing economic security for all the people.

The Interruption of Reform. Roosevelt was still urging further reforms to strengthen the nation when war was thrust upon Europe by the Nazi and Communist dictatorships in 1939. Whether the voluminous legislation of the New Deal would have solved the economic and social problems revealed by the Great Depression was never answered, for recovery measures and reform plans were interrupted by the Second World War. As F.D.R. phrased it: "Dr. New Deal had been replaced by Dr. Win-the-War."

REVIEW QUESTIONS

1. Explain President Hoover's reaction to the impact of the Great Depression.
2. Why did the Roosevelt administration make the agricultural program so important a part of its general recovery schemes?
3. Upon what economic theories did the New Dealers base their arguments in support of a "managed currency"?
4. How much justification was there for the charge that the recovery program constituted a denial of the American system of free enterprise?
5. What features of the New Deal seem to have contributed to the strength of organized labor in the United States?
6. If you had been a member of the Senate would you have supported Roosevelt's proposal for reorganization of the Supreme Court? Why?
7. Was the government wise in resorting to "deficit financing" after 1933? Give your reasons.
8. Compare Roosevelt's conception of the function of government with that of Woodrow Wilson.
9. In what ways was the legislative program of the New Dealers an extension of earlier reform movements?

Chapter XIII

THE IMPACT OF WORLD POWER

In the period between the First and Second World Wars, the United States gradually assumed a position of world leadership commensurate with its wealth and industrial power. When the aggressive policies of Germany, Italy, and Japan brought war to Europe and Asia, the American people turned from isolationism to aid the democracies.

ECONOMIC LEADERSHIP

The First World War had pushed the United States rapidly toward a position of primacy in industrial production and international trade.

Sources of Material Strength. The statistics of economic expansion were impressive, indicating that the center of financial and industrial power had shifted from western Europe to the United States.

ABUNDANT NATURAL RESOURCES. By 1920 the nation was producing 40 per cent of the world's coal, 68 per cent of its petroleum, and approximately 45 per cent of its pig iron.

EXPANDING INDUSTRIAL PLANT. In manufactured goods Americans outdistanced all rivals; by 1928 their factories were producing slightly less than 50 per cent of the total industrial production of the world.

MOUNTING INVESTMENTS. The First World War literally transformed the country from a debtor into a creditor nation. Europe needed not only America's agricultural products but also its manufactured goods. To pay for them, the warring countries borrowed from the United States. By the time the war ended, private and government loans to foreign nations had reached a total of 12.5 billion dollars.

Changes in Foreign Trade. As American exports rose rapidly, exceeding the imports from abroad, foreign debtor nations found it difficult to make payments for goods bought on credit.

TARIFF WARS. From all parts of the world came protests against American tariffs which remained high during the 1920's (see pp. 157–158). When the Smoot-Hawley Tariff of 1930 further increased the duties on most imported goods, many nations passed bills in retaliation placing restrictions on the passage of American-made goods through their customs offices.

LONDON ECONOMIC CONFERENCE. During June and July of 1933 a conference was held, under the auspices of the League of Nations, to consider monetary and tariff problems. The United States sent a delegation, headed by Secretary Hull, but refused to co-operate with the other nations in currency stabilization, having gone off the gold standard (see p. 177). The gold-block nations were angered by the United States attitude, and the conference adjourned without results.

RECIPROCAL TRADE AGREEMENTS. Secretary Hull feared both the political and economic effects of trade wars. He proposed a series of reciprocal trade agreements with the nation's best customers in Europe, Asia, and South America. Congress agreed (1934) that the President, with the advice of certain qualified experts in the governmental service, might negotiate such agreements without congressional approval provided that the agreements did not vary from existing duties by more than 50 per cent. Several years later agreements were in effect with a list of nations which included Great Britain, France, Belgium, the Netherlands, Canada, and Latin-American countries.

TOWARD INTER-AMERICAN SOLIDARITY

In Latin America, the United States used its influence to promote greater understanding among all the American republics. It did so with a realization that its own national defense was a hemispheric problem.

Better Relations With Mexico. The attempts of the Obregon and then the Calles government in Mexico to enforce a provision of the 1917 constitution that all mineral resources belonged to the Mexican government alarmed United States oil companies and other American investors.

SECRETARY KELLOGG'S WARNING. President Calles' decision in 1925 to dispossess foreign oil and mining companies brought a warning from Secretary of State Kellogg that "the government of Mexico is now on trial before the world."

AMBASSADOR MORROW'S MISSION (1927–1930). As tensions mounted President Coolidge named his close friend, Dwight W. Morrow, to be ambassador to Mexico. Morrow's sympathetic handling of a delicate situation won him tremendous acclaim both in the United States and in Mexico. He not only succeeded in securing satisfactory modifications of the Petroleum Law (which restricted foreign corporations), but he also mediated between the Roman Catholic hierarchy in Mexico and the anticlerical government.

SECRETARY HULL'S PEACEFUL PERSUASION. The experiments in state socialism undertaken by the Mexican government after 1934 disturbed the United States, but the State Department refrained from interference. When Mexico expropriated foreign-owned properties in 1938, Secretary Hull admitted the right of a sovereign state so to do and then reminded Mexico that she must compensate the dispossessed owners at "fair, assured, and effective values." Mexico refused Hull's suggestion of arbitration and insisted that she would reimburse the owners in her own way and at her own convenience; but in 1941 a settlement was reached which proved satisfactory to American investors.

Conciliatory Diplomacy. Presidents Coolidge, Hoover, and Franklin Roosevelt tried to promote a better understanding between the republics of Central and South America and the United States.

PAN-AMERICAN CONFERENCES. In 1923 at Santiago, Chile, an Inter-American Conference adopted the principle that peaceful means should be found to settle any dispute between American republics. Five years later at Havana, Cuba, President Coolidge stated: "All nations here represented stand on an equal footing." The participating countries signed a general treaty providing for the arbitration of almost all disputes in this hemisphere.

THE CLARK MEMORANDUM. In 1928 Under-Secretary of State J. Reuben Clark prepared a memorandum that clarified the current American interpretation of the Monroe Doctrine. Approved by the Coolidge and Hoover administrations, it specifically repudiated the Theodore Roosevelt Corollary (see p. 118) and gave assurance that the United States was abandoning its role as a policeman keeping order in Latin-American countries. It was greeted with satisfaction in South America.

THE GOOD NEIGHBOR POLICY. In his first inaugural address Franklin Roosevelt indicated that his administration was eager to adopt a new policy toward Latin America. Said the President: "In the field of foreign relations I would dedicate this nation to the policy of the good neighbor."

Montevideo Conference (1933). Secretary of State Cordell Hull announced at this Pan-American Conference that "no state has the right to intevene in the internal or external affairs of another." President Roosevelt supported Hull by declaring that in the future the United States would oppose any armed intervention in other countries.

Abrogation of the Platt Amendment. In 1934 the State Department announced the abrogation of the Platt Amendment (see p. 102) so far as the intervention of the United States in Cuban affairs was concerned.

Haiti and Nicaragua. By January, 1935, the last American marines had been withdrawn from Haiti and Nicaragua. Three years later, to forestall German financial interests, the United States through the Export-Import Bank virtually underwrote a loan of $5,000,000 to Haiti for a public works program.

Dominican Republic. In 1940 President Roosevelt terminated the customs receivership which the United States had exercised in the Dominican Republic ever since 1905.

HEMISPHERIC DEFENSE. In the countries of South America the efforts of the United States were largely directed toward curbing the economic penetration of Germany and Italy by developing a system of hemispheric defense.

The Lima Conference (1938). The Eighth Pan-American Conference was held at Lima, Peru, late in December, 1938. The twenty-one American republics affirmed their continental solidarity and announced that any threat to peace in the Western Hemisphere would lead to immediate consultation between all governments.

Panama Declaration. With the outbreak of war in Europe in September, 1939, the American states undertook to define their neutral position. The conference at Panama City in October, in harmony with the desire of the Roosevelt administration to keep the war out of the Americas, adopted a resolution establishing a three-hundred-mile safety zone around the Western Hemisphere wherein belligerent activities were to be barred.

Act of Havana. In July, 1940, the foreign ministers of the Latin-

American countries and the United States affirmed their position that an act of aggression against any one state would be considered an attack on all of them. This act also provided for the taking over by the American republics of any European possession in the New World that was in danger of aggression. When war came in 1941, there was an inter-American partnership to protect the Western Hemisphere.

Act of Chapultepec. In 1945 the American republics, with the exception of Argentina, signed an agreement providing for mutual assistance and collective security during the Second World War. Argentina later entered the war and was admitted to the pact.

THE FUTILE SEARCH FOR PEACE

For twenty years after the First World War the United States found it difficult to co-operate with other nations in any form of collective action to promote peace. The trend of opinion toward economic nationalism and political isolation was strong.

War Debts in Reparations. Relations with European nations early in the 1920's were seriously affected by efforts to collect the sums which Americans had loaned to the governments of the Allied Powers during and immediately after the war.

FOREIGN DEBT COMMISSION (1922). Many Americans believed that for selfish, as well as sentimental, reasons that United States should cancel the war debts. Congress, however, created a World War Foreign Debt Commission which negotiated agreements with the various nations on the basis of each debtor's ability to pay. The total funded indebtedness of seventeen nations was fixed at $10,350,000,-000, a considerable scaling down of the original loans and accrued interest. Payments were spread over a period of sixty-two years.

THE DAWES PLAN (1924). Although the United States refused to admit that payment of the war debts was contingent upon collection of reparations from Germany by the Allies, such was in reality the case. When Germany defaulted on reparations payments, the United States participated in formulating the Dawes plan, whereby the German obligations were materially reduced and German industries were extended long-term credits.

THE YOUNG PLAN (1930). Revision of the German reparations agreement became necessary in 1929. A commission of experts, headed by Owen D. Young, arranged new terms partially contingent upon the American policy concerning the reduction of Allied war debts. It set up a Bank for International Settlements to facilitate reparations payments and other processes of international finance.

THE MORATORIUM OF 1931. So alarming was the financial weakness of Germany and Austria in the spring of 1931 that President Hoover proposed "postponement during one year of all payments on intergovernmental debts, reparations, and relief debts, both principal and interest." This moratorium was not extended in 1932, but several nations failed to make payments on their debts to the United States, and the following year almost all of them defaulted.

The Movement to Ban War. After the First World War there was a spirited revival in the Western world of the crusade against war.

PLANS FOR DISARMAMENT. Despite its isolationist attitude, the government of the United States participated in several conferences designed to limit armaments.

The Washington Conference (1921–1922). At President Harding's invitation, delegates from Great Britain, France, Italy, Japan, China, Belgium, the Netherlands, and Portugal met in Washington to discuss reduction of naval armaments and problems of the Pacific. The conference drafted nine treaties the most important of which were: (1) a five-power treaty providing for a ten-year "naval holiday" in the construction of capital ships, fixing the relative tonnage of Great Britain, the United States, Japan, France, and Italy at 5 :5 :3 :1.67 :1.67, limiting the total tonnage of capital ships according to this ratio, and generally maintaining the status quo of naval bases and fortifications in the Pacific; (2) a four-power treaty binding the signatories (the United States, Great Britain, Japan, and France) to respect one another's rights in the Pacific and to confer in the event that any question threatened to disrupt harmonious relations; and (3) a nine-power treaty guaranteeing the political and territorial integrity of China and the "open door" for trade. (A second nine-power treaty restored tariff control to China.)

The Geneva Conference (1927). At President Coolidge's suggestion the signatories of the Washington naval treaty were invited to confer at Geneva in 1927. Delegates from Great Britain, the United States, and Japan spent six weeks in fruitless discussions regarding restrictions on ship-building.

The London Conference (1930). The dangers of a new race in naval armaments caused Great Britain to invite the five powers to discuss naval armaments in 1930. France and Italy withdrew from the conference; but the United States, Great Britain, and Japan signed a treaty establishing naval parity between the United States and Great Britain, fixing ratios for the building of auxiliary craft, and extending the ban on battleship construction to 1936.

General Disarmament Conference (1932). President Hoover sent a distinguished delegation to the general disarmament conference of thirty-one nations which met at Geneva on February 5, 1932. Before its first recess in July it adopted a resolution setting forth certain principles which were regarded as basic in meeting concrete problems of disarmament. The prolonged deliberations were doomed when Japan, convinced that she could not secure satisfactory concessions from Great Britain and the United States, formally announced (December, 1934) that she would not renew the naval agreement originally signed at the Washington Conference of 1921. A new race to build naval armaments loomed on the horizon.

THE PACT OF PARIS (1928). Popularly known as the Kellogg-Briand Pact (from its originators, United States Secretary of State Frank B. Kellogg and French Premier Aristide Briand), this agreement signed by fifteen nations represented an attempt to outlaw war. Forty-eight nations in addition to the original fifteen subscribed to the covenant, which provided (1) that the signatory powers renounce war as an instrument of national policy and (2) that they agree to settle all international disputes by pacific means. The Pact gave some impetus to the use of arbitration treaties as means of settling disputes.

THE WORLD COURT. Three distinguished American jurists served upon this tribunal: John Bassett Moore (1921–1928); Charles Evans Hughes (1928–1930); and Frank B. Kellogg (1930–1935). On January 27, 1926, at the prompting of President Coolidge, the Senate accepted the protocol of membership with five reservations. Not all of these reservations were acceptable to the members of the Court; American co-operation was therefore delayed. Elihu Root participated in 1929 in the formulation of a revised protocol which seemed to be more satisfactory, but after long delay the Senate finally refused to ratify (January, 1935). In 1945 the functions of the World Court were taken over by the International Court of Justice established under the United Nations. United States membership in this Court was promptly ratified by the Senate.

THE LEAGUE OF NATIONS. The United States gradually abandoned its earlier refusal to recognize the existence of the League of Nations. It co-operated constantly in the nonpolitical phases of the League's work; it participated in the preliminary plans for the League's general disarmament conference; and it indicated officially its willingness to act with the League in an effort to make effective the provisions of the Kellogg-Briand Pact.

Trying to Avoid Europe's Quarrels. With the rise of Adolf Hitler to power in Germany in 1933, the United States Congress tried constantly to minimize the possibility of America's becoming involved again in any war in Europe.

NYE INVESTIGATION (1934). A Senate investigating committee, headed by Gerald P. Nye of North Dakota, revealed that enormous profits had been made during the First World War by United States financiers and arms manufacturers. It suggested that pressure from these groups had forced the nation into the war.

JOHNSON ACT (1934). Sponsored by Senator Hiram Johnson of California, this act forbade the sale in the United States of securities issued by any government which had defaulted in the payment of its obligations to this country. Since virtually every European nation except Finland belonged in the category of a defaulter, the law was regarded as an effective device to prevent the financial involvement of the United States or its people in the plans of any European nation seeking to finance war expenditures.

THE NEUTRALITY ACTS. Between August, 1935 and May, 1937, Congress passed three neutrality acts in an effort to meet all possible contingencies and to insure neutrality in the event of war anywhere in the world. The acts varied chiefly in the provisions affecting the discretionary powers of the President. Each succeeding act indicated a growing inclination on the part of Congress to keep control of foreign policy in its own hands. The Act of 1937, designed to be permanent, compelled the President to take certain actions when a state of war existed. Among the compulsory prohibitions were: (1) travel by Americans on belligerent ships; (2) use of American merchantmen to transport implements of war to belligerents; (3) export of "arms, ammunition, and implements of war" to belligerents. The President might prohibit: (1) the use of American ports as supply bases for belligerent warships or armed merchant ships; (2) the transport of any commodities on an American ship to a belligerent; (3) the export of goods to a belligerent, unless title had first been transferred to a foreign government.

ARMS EMBARGO REPEAL. When war broke out over the Polish situation late in 1939, the administration urged Congress to reconsider certain of the mandatory features of the existing neutrality legislation. The point at issue was the compulsory embargo on "arms, ammunition, and implements of war." After spirited debate Congress modified the Neutrality Act so as to repeal the arms embargo, open the munitions trade to belligerents on a cash-and-carry basis, and bar American merchant shipping from war zones to be designated by presidential proclamation.

RESISTANCE TO AGGRESSION

Despite elaborate neutrality legislation, the Roosevelt administration moved steadily, though at times hesitantly, to prepare the nation for the impact of what might become a second world war.

Attitude toward the Axis Powers. Many Americans believed that the Treaty of Versailles had been too severe in the penalties imposed upon Germany; but as they watched the rise of National Socialism under Hitler, they came to regard the Nazi regime as uncompromisingly dictatorial in its domestic policies and unjustifiably aggressive in its foreign relations. Fascist Italy, under Mussolini, was also a threat to world peace.

STEPS TOWARD WAR. In 1935 Italy, defying the League of Nations, invaded Ethiopia and the following year joined Germany (which had withdrawn from the League in 1933) to form the Rome-Berlin Axis. In the spring of 1938 Germany forcibly annexed Austria. Several months later, at the Munich Conference, Great Britain and France agreed to German annexation of the Czechoslovakian Sudetenland, in the hope of averting a general war. Shortly thereafter Germany took over the whole of Czechoslovakia. In August, 1939, Germany and the Soviet Union announced the conclusion of a nonaggression pact between the two nations. The stage was now set for the Second World War, which began September 1, 1939, with the German invasion of Poland (whose independence Great Britain and France had guaranteed).

WAR IN EUROPE. During the winter of 1939–1940 there was little action on the Western front. However, the Soviet Union took advantage of the situation to invade the Baltic states: Estonia, Latvia, Lithuania, and Finland. The Finns put up valiant resistance but were defeated by overwhelming Soviet military power. In the spring of 1940, the highly mechanized German army overran Denmark, Norway, Luxembourg, the Netherlands, and Belgium. Italy then entered the war on the German side. France surrendered in June, and the British expeditionary army was forced to evacuate the Continent. American public opinion was aroused against the ruthless German invasion of neutral countries and applauded the heroism of England, which fought on alone despite heavy bombings by the Nazi *Luftwaffe*.

QUARANTINE OF AGGRESSORS. In 1937 Roosevelt suggested that the United States take the lead in persuading all peace-loving nations to "quarantine" the aggressor through economic boycott in the event of international strife. Finding little support in Congress, he undertook to persuade Germany and Italy that their just demands could be satisfied around the conference table rather than by military victories. When his pleas to the dictators for peaceful negotiation brought no results, he advised Congress that there were means "short of war" to curb the spread of totalitarian power.

ISOLATIONISTS. The chief critics of the presidential policy came to be known as isolationists, for they recommended that the nation refrain from words as well as deeds which might involve it in any European or Asiatic struggle for power. By the spring of 1941 this group was devoting its efforts to keeping the United States out of the Second World War. Its leaders in Congress were Senators Burton K. Wheeler, Gerald P. Nye, Robert A. Taft, and Bennett Clark, while Charles A. Lindbergh, supported by General Robert E. Wood of the "America First" Committee, had won a considerable popular following by urging a negotiated peace between Great Britain and the Axis.

Strife in the Far East.

Defying the League Covenant, the Washington treaties, and the Kellogg-Briand Pact (as well as bilateral agreements with the United States), Japan attempted by military aggression to secure control of the Far East. The United States government denounced Japan's actions but was unwilling to apply force to prevent them.

STIMSON DOCTRINE. In 1931 Japan occupied Manchuria and set up a puppet government there. Secretary of State Stimson informed

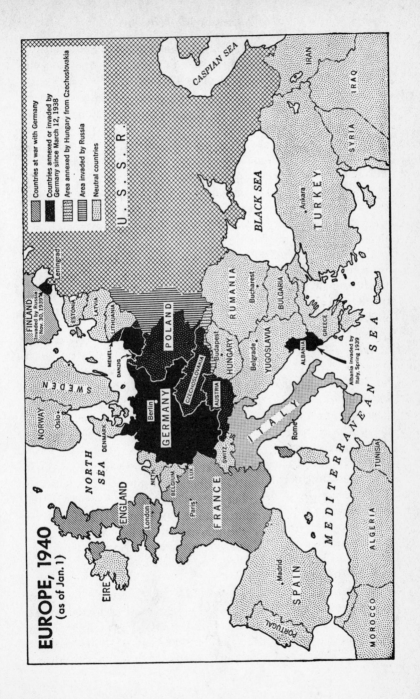

EUROPE, 1940
(as of Jan. 1)

Countries at war with Germany
Countries annexed or invaded by Germany since March 12, 1938
Area annexed by Hungary from Czechoslovakia
Area invaded by Russia
Neutral countries

CASPIAN SEA

U. S. S. R.

Leningrad

FINLAND
Invaded by Russia
Nov. 30 1939

ESTONIA

LATVIA

LITHUANIA

MEMEL

DANZIG

POLAND

CZECHOSLOVAKIA

Berlin

GERMANY

AUSTRIA

Budapest

HUNGARY

RUMANIA

Bucharest

BULGARIA

BLACK SEA

TURKEY

Ankara

IRAN

SYRIA

IRAQ

Belgrade

YUGOSLAVIA

GREECE

ALBANIA

Albania invaded by
Italy, Spring 1939

NORWAY

Oslo

SWEDEN

DENMARK

NORTH
SEA

ENGLAND

London

EIRE

NETH.

BELGIUM

LUX.

Paris

FRANCE

SWITZ.

ITALY

Rome

MEDITERRANEAN SEA

TUNISIA

SPAIN

Madrid

PORTUGAL

MOROCCO

ALGERIA

China and Japan (January, 1932) that the United States would not recognize any agreement that violated the "open-door" policy or the political and territorial integrity of the Chinese republic. The League of Nations accepted the principle of nonrecognition, causing the withdrawal of Japan from the League; but it took no concrete measures to implement this policy.

BRUSSELS CONFERENCE. With the Japanese invasion of China in July, 1937, American opinion became strongly anti-Japanese. In November of that year, representatives of the United States joined with delegates from eighteen other nations in denouncing Japan as a treaty-breaker and an aggressor. However, the leaders of these nations were too much concerned over the European situation to take punitive action in the Far East.

THE "OPEN DOOR." One year later Japan felt strong enough to warn the rest of the world that the "new order in Asia" would not be based upon the principle of the "open door" in trade and industry. The American State Department refused to accept any such unilateral abrogation of Japan's previous agreements.

THE "WAR OF NERVES." By 1939 Japan and the United States were carrying on a verbal war in which each was trying to wear down the other through nervous tension. In July of that year the American State Department gave the necessary six-months' notice to terminate the reciprocal commercial treaty which had been negotiated in 1911. Japanese purchases of gasoline, scrap iron, and other war materials in the United States continued, but the control over them became increasingly rigorous.

AID TO CHINA. Resentment against Japan served to quicken American sympathy for China. Contributions to the relief of Chinese victims of the war were but one evidence of that sympathy. By 1940 the American government had loaned almost $70,000,000 to the Chinese government for the purchase of badly needed supplies. President Roosevelt refrained from invoking the Neutrality Act (on the ground that there had been no declaration of war) to make such aid possible.

NETHERLANDS EAST INDIES. As soon as German troops had overrun the Netherlands in the spring of 1940, Japan began a drive to secure a larger portion of the products from the Dutch colonial empire in the South Pacific. The British at Singapore and the American fleet at Pearl Harbor in the Hawaiian Islands probably prevented any overt act at that time, but Japanese desire to acquire the islands was obvious.

The Arsenal of Democracy. Though a large majority of Americans were anxious to avoid any involvement in the Second World War, they were eager that Great Britain and France should win.

CONTROL OF THE ATLANTIC. The revision of the Neutrality Act, late in 1939, enabled Great Britain and France to place orders for munitions and other war supplies in the United States. Delivery, however, depended upon the ability of the Allies to get their ships across the Atlantic safely, and the United States Navy steadily increased its activity in protecting such shipments in the North Atlantic. By the spring of 1941 America had established a naval base in Greenland and had made sure that control of the Atlantic would not pass to any hostile nation.

INDIRECT SALES. After the collapse of France, the United States, through a system of indirect sales, released to the Allies considerable stores of munitions remaining from the First World War. To facilitate his program of aid to the Allies, President Roosevelt named Henry L. Stimson of New York to be Secretary of War and Frank Knox of Illinois to be Secretary of the Navy. Both men were Republicans and both were strongly pro-Ally.

TRANSFER OF DESTROYERS. Because of the success of German attacks upon British commerce in the Atlantic, the British Navy was in need of additional destroyers. In September, 1940, the administration announced the transfer of fifty over-age destroyers to Great Britain in exchange for ninety-nine-year leases on eight naval and air bases on British possessions in the Western Hemisphere.

LEND-LEASE BILL. Early in 1941 Congress, over the protests of the isolationist leaders, authorized the sale, loan, lease, transfer, or exchange of war materials to any country whose defense the President considered vital to the defense of the United States. The amount of aid which could be given was limited, but the President was allowed considerable discretion in placing a valuation upon such goods and in arranging the terms of the transfer. By 1942, thirty-five countries in addition to the British Commonwealth had thus received assistance. In June, 1941, Hitler repudiated the German-Soviet pact, and the German army invaded Russia. American Lend-Lease aid was then extended to the Soviet Union.

INTERVENTIONISTS. A well-organized minority in the nation had become convinced that the best defense for the United States lay in the victory of Great Britain over Germany. They were prepared to intervene in the war at that time in order to make certain of German defeat.

National Defense Program. With the German invasion of the Low Countries, Americans were shocked into a realization of the implications for them of total war. Their earnest endeavor to prepare for full national defense began at that time.

Hemisphere Strategy. German conquests raised questions in the United States concerning the fate of Dutch, French, and possibly British possessions in the Western Hemisphere.

Rephrasing the Monroe Doctrine. In a joint resolution, Congress declared (June, 1940) that the United States would not countenance the transfer of any American territory from one non-American nation to another.

Canadian Co-operation. Implementing his statement in 1938 that the United States would not permit the domination of Canada by any foreign empire, President Roosevelt joined Canadian Prime Minister MacKenzie King in creating a Permanent Joint Board to study the defense needs of the northern part of the North American Continent.

Rearmament Appropriations. During 1940 Congress appropriated approximately eighteen billion dollars for armaments. The bulk of this huge sum was earmarked for two purposes: the construction of a two-ocean navy superior to any possible combination of naval power, and the creation of an army of 1,200,000. These two branches were to be supported by an air fleet of 35,000 planes.

Compulsory Military Service. The first peacetime conscription was authorized by Congress in September, 1940. All men between the ages of twenty-one and thirty-five inclusive were compelled to register, and from the registrants 800,000 were selected by lot for a year's military training. The National Guard also was called out for intensive instruction in modern warfare.

Industrial Mobilization. In May, 1940, the President, acting under the authority conferred by a statute of 1916, appointed an Advisory Commission to the Council of National Defense. The seven members of the Commission were severally responsible for the following divisions: industrial materials, production, transportation, labor, agriculture, price stabilization, and consumer protection. Their task was to carry the defense program from the appropriation stage into action, but they could not enforce their recommendations.

Foreign Policy and the Election of 1940. President Roosevelt's close advisers stated that his reluctance to run for a third term had been overcome by his conviction that it would be detrimental to the country to change administrations in the midst of world-wide war.

The Nominating Conventions. The Republican convention at Philadelphia on June 24 passed over such well-known political figures as Senator Robert A. Taft of Ohio and Thomas E. Dewey, district attorney of New York. It nominated Wendell L. Willkie, a newcomer to the politicians, who had just transferred his membership from the Democratic to the Republican party. Willkie, as president of the Commonwealth and Southern Corporation, had been a cogent critic of New Deal policies. His big-business connections were balanced by the nomination of Charles L. McNary, senator from Oregon and friend of the farmers, for Vice-President. The Democrats, in rather sullen mood, permitted the administration leaders at Washington to indicate that the ticket should be Roosevelt and his Secretary of Agriculture, Henry A. Wallace.

The Platforms. There had been many forecasts that the campaign would turn on foreign policy, but the platforms offered the voter little choice. Both parties favored a strong national defense, all aid to Great Britain "short of war," and protection of the Western Hemisphere against totalitarian aggression; each promised to keep the United States out of the European conflict. The Republican pronouncements attacked the New Deal methods as wasteful, bureaucratic, and dictatorial but supported many of its reform measures. They accused the Roosevelt supporters of stirring class antagonism for political advantage. The Democrats stood on the New Deal record and their defense achievements. They virtually repudiated conservative support and promised to extend social legislation.

The Election. The balloting on November 5 resulted in a third victory for Roosevelt, not so widespread, however, as the result in 1936. Though Willkie secured almost 45 per cent of the popular vote, he received only eighty-two votes in the electoral college, representing ten states chiefly in the farm belt of the Middle West. The Democrats carried both houses of Congress and to the surprise of most politicians increased their majority in the House of Representatives. Though the campaign had stirred the country deeply, Willkie promptly called for national unity despite differences of opinion on domestic policies. He was especially insistent that partisanship play no part in modifying the nation's decision to aid Great Britain and to resist to the utmost totalitarian aggression.

All Aid "Short of War." The year after Roosevelt's re-election was marked by a bitter battle between the isolationists and the interventionists which in the end was won by the latter.

GREENLAND AND ICELAND. By an agreement with Denmark, the United States established a protectorate over Greenland (April, 1941). American marines were ordered to occupy Iceland (July, 1941) by agreement with the Icelandic government, which had proclaimed its independence after the German occupation of Denmark. In each instance it was asserted that the island lay in waters necessary to the defense of the United States.

"FROZEN ASSETS." On June 14, 1941, German and Italian assets in the United States were "frozen" by order of the United States Treasury. About a month later the same treatment was accorded to Japanese assets in the United States.

"SHOOT AT SIGHT." The German government tried to prevent America from sending aid to Great Britain and Russia by sinking merchant vessels, which were being convoyed by British warships and such other warships as had escaped from the ports of countries already occupied by the Nazis. When a submarine attack sank the American destroyer *Reuben James,* with the loss of seventy-six of her crew (October 30, 1941), President Roosevelt ordered naval commanders to "shoot at sight" on any Axis submarine coming into American defense waters. Shortly thereafter Congress enacted a law authorizing the arming of merchant ships.

THE ATLANTIC CHARTER. Meanwhile the United States and Great Britain had defined the objectives of the war in a joint statement, which caused the Axis propagandists to insist that the two countries were already in alliance. Known as "The Atlantic Charter," this statement was the result of conversations between President Roosevelt and Prime Minister Churchill at meetings aboard their respective battleships in the North Atlantic (August 14, 1941). It consisted of the following chief points: (1) neither nation would seek territorial or other aggrandizement after the war; (2) both nations would undertake to disarm any nation which threatened aggression, to respect the right of all peoples to choose their own form of government, to assist in arranging for all nations equal access to the trade and raw materials of the world, to encourage co-operation among the nations for the improvement of labor standards and for social security, and to work for a peace which would make the seas highways of peaceful commerce open to all. It expressed the hope that the peace settlement would enable people throughout the world to "live out their lives in freedom from fear and want."

REVIEW QUESTIONS

1. How did the Roosevelt administration modify the policy of the United States toward Latin America?
2. Why was the American government hostile toward the Japanese attempt to create a "new order" in Asia?
3. If you had been a member of Congress, would you have voted for the repeal of the arms embargo? Give your reasons.
4. In what ways have the commercial policies of the United States affected its international relations?
5. Why did President Roosevelt proclaim an unlimited national emergency in May, 1941?
6. Discuss the arguments for and against universal military service.
7. Do you think that the "third-term" tradition was an important factor in the election of 1940? Why?
8. How did the First World War affect the economic position of the United States?
9. Explain the isolationist sentiment in the country after the First World War.
10. Why did Latin-American statesmen applaud the announcement of the Clark Memorandum?

CHAPTER XIV

THE SECOND WORLD WAR

Late in 1941, the Japanese attack on Pearl Harbor brought the United States into the Second World War. American industry, agriculture, and labor were mobilized to support the armed forces in the war against the Axis nations. On the European front, invasions of Africa and Italy prepared the way for the 1944 landings in France. Although the Germans fought stubbornly, their resistance was crushed within a year by the military might of United Nations forces. The defeat of Japan, hastened by use of the atomic bomb, followed several months later.

THE COLLAPSE OF NEUTRALITY

While most Americans were watching the first successful campaigns of the Germans in Soviet Russia, the United States was plunged into the war by the treacherous attack of Japan in the Pacific.

Japanese Aggression. Late in 1940 the Japanese government became a member of the Axis when it signed a ten-year pact with Germany and Italy which gave the Asiatic power a free hand to establish its new order in Greater East Asia.

THREATS IN THE SOUTH PACIFIC. During 1941 the Japanese militarists, now in complete control, regardless of the ministry of the moment, grew more truculent. They interfered in the political and economic affairs of Thailand and Indo-China, ruthlessly pressed the war against China, staged a naval demonstration in the gulf of Siam, and seized the Spratly Islands, only seven miles from the Philippines.

APPEASEMENT OR COERCION? Unprepared and unwilling to fight Japan in the Pacific, while the fate of Europe hung in the balance, the United States government continued a policy of appeasement until midsummer of 1941. On July 25, having secured the co-operation of the British government and the Dutch government in exile, the State Department finally forbade the export to Japan of scrap iron, aviation gasoline, and other war materials.

DIPLOMATIC HOCUS-POCUS. The Japanese government kept up a pretense that it desired to reach a peaceful settlement of all outstanding differences between the United States and Japan.

Nomura's Mission. Admiral Kichisaburo Nomura, the Japanese ambassador to the United States, tried in vain to convert Secretary Hull to the idea of an *entente cordiale* between the two nations in the Pacific. He demanded that the United States recognize Japanese control of China.

Saburo Kurusu. After the extreme jingoist, General Tojo, became premier in October, 1941, Saburo Kurusu came to the United States as a special envoy on a mission of peace; but the peace which he offered meant that the United States would be expected to abandon China to its fate, to recognize the dominance of Japan in its "Co-prosperity Sphere for Greater East Asia," and to reopen trade in all commodities which the Japanese desired. Secretary Hull made counterproposals for the United States, including withdrawal of Japan from China and Indo-China, a multilateral nonaggression pact in the Far East, and support of the Chinese republic.

"A DATE WHICH WILL LIVE IN INFAMY." While Nomura and Kurusu were still discussing with Secretary Hull the possibilities for a peaceful settlement in the Pacific, Japanese airmen carried out a "sneak attack" on American warships and defense installations at Pearl Harbor in the Hawaiian Islands, inflicting heavy damage. On the same day, Japanese forces attacked the Philippines, Guam, Hong Kong, and the Malay Peninsula. Next day, December 8, 1941, President Roosevelt asked Congress to declare a state of war between the United States and the Japanese Empire. Three days later Germany and Italy declared war upon the United States.

Preparing for a Global War. The attack on Pearl Harbor quickly quieted the arguments over American foreign policy and united the nation in a solemn determination to meet successfully the greatest crisis in its history.

THE INDUSTRIAL FRONT. By the spring of 1943 the American people had converted their peacetime industrial establishment into the "mightiest wartime arsenal" that the world had ever seen. The task was supervised by a War Production Board of nine men, with an able administrator, Donald Nelson, as chairman. Within a year after Pearl Harbor the nation produced forty-seven billion dollars' worth of war material, including 32,000 tanks, 49,000 airplanes, and 8,200,-000 tons of merchant shipping. The manufacture of many peace-time commodities was either curtailed or prohibited in order to facilitate war production, but the net income of American corporations rose from $17,000,000 in 1940 to $28,000,000 in 1943.

THE FARMERS' PROBLEMS. Despite the bumper crops of 1942, it was difficult to meet the extraordinary demand for foodstuffs. The military and naval establishments were taking 25 or 30 per cent of the total American meat supply. In fifteen months the United States sent to China, Great Britain, and Russia more than seven billion pounds of food in various forms. To continue this program of helping its Allies and supplying its armed forces required careful planning, especially since the farmers were handicapped by a dwindling labor supply and the lack of new machines and machine parts. Domestic consumption was partly controlled through the ration schedules imposed by the Office of Price Administration (OPA), but the entire food problem was directly under the supervision of a Food Administrator appointed by the President. The complicated and difficult tasks imposed on the OPA were generally well handled. The index of consumers' prices rose from 105.2 in 1941 to 123.6 in 1943 and then tended to find a level at 125.5 for 1944–1945.

MOBILIZING MANPOWER. Although the activities of individual citizens were more strictly supervised by the government than at any other time in United States history, the American people escaped the kind of regimentation which characterized most of the nations at war.

Military Forces. Attempts to provide the men and women needed to serve in the armed forces were often inconsistent because local draft boards disagreed on interpretations of the Selective Service Act announced from time to time by Selective Service Director Lewis B. Hershey and his associates. Despite this confusion the armed forces were increased from 1,800,000 in 1941 to more than 11,000,000 in 1945. Almost 260,000 women enlisted for noncombatant work in every branch of the military service.

The Armies of Labor. Organized labor generally refrained from strikes and jurisdictional disputes during the first year of the war. When labor strife did flare up in 1943, Congress finally passed the Smith-Connally Bill, prohibiting strikes in plants which were working on war contracts and authorizing the President to seize plants where labor disturbances impeded defense production. American labor, however, scarcely needed such legislation to spur it on to great efforts. Its production record from 1940 to 1944 surpassed any previous record in the nation's history. At the same time, average weekly earnings rose from $25.20 to $46.08, while the length of the work-week also increased from 38.1 to 45.2 hours.

War Manpower Commission. The national manpower program was placed under the War Manpower Commission, with Paul V. McNutt of Indiana as chairman. The Commission handled the task of apportioning the work of some 70,000,000 men and women (almost 20,000,000 of whom were women) in the labor force.

The War Labor Board. An attempt—not successful—was made to stabilize wages through the rulings of the National War Labor Board. After an increase amounting to 15 per cent was granted in 1942 to CIO United Steel Workers, a similar formula (Little Steel Formula) was used in many other industries.

Relocation Order. On February 19, 1942, President Roosevelt issued an executive order authorizing the Secretary of War to exclude any persons from military areas. Under this order, more than 100,000 Japanese-Americans were evacuated from the West Coast to inland relocation centers. This action, though upheld by the Supreme Court, was later condemned by President Truman's Commission on Civil Rights as unjustified interference with physical freedom.

WARTIME TRANSPORT. If the United States had any secret weapon during the early war years, it was the marvelous efficiency of its transportation facilities.

The Railroads. During the First World War it had been necessary for the government to assume control of the American railroads. In 1942, however, they carried 30 per cent more freight and 40 per cent more passengers than they had carried the previous year. This was done with 20,000 fewer locomotives and 600,000 fewer freight cars than they had in 1918. Railroad operators and employees, working harmoniously under the general direction of Joseph B. Eastman, head of the Office of Defense Transportation, carried unprecedented numbers of troops and supply units and hauled, in addition, the gasoline and fuel oil which could not be shipped in tankers while the Axis submarines were taking their heavy toll.

The War Shipping Board. The United Nations* had two an-

---

* The term United Nations came into existence following the promulgation of the United Nations Declaration in 1942.

swers to the menace of Axis submarines: first, improved methods used by the Allied navies in hunting and destroying both "wolf packs" and lone raiders; and second, the tremendous output of American shipyards. With the approval of the War Shipping Board, Henry J. Kaiser demonstrated the possibilities of the prefabricated vessel, which could be constructed in seventy-eight days or less. Speed made possible the "victory fleet" which kept the service of supply more than adequate after the first few months of war.

Airways. The commercial airlines, though subordinating their plans to the war needs, managed to maintain many of their normal schedules. Most of the airplane construction was for military purposes. By the spring of 1943 the monthly output was over 5,500 planes, as compared with an average of 200 in 1939. The glider industry provided much of the transport space for the Allied air-borne invasions of 1943 and 1944.

FINANCING THE WAR MACHINE. Between January, 1940 and January, 1943, the appropriations for national defense and war amounted to approximately $220,000,000,000, or slightly more than the cost of government from George Washington's inauguration to 1940. From 1941 to 1945 the national debt rose from about $47,000,000,000 to $247,000,000,000.

Taxes. By the second year of the war it was estimated that war's daily cost to the American people was $1.15 for every man, woman, and child in the population, while receipts from taxes were scarcely forty cents per person. Successive tax bills were designed to increase the proportion of the cost of the war which would be met through taxation. This was accomplished by lowering the individual exemptions, thus adding millions of new taxpayers to the lists, increasing the rates of the normal tax and surtax on incomes, and virtually confiscating all corporate earnings which represented excess profits from the war. Congress finally accepted in 1943 a plan to place collection of federal income taxes on a pay-as-you-go basis (suggested by Beardsley Ruml, who was then treasurer of Macy's Department Store).

War Bonds. Despite the increased revenues from taxes, the government relied upon war-savings stamps and war bonds to meet the bulk of the war costs. Prior to July, 1945, the Treasury Department conducted seven successful war-bond drives with total subscriptions of $61,000,000,000.

THE MILITARY STRATEGY

Less than a month after the entrance of the United States into the Second World War, representatives from twenty-six countries signed the United Nations Declaration, pledging themselves to joint action until victory over the Axis had been achieved and to a peace based upon the principles of the Atlantic Charter.

Retreat in the Pacific Area. The first half of 1942 was marked by a series of major disasters to the United Nations in the Pacific.

JAPANESE DRIVE AGAINST THE ENGLISH AND DUTCH. The whole Western world was astonished at the speed of the Japanese advance after Pearl Harbor. Within eight weeks Japan had secured the entire Malay Peninsula. The great British naval base of Singapore fell on February 15, 1942; three weeks later the Japanese had overrun the Netherlands East Indies and by early May British forces had retreated across Burma into India. Japanese bases on New Guinea and in the Bismarck and Solomon Islands were growing in strength.

THE FALL OF THE PHILIPPINES. Under the command of General Douglas MacArthur, American and Filipino troops heroically defended the Bataan peninsula and the fortress of Corregidor until resistance was no longer possible. At the order of President Roosevelt, MacArthur transferred his headquarters to Australia on February 22, but his men under General Jonathan Wainwright held Corregidor until May 6, 1942.

THE ALEUTIANS. Shortly after the Japanese secured the Philippines, their forces far to the north moved into the Aleutian Islands, occupying Attu, Agattu, and Kiska, which they held for more than a year before American forces ousted them in 1943.

The Road Back. By the early autumn of 1942 the Japanese had occupied a million square miles of territory in their triumphant advance, but there the road ended. Their retreat was humiliating and costly in life and treasure.

THE CORAL SEA AND MIDWAY. American bombers, commanded by General James Doolittle, dropped several tons of bombs on Kobe, Yokohama, and Tokyo on April 18, 1942. A few weeks later American naval and air forces in the Coral Sea stopped an invading force apparently aimed at Australia. The first real defeat for the Japanese war lords, however, was the rout of a strong Japanese naval force proceeding toward Midway Island (June, 1942).

GUADALCANAL AND TULAGI. On August 7, 1942, the United Nations launched their counteroffensive in earnest, when American marines, supported from the air and sea, landed at Tulagi and on Guadalcanal Island in the Solomons. For the next two years the story in the western Pacific told of the Japanese avoiding battle and suffering costly defeats as island after island fell to the United Nations forces. Americans, under General MacArthur and Admirals Chester W. Nimitz and William F. Halsey, played a major role in these victories, but they were ably supported by their allies. From the Solomons they moved into the Marshalls, Gilberts, Carolines, and Marianas; they took Guam and Saipan and prepared for the reconquest of the Philippine Islands.

THE SUPERFORTRESSES. In the spring of 1944 American airplane factories began to produce special bombers, designed for long flights with heavy bomb loads. Based on airfields in China, which Chinese labor had built almost without tools, these "superfortresses" undertook to destroy Japan's industrial centers.

CHINA. While the United Nations moved northward and westward across the Pacific islands, the Chinese kept up their heroic resistance. They were heartened by increasing air support from General Claire Chennault's forces and by the campaign of Chinese and American troops to reopen the Burma Road. At the same time British Empire forces were gradually clearing the Japanese out of Burma.

The Invasion of Fortress Europe. The destruction of Japan's empire was subordinated in the strategy of the United Nations to the defeat of Nazi Germany.

THE BATTLE FOR TUNIS. On November 8, 1942, a British-American armada landed on the coasts of French Morocco. Within three days General Dwight D. Eisenhower had so disposed his forces that he controlled all Morocco and Algeria to the Tunisian frontier. The Germans fought stubbornly for six months before they yielded to superior forces in May, 1943.

THE ITALIAN CAMPAIGN. During the summer of 1943 the Fifth American Army, commanded by General Mark Clark, and the Eighth British Army, under General Bernard Montgomery, occupied Sicily and several smaller Mediterranean islands. The invasion of the Italian mainland began in September, 1943, more than a month after the Italians had ousted Mussolini and his Fascist regime. The campaign in Italy, despite this revolt, was long and costly. Not until the first week in June, 1944, did the United Nations liberate Rome from the Nazi's control.

DESTROYING NAZI POWER. From the moment the United States entered the war its energies were primarily directed toward the liberation of Europe from Hitler's tyrannical "new order."

"Softening" Germany. During 1943 the bombing of Germany reached gigantic proportions. The *Luftwaffe* was knocked out of the sky and its production centers were repeatedly bombed and burned; the Ruhr Valley and the industrial Rhineland were all but paralyzed; Berlin, Hamburg, Munich, and Cologne suffered more than English cities had suffered earlier in the war.

Russian Offensives. While the R.A.F. and American Air Force were attacking Germany's airplane, ball-bearing, and oil-refining industries, the Russian armies had launched huge offensives all along the front from the Baltic to the Black Sea. Their primary objective was the destruction of the German armies, but in the process they regained, by the summer of 1944, all the territory which the Germans had occupied and opened routes into the Danube valley.

The Invasion Forces. During 1943 the British and American navies conquered the submarine and opened the sea lanes to the transport of troops and supplies. By June 1, 1944, Secretary of War Stimson stated that more than two million American troops were in Great Britain awaiting the moment for invasion of that part of Europe which lay behind Hitler's Atlantic Wall.

THE BATTLE OF FRANCE. In the early hours of June 6, 1944, United Nations troops, on orders from their Supreme Commander, Dwight D. Eisenhower, left their bases in Great Britain and crossed the Channel to storm the French beaches in the vicinity of Cherbourg. Preceded by air-borne paratroopers and protected by an awesome bombardment from the huge battle fleet, they soon established beachheads and, with the aid of the air forces, connected their landings into one battle front. Within twelve weeks of these successful landings, the Allied armies had conquered Normandy, overrun Brittany, chased the Germans north of the Seine, and assisted the French Forces of the Interior in liberating Paris. In August new landings were made with slight loss, on the Mediterranean coast of France near Marseilles. On August 26, General Eisenhower announced that the Seventh German Army had been destroyed and warned the residents of Alsace, Lorraine, and Luxembourg that they would soon be in the path of the retreating Nazis. The Battle of France had been won.

THE CONQUEST OF GERMANY. German resistance just west of the Rhine proved to be surprisingly determined but was overcome by Allied military power.

European and African Fronts in World War II

Reproduced by permission of publisher from C. L. Lord and E. H. Lord, *Historical Atlas of the United States*. New York: Henry Holt & Co., 1953.

The Battle of the Bulge. In December, 1944, the Germans mounted an offensive that created a huge bulge in the Allied lines. After yielding some valuable ground, the American and British troops stood firm. One young American general, Anthony McAuliffe, when the Germans pressed him to surrender gave the simple but memorable reply: "Nuts!"

The Remagen Bridge. While incessant bombing pounded the German railroads into rubble, the American First Army reached the Remagen Bridge, crossing the Rhine southeast of Cologne. On March 8, 1945, the first troops crossed the river and moved into the interior of Germany.

V-E Day. For the next two months the United Nations armies in the west advanced steadily, while the Russians cut through Austria and closed in on Berlin. Hitler and other Nazi high officials, aware that the end was near, either committed suicide or went into hiding. On May 7, at Reims, France, a representative of the German General Staff (which had taken over after Hitler's death) accepted the terms of "unconditional surrender." V-E Day was announced to an expectant world.

Political Interlude. Both Republican and Democratic leaders tried to keep the discussions of postwar foreign policy free from the partisanship of the political campaign of 1944.

Republican Nominations. During the preconvention primaries Wendell Willkie, who had lost to Roosevelt in 1940, came to the conclusion that he could not again secure the Republican nomination. His position in the party, however, was still strong, and he used his influence to counteract the "isolationist" views of such Republicans as Colonel Robert McCormick of the *Chicago Tribune.* Those who were reluctant to make any positive commitments concerning the role of the United States in the postwar world probably would have preferred Governor John Bricker or Senator Robert A. Taft of Ohio, as the party nominee. They yielded, however, to the apparent popularity of Governor Thomas E. Dewey of New York and nominated him with but one dissenting vote in the convention, which was held at Chicago in June. Governor Bricker was unanimously chosen for the second place on the ticket.

Democratic Convention. When the Democrats assembled in Chicago in July, they knew that President Roosevelt was willing to be nominated for a fourth term. This they proceeded to do on the first ballot, though the opponents of a fourth term cast some ninety votes for Senator Harry F. Byrd of Virginia. Most of them came from Southern delegations. The drama of the convention came in the fight of Vice-President Wallace for renomination. Though he led on the first ballot, his defeat was finally brought about by an understanding between certain Southern delegates and the leaders of several powerful political machines in Northern cities. Senator

Harry Truman of Missouri was named in a stampede on the second ballot.

THE ELECTION. More than 45,531,000 Americans voted on November 7, 1944, giving President Roosevelt a plurality of slightly over 3,000,000 votes. In the electoral college the President had 432 votes to 99 for Governor Dewey. The greatest Republican strength was in rural counties. President Roosevelt's sudden death on April 12, 1945, elevated Vice-President Truman to the presidency (see p. 221).

Victory in the Pacific. With the collapse of the Nazi regime and the military defeat of Germany, the American government strove to speed up the war against Japan.

THE ASSAULT ON JAPAN. During the spring of 1945 General MacArthur's troops continued to clean up sporadic Japanese resistance in the Philippines and co-operated with the Australians in the attack on Borneo. To the north the combined operations of navy, marines, army, and air forces won Iwo Jima and broke the resistance on Okinawa. The bases for the final assaults on Japan's home islands had been prepared in the early summer of 1945.

THE ATOMIC BOMB. The most devastating weapon of this or any previous war was perfected by the co-operative efforts of scientists of the United Nations. On August 6, 1945, American airmen dropped the first atomic bomb on Hiroshima. Three days later a second bomb was dropped on Nagasaki. Both cities were virtually obliterated.

UNCONDITIONAL SURRENDER. During the Berlin Conference, which assembled on July 17, 1945, the United States and Great Britain sent an ultimatum to Japan demanding unconditional surrender. At the same time Premier Stalin informed President Truman that the Soviet Union would soon enter the war against Japan. Two days after the atomic bomb was first used, Russia moved its forces against the Japanese in Manchuria. Almost immediately the Tokyo radio broadcast an appeal for peace. After an exchange of notes between the two nations, President Truman announced on August 14 that hostilities had ceased. It was agreed that the Supreme Allied Military Commander would rule Japan through the emperor, Hirohito, pending demilitarization and government reforms. General Douglas MacArthur was named Supreme Allied Military Commander.

OCCUPATION OF JAPAN. In the early morning of August 29th the peaceful occupation of the Japanese home islands began. Three days later, aboard the battleship *Missouri,* the Japanese signed the surrender documents before the representatives of nine of the United

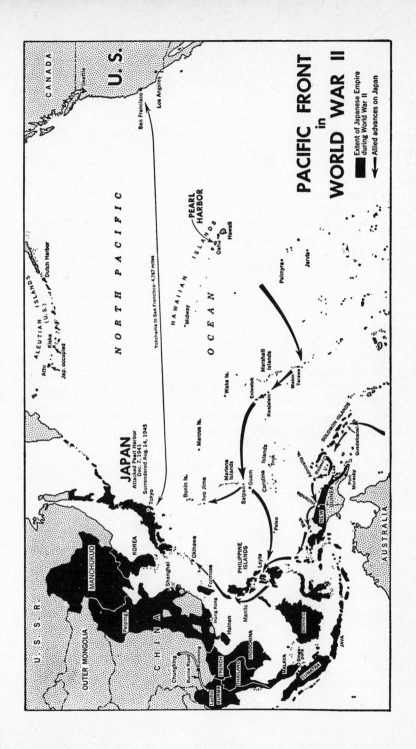

PACIFIC FRONT
in
WORLD WAR II

■ Extent of Japanese Empire
during World War II
→ Allied advances on Japan

Nations. As the occupation forces moved into control of strategic positions in Japan, it became clear that bombing from the air and naval bombardment had brought that nation to the point of collapse even before the atomic bomb was used.

REVIEW QUESTIONS

1. Should the United States have imposed economic restrictions on Japanese trade earlier than 1941? Why?
2. For what purpose was the Office of Price Administration created?
3. Why was there considerable criticism of the Roosevelt administration's policy of extending large-scale aid to Russia through the agency of Lend-Lease?
4. What changes in its tax program were made by the federal government in order to meet the heavy expenses of the war?
5. Was the administration wise in deciding that the war in the Pacific should be regarded as secondary to the war against Axis Europe?
6. Why were the initial landings in North Africa accomplished with relatively little loss to the Allies?
7. Should the governmental regulations concerning the utilization of civilian manpower have been more strict during the war years?
8. What was the strategy of the Allied forces in the Pacific after the fall of the Philippines? Why was it successful?
9. What have been some of the long-range effects of the use of the atomic bomb to destroy Hiroshima and Nagasaki?

CHAPTER XV

THE QUEST FOR PEACE
AND SECURITY

Conferences among Allied leaders during the Second World War, followed by the establishment of the United Nations, inspired hopes for a lasting peace based on world-wide co-operation. After the war, however, tensions increased between the Eastern Communist powers, led by the Soviet Union, and the Western democracies, led by the United States. Armed conflict between the two sides occurred in Korea, and the threat of further outbreaks caused the maintenance of large military establishments and the development of new weapons to continue.

CREATING THE UNITED NATIONS ORGANIZATION

Even before the United States became a belligerent, the nations that were fighting the Axis powers had begun to discuss the nature of the peace they desired and how it could be achieved.

International Planning for a Peaceful World. Roosevelt and Churchill, developing a close personal friendship, exchanged views almost daily by letter or telephone conversation. They met in six formal conferences over a period of three years, discussing their plans for international co-operation after the war.

THE CASABLANCA CONFERENCE. On the Atlantic coast of North Africa (January, 1943) Roosevelt and Churchill served notice that the war would continue until a peace could be based on the "unconditional surrender" of the enemy countries.

THE DECLARATION OF MOSCOW. Late in October, 1943, Secretary of State Hull flew to Moscow to meet Foreign Secretary Eden of Great Britain and Foreign Secretary Molotov of the Soviet Union. The three men issued a statement, known as the Moscow Declaration, that a new world organization for the maintenance of peace and security would be established after the war.

CAIRO CONFERENCE. A month later, Roosevelt and Churchill, on their way to a conference with Stalin in Teheran, met for the first time with the nationalist defender of China, Chiang Kai-shek. There they promised formally that any territory which the Japanese had taken from China since the First World War would be restored to the republic of China.

TEHERAN CONFERENCE. In the capital of Iran, Roosevelt, Churchill, and Stalin met for the first time (November, 1943). In a joint declaration at the close of their conference, the three men declared: "We leave here, friends in fact, in spirit and in purpose." They agreed to work together, not only for victory in war but also for peace in the postwar era.

MOMENTOUS YALTA. This was the most fateful of all the wartime conferences. Roosevelt, Churchill, and Stalin and their foreign ministers attended at Yalta in the Crimea (February, 1945).

Decision for World Organization. It was agreed to call a special conference of all "peace-loving nations" to draft a charter for a postwar association of nations to preserve the peace of the world. The voting procedure for the Security Council was formulated at Yalta.

Agreements on Poland and Yugoslavia. It was agreed that the Curzon line should be Poland's eastern boundary, with Poland to receive compensating territory in the north and west; that free elections should be held in Poland; and that the Tito government of Yugoslavia should be more broadly based.

Secret Commitments. Some provisions of the Yalta agreements were not made public immediately. These secret clauses included provisions: (1) that the Soviet Union would enter the war against Japan soon after Germany's surrender; (2) that Outer Mongolia would be recognized as independent of Chinese control; (3) that the Soviet Union might occupy part of Korea; (4) that the Soviet Union might recover the privileges which it had enjoyed in Manchuria before the Russo-Japanese War (1905); and (5) that the Ukraine and Byelorussia would be separately recognized in the United Nations. Later events proved that these concessions to the Russians constituted a costly mistake, but that could not be known to the negotiators at Yalta, who expected that Soviet aid might be necessary to end the war with Japan.

Hopes for a People's Peace. President Roosevelt returned from Yalta, weary but convinced that the nations allied with the United States would find a way to control irresponsible force.

THE "TOWN MEETING OF THE WORLD." Many agreed that the causes of international conflict could be checked, if five nations—the United States, the Soviet Union, Great Britain, France, and China—would continue to co-operate.

Economic Co-operation. Before the war ended, representatives of the nations allied against Germany, Italy, and Japan had joined in plans for the postwar period. At Atlantic City (November, 1943) the United Nations Relief and Rehabilitation Administration (UNRRA) discussed relief measures for the people of occupied Europe and Asia. At Bretton Woods, in New Hampshire, delegates formulated (July, 1944) plans to handle international banking and currency problems after the war.

Dumbarton Oaks Conference. Late in 1944 Secretary Hull invited representatives of Great Britain, the Soviet Union, and China to join delegates from the United States for a series of discussions concerning an international association after the war.

The San Francisco Charter. Despite the sudden death of President Roosevelt on April 12, 1945, the United Nations went forward with plans to carry out the decision reached at Yalta. On April 25, 1945, there met in San Francisco two hundred representatives of forty-six nations. After two months of deliberation they completed the draft of the Charter of a World Security Organization.

Potsdam Conference. This conference was attended in July and August of 1945 by Truman, Stalin, and Clement Atlee (who replaced Churchill as Prime Minister while the conference was in process). They called upon Japan to surrender and announced plans for the occupation, demilitarization, and democratization of Japan and Germany.

THE STRUCTURE OF THE UN (United Nations Organization). By the close of 1945 fifty-one nations had ratified the United Nations Organization Charter; and the first meeting of the Assembly was held in London on January 10, 1946.

The Security Council. The Security Council consisted of five permanent members—the United States, the Soviet Union, Great Britain, France, and China—and six members elected by the General Assembly for two-year terms. Each of the permanent members had a right to veto any decision. The Security Council was entrusted

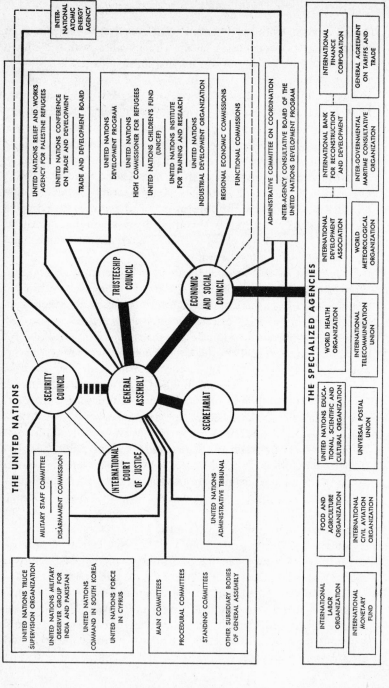

THE UNITED NATIONS AND RELATED AGENCIES

As of 1968

THE UNITED NATIONS

INTERNATIONAL ATOMIC ENERGY AGENCY

UNITED NATIONS TRUCE SUPERVISION ORGANIZATION
UNITED NATIONS MILITARY OBSERVER GROUP FOR INDIA AND PAKISTAN
UNITED NATIONS COMMAND IN SOUTH KOREA
UNITED NATIONS FORCE IN CYPRUS

MAIN COMMITTEES
PROCEDURAL COMMITTEES
STANDING COMMITTEES
OTHER SUBSIDIARY BODIES OF GENERAL ASSEMBLY

MILITARY STAFF COMMITTEE
DISARMAMENT COMMISSION

UNITED NATIONS ADMINISTRATIVE TRIBUNAL

SECURITY COUNCIL

INTERNATIONAL COURT OF JUSTICE

TRUSTEESHIP COUNCIL

GENERAL ASSEMBLY

ECONOMIC AND SOCIAL COUNCIL

SECRETARIAT

UNITED NATIONS RELIEF AND WORKS AGENCY FOR PALESTINE REFUGEES
UNITED NATIONS CONFERENCE ON TRADE AND DEVELOPMENT
TRADE AND DEVELOPMENT BOARD

UNITED NATIONS DEVELOPMENT PROGRAM
UNITED NATIONS HIGH COMMISSIONER FOR REFUGEES
UNITED NATIONS CHILDREN'S FUND (UNICEF)
UNITED NATIONS INSTITUTE FOR TRAINING AND RESEARCH
UNITED NATIONS INDUSTRIAL DEVELOPMENT ORGANIZATION

REGIONAL ECONOMIC COMMISSIONS
FUNCTIONAL COMMISSIONS

ADMINISTRATIVE COMMITTEE ON COORDINATION
INTER-AGENCY CONSULTATIVE BOARD OF THE UNITED NATIONS DEVELOPMENT PROGRAM

THE SPECIALIZED AGENCIES

INTERNATIONAL LABOR ORGANIZATION
INTERNATIONAL MONETARY FUND

FOOD AND AGRICULTURE ORGANIZATION
INTERNATIONAL CIVIL AVIATION ORGANIZATION

UNITED NATIONS EDUCATIONAL, SCIENTIFIC AND CULTURAL ORGANIZATION
UNIVERSAL POSTAL UNION

WORLD HEALTH ORGANIZATION
INTERNATIONAL TELECOMMUNICATION UNION

INTERNATIONAL DEVELOPMENT ASSOCIATION
WORLD METEOROLOGICAL ORGANIZATION

INTERNATIONAL BANK FOR RECONSTRUCTION AND DEVELOPMENT
INTER-GOVERNMENTAL MARITIME CONSULTATIVE ORGANIZATION

INTERNATIONAL FINANCE CORPORATION
GENERAL AGREEMENT ON TARIFFS AND TRADE

with the maintenance of international peace and security and was empowered to take enforcement action for this purpose.

The General Assembly. The General Assembly, which included representatives of every signatory nation, was dominated by the smaller nations of the world. It was given powers of debate, recommendation, and supervision of special agencies. It handled matters on which the Security Council failed to overcome the veto, so frequently used after 1946 by the Soviet Union.

The Secretary-General. The Secretary-General, as chief administrator of the organization, was charged with putting into effect decisions reached by the Council and the General Assembly. His influence became powerful in the deliberations of both bodies.

International Court of Justice. Fifteen justices were named to constitute the panel for the International Court of Justice with its headquarters at the Hague.

Special Agencies. The UN, on the basis of international agreements, set up several agencies, to deal with nonpolitical problems. Among these agencies were the International Labor Organization (ILO), the Food and Agriculture Organization (FAO), the United Nations Educational, Scientific and Cultural Organization (UNESCO), the International Civil Aviation Organization (ICAO), and the World Health Organization (WHO).

International Atomic Energy Commission. This body, created by the Security Council in 1946, consisted of eleven member nations. It was expected to enjoy "broad privileges of movement and inspection, including rights to conduct surveys by ground and air." Its effectiveness, as an international authority controlling the uses of atomic energy for military purposes, was destroyed by Russia's insistence on vetoing any recommendations unacceptable to the Soviet Union.

THE TRUMAN ADMINISTRATIONS

As he assumed the heavy duties of the presidency, Harry Truman remarked that he felt as if "the moon, the stars, and all the planets" had fallen on him; but he quickly showed a decisiveness that reassured his fellow-countrymen.

Choice of Advisers. The new President relied upon his former associates in Congress and his close personal friends for advice in the early days of his administration.

THE STATE DEPARTMENT. Deeply concerned over the grave international situation, he paid special attention to the State Department. James F. Byrnes, long a senator from South Carolina, became Secretary of State. He guided foreign policy until 1947, when General George C. Marshall, whom Truman greatly admired, succeeded him. As General Marshall's health failed, he was replaced by Dean Acheson of New York, who had previously served in the State Department under Secretary Hull.

CHANGING PERSONNEL. Cabinet changes were numerous during the Truman years, as the President sought efficient assistants, who could also be politically helpful. With the death of Chief Justice Stone, Fred H. Vinson of Kentucky, then Secretary of the Treasury, was named Chief Justice of the Supreme Court. President Truman called his Missouri friend, John W. Snyder, to Washington to be Secretary of the Treasury. In 1947 Truman issued a Loyalty Order to oust from executive departments persons whose activities or associations were disloyal to the United States. A Loyalty Review Board was created to carry out this policy.

Presidential Succession. An act of 1947 revised the line of succession to the presidency. The Speaker of the House and the president *pro tempore* of the Senate were placed next in line after the Vice-President; cabinet officers followed in order of rank. The Twenty-second Amendment, passed by Congress in 1947 and ratified in 1951, prohibited a President from being elected for more than two terms.

Reorganizing the Military Departments. After months of rather bitter debate among the representatives of the armed services, Congress created a Department of Defense by a merger of the War and Navy Departments. In 1947 President Truman named Secretary of the Navy James V. Forrestal as head of the new department. At the same time secretaries were designated for the army, navy, and air force interests within the Defense Department. The draft, which had been allowed to lapse for a year, was re-established by the Selective Service Act of 1948. This act provided for the induction of enough men to provide an adequate defense establishment.

Formulating Policies. As he undertook his new tasks, President Truman was confronted by what he later called "a year of decisions."

PRICE CONTROLS AND OPA. Congress acted quickly to remove wartime restrictions on prices, over the opposition of President Truman, who wanted them retained as anti-inflationary measures.

Soaring Prices. After the Republicans won the congressional elections of 1946, price controls were either revoked by presidential order or were allowed to lapse. Prices, meanwhile, had been rising rapidly as consumers tried to buy commodities that were in short supply.

Checks to Inflation. Danger of a runaway inflation was averted because industry quickly poured out the goods that purchasers were demanding, and because the American people had accumulated savings during the war which helped them meet rising living costs.

ATOMIC ENERGY ACT (1946). This act created the Atomic Energy Committee and empowered it to control ownership and production of fissionable materials and to conduct atomic research.

LABOR-MANAGEMENT PROBLEMS. Rising prices soon brought widespread demands for wage increases.

An Epidemic of Strikes. When wages lagged behind prices, workers turned to the strike to compel employers to meet their demands. During 1946 approximately 1,650,000 people were on strike. United States Steel and General Motors plants were idle for months.

Seizing the Coal Mines. Truman acted promptly in the spring of 1946, when John L. Lewis ordered the bituminous coal miners to walk out. The President seized the mines. The government won in the courts, after the union had struck against government operation of the mines, and Lewis agreed to a compromise contract with the mineowners.

The Taft-Hartley Act. In an attempt to reduce the number of industrial disputes and to curb "unfair" labor practices, Congress passed the Taft-Hartley Act, over President Truman's veto, in 1947. Unions were placed under supervision so far as their finances and their relations with nonunion laborers were concerned. Union officers were compelled to sign affidavits that they were not members of the Communist party. Concerning strikes, the law provided (1) that unions and management had to give sixty days notice of a decision to terminate a labor contract and (2) that the government could secure an injunction postponing for eighty days any threatened strike or shutdown which might endanger public health or safety. The act prohibited the closed shop, unfair practices of labor unions (e.g., "featherbedding" and excessive initiation fees), and union contributions to federal political campaigns.

The Surprising Election of 1948. The presidential campaign of

1948 resulted in a political upset that confounded the professional forecasters of election returns.

THE NOMINATING CONVENTIONS. At the Republican national convention, held in Philadelphia, June 21–24, the supporters of Taft, Stassen, and Vandenberg were unable to find any plan which could prevent the nomination of Governor Thomas E. Dewey of New York, who had been the unsuccessful Republican standard-bearer in 1944. The Democrats, meeting at Philadelphia, July 12–15, somewhat reluctantly accepted President Truman as their candidate after Dwight D. Eisenhower, then president of Columbia University, had made it clear that he was not available. Some conservative Southern Democrats, who opposed President Truman's civil rights program, formed the States' Rights Democratic party (Dixiecrats) and nominated Governor J. Strom Thurmond of South Carolina. The extreme left-wing faction of the Democratic party organized a Progressive party and chose Henry A. Wallace as its candidate.

THE CAMPAIGN. Neither Governor Dewey nor his running mate, Governor Earl Warren of California, was inclined to be specific about the issues confronting the country. Just what a Republican victory would have meant in terms of domestic policies remained unclear. President Truman, strongly supported by his vice-presidential candidate, Senator Alben Barkley of Kentucky, proposed that the New Deal be continued and that the idea of the "welfare state" be translated into more effective legislation.

TRUMAN'S VICTORY. Though President Truman ran behind his ticket in many Democratic districts, he carried twenty-eight states with 304 electoral votes. Governor Dewey won sixteen states with 189 votes, while Governor Thurmond received thirty-eight votes from four Southern states. Wallace received no electoral votes.

The "Fair Deal." Both before and after the 1948 election President Truman advocated legislation to continue the "welfare state" of the New Deal. He called his program the "Fair Deal."

THE LEGISLATIVE PROGRAM. The President emphasized extension of social security benefits to more wage earners, provision for national health insurance, increased funds for public housing and slum clearance, and federal aid for schools. In an attempt to establish equality of civil rights he supported federal laws against lynching and for equal job opportunities.

BIPARTISAN OPPOSITION. A coalition of Republicans and Southern Democrats prevented the passage of much of the "welfare" legislation; and a stubborn filibuster led by Southern Democrats in the Senate defeated the civil rights program. Congress was also reluctant to carry out the President's campaign pledge that the Taft-Hartley labor act would be repealed. Several substitute bills were brought to a vote, but none commanded a majority, and the Taft-Hartley Act remained on the statute books.

SOCIAL LEGISLATION. Though the Eighty-first Congress failed to accept the major provisions of President Truman's "Fair Deal" program, it enacted several measures which had the strong support of the administration. A minimum-wage bill increased the standard from forty to seventy-five cents an hour. An appropriation of more than $2,700,000,000 was voted for slum clearance and low-rent housing. In the session of 1950 the Social Security Act (originally passed in 1935) was modified to include new groups of wage earners and to provide old-age pensions for many who were self-employed.

TENSIONS AND STRIFE IN THE COLD WAR

During 1946 and 1947 relations between the Soviet Union and the Western powers—Great Britain, France, and the United States—steadily deteriorated. The Russians had dropped an "iron curtain," as Winston Churchill pointed out, which was difficult to penetrate.

The War Criminals. On one point the wartime allies could agree—the punishment of those in Germany and Japan who had been responsible for aggressive war and who had committed crimes against humanity. Those considered to have violated international law were tried by international tribunals.

THE NUREMBERG TRIALS. At the insistence of the United States, the leaders of Nazi Germany were accorded fair trials under proper judicial processes. With Justice Robert H. Jackson of the United States Supreme Court as chief prosecutor, the trials were conducted by an International Tribunal, sitting at Nuremberg, Germany, in 1946. Twelve of the defendants, including Goering, were sentenced to death, seven received prison terms, while three were acquitted. Lesser offenders were tried by German denazification courts and by Allied military governments.

JAPAN'S WAR CRIMES TRIALS. A number of Japanese who had led the extreme militarists in that country were tried and sentenced by an international tribunal. Premier Tojo was sentenced to death and hanged. Many Japanese military officers were tried by special courts for violating the rules of war.

The Occupied Countries. The problem of administering the conquered nations—Germany and Japan—and of guiding their people into normal relations with the Western world proved to be a long and difficult task.

GERMANY. Conquered Germany was divided into zones of occupation, assigned to the military forces of the United States, the Soviet Union, Great Britain, and France respectively. Secretary Byrnes and his associates slowly formulated the general principles underlying American policy. As announced at Stuttgart, Germany, in September, 1946, it provided for the long-term military occupation of the defeated country but promised that the German people would be assisted in their efforts to find an honorable place among the free and peace-loving nations of the world. The tremendous task of working out the details of this assistance fell upon the shoulders of General Lucius Clay and his associates in the Military Government until May, 1949, when John J. McCloy was appointed first United States civilian High Commissioner to the new Federal Republic of Germany and also military governor of the United States occupation zone.

JAPAN. Ruling through Emperor Hirohito of Japan, General Douglas MacArthur tried to start the Japanese people along the democratic way. By July, 1947, the General was able to announce that Japanese military forces had been disarmed, demobilized, and absorbed in peaceful pursuits and that Japan's remaining war potential was completely neutralized. In that year a new constitution was adopted, providing for democratic elections and limiting the powers of the emperor.

KOREA. North Korea was to be occupied by the Soviet Union, South Korea by the United States. A Communist administration gained control in the north, and a republic, with Syngman Rhee as first president, was established in the south. By mid-1949 all occupying forces had been withdrawn.

Drafting the Peace Treaties. The process of framing satisfactory peace treaties proved to be tortuous and tedious. Procedural difficulties developed in the Council of Foreign Ministers of the four great powers—the United States, the Soviet Union, Great Britain, and France. As tension increased between East and West, it became impossible to continue a joint policy toward former enemy nations.

AXIS SATELLITES. In 1947, after more than a year of negotiations, the Council of Foreign Ministers concluded peace treaties with Italy, Rumania, Hungary, Bulgaria, and Finland. The treaties provided for reparations, demilitarization, and territorial adjustments. It was not until 1955 that a peace treaty was signed with Austria, restoring that nation to full sovereignty and prohibiting economic or political union with Germany.

GERMANY. Progress toward a peace treaty with Germany proved even more difficult because of the impasse over economic and political terms between the Western powers on one side and the Soviet Union on the other. In 1948 the Federal Republic of Germany—comprising the occupation zones of the United States, Great Britain, and France—was proclaimed. In May, 1952, these nations, acting without the concurrence of the Soviet Union, authorized their foreign ministers to sign a convention with the Federal Republic which restored its independence and recognized it as an equal partner in the West European alliance. Full sovereignty was restored to West Germany in 1955. Meanwhile, East Germany, under Soviet control, was proclaimed the German Democratic Republic and kept isolated from the West. The occupation of Berlin remained divided between East and West.

JAPAN. In 1951, a peace treaty with Japan, prepared under the direction of John Foster Dulles (then Republican adviser to the State Department), was signed by forty-nine nations; the Soviet Union refused to sign. This treaty restored Japan to full sovereignty but stripped her of her former empire. At the same time the United States and Japan signed a bilateral defense treaty.

Checking the Communist Menace. Underlying the struggle for power between the Soviet Union and the western democracies, led by the United States, was the knowledge that an atomic war could bring doom to mankind.

POLICY OF THE TRUMAN ADMINISTRATION. In March, 1947, President Truman asked Congress to approve a program of large-scale aid for the peoples of Europe who were then trying to maintain a democratic way of life in a world that seemed to be surrendering to Communist totalitarianism. This point of view became known as the Truman Doctrine.

Aid to Greece and Turkey. Specifically, the President called for financial aid to Greece and Turkey, pointing out that Russian penetration in that area would endanger Anglo-American interests in the Near and Middle East. Congress acted promptly, authorizing commodity shipments, financial aid, and military support.

The Marshall Plan. In June, 1947, Secretary of State Marshall pointed out that the United States was anxious to co-operate with Europe, if the European nations were ready to formulate a program for mutual reconstruction. Sixteen western European nations accepted this offer and sent representatives to Paris, where a corps of experts worked out the details for international co-operation along economic lines. The Soviet Union and its satellites refused to attend. By October, 1947, the proposals were sufficiently specific to be submitted to the United States for approval.

Economic Co-operation Act of 1948. A proposal to enact the Marshall Plan was submitted to Congress by President Truman on December 19, 1947. It had been carefully formulated by the administration leaders, but it met with strong opposition in both House and Senate. The modified version which was finally accepted in the spring of 1948 resulted from the hard work of Republicans and Democrats in the Senate Committee on Foreign Relations, under the guidance of Republican Senator Arthur Vandenberg of Michigan. During the administration of Paul G. Hoffman (April, 1948—September, 1950) the ECA spent more than $10,000,000,000 in Europe to aid the countries which had accepted the Marshall Plan.

The Results of the Europe Recovery Program. The impact of the Marshall Plan—the European Recovery Program—on European countries was soon noticeable. It spurred economic co-operation among them and stiffened their resistance to Communist aggression. In 1949 the Benelux states—Belgium, the Netherlands, and Luxembourg—established a customs union; and a year later Robert Schuman, foreign minister of France, got favorable consideration for his plan to internationalize the steel industry of the Ruhr.

Point Four. In his 1949 inaugural address, President Truman announced the "Point Four" program of technical aid to improve production and living standards in underdeveloped areas if the world. The first appropriations for an International Development Fund to carry out this program were made by Congress in September, 1950.

CONTINUANCE OF THE COLD WAR. Evidence of increasing tension

between West and East was recorded in the zones of military occupation in Germany.

The Berlin Airlift. In the summer of 1948 the Soviet Union stopped all rail and road traffic between Berlin and the western German occupation zones. The Western powers, led by the United States, responded by keeping an air corridor open between their zones in Germany and their respective sections of Berlin, along which they could fly cargoes of food, fuel, and other supplies into the city. For ten months and twenty-three days this airlift was maintained, demonstrating the determination of the Western powers not to be forced into a policy of appeasing the Soviet Union. Finally, the Russians agreed to terminate the Berlin blockade in return for a Western agreement to lift the counterblockade and to arrange an early meeting of the Council of Foreign Ministers. This compromise became effective on May 12, 1949.

The North Atlantic Pact. Some observers felt that the change in Russian policy, marked by the calling of a meeting of the Council of Foreign Ministers, had in part been induced by the success of Western diplomats in formulating and signing (April 4, 1949) the North Atlantic Security Treaty. Twelve nations on either side of the Atlantic—including Great Britain, France, Belgium, the Netherlands, Norway, Canada, and the United States—adopted a defensive pact whereby they would regard an aggressive attack upon any one of their number as an attack upon all.

NATO. The defensive pact was given form in the North Atlantic Treaty Organization, and in December, 1950, President Truman called General Eisenhower from his post as president of Columbia University, to be Supreme Commander of the Western forces in defense of Europe. For more than a year Eisenhower built carefully but rapidly the structure of the military forces of the Western world and won wide support for a political, as well as an economic, union among the states of Western Europe. When he decided to enter politics in 1952 he was succeeded by General Matthew Ridgway, who had been commander of UN forces in Korea. General Alfred M. Gruenther succeeded Ridgway in 1953; he was succeeded in 1956 by General Lauris Norstad. In December, 1957, the first NATO heads-of-government meeting was held in Paris. The representatives agreed that NATO should stockpile nuclear missiles and announced plans for closer economic and political co-operation.

Satellites of the Kremlin. After the Second World War, Poland,

Hungary, Czechoslovakia, Rumania, Bulgaria, and Albania came under the dictatorial control of Moscow. Marshal Tito's Communist regime in Yugoslavia frequently followed a nationalistic line that was denounced by the Kremlin leaders and thereby secured economic aid from the Western powers. An attempted revolt in Hungary was crushed by the Soviet Union in 1956.

Communist Penetration in Asia. The governments of many Asiatic countries were harassed after the Second World War by the infiltration of Communism. In the Republic of the Philippines Communist-led "Huks" spread terror; Indo-China was split asunder by Communistic subversion; in Malaya, Burma, Indonesia, Siam, and other areas the Communists threatened established governments.

CIVIL WAR IN CHINA. Moscow's greatest success, however, was in aiding the Chinese Communists, led by Mao Tse-tung, to defeat the Nationalist Chinese under Chiang Kai-shek.

Marshall's Mission. In 1946 President Truman sent General George C. Marshall to China to attempt to bring about a settlement between the Communist and Nationalist factions. Marshall managed to arrange a truce, after a year of frustrating work, but it was broken as soon as he returned to the United States.

Withdrawal of American Forces. When General Marshall became Secretary of State (1947) he recommended the withdrawal of the remaining military and naval forces of the United States stationed in China, maintaining that support of Chiang Kai-shek's regime would require more men and materials than the American people could supply. United States economic aid to Nationalist China continued until its defeat on the mainland.

Formosa. When Chiang Kai-shek fled the mainland of China and set up the Nationalist government on the island of Formosa, the United States promptly recognized the Formosan regime as the true government of China (January, 1949). China proper was now controlled by the Communists, whom the American government refused to recognize. The United States guaranteed the safety of Formosa from external aggression by the Chinese Communists.

THE KOREAN WAR. After the Second World War, Korea, which had long been dominated by Japan, was divided into two parts along the 38th parallel.

The Republic of South Korea. Free elections, under the UN, resulted in the creation of the Republic of Korea, with Dr. Syngman

Rhee as president. Dr. Rhee was an ardent nationalist, who hoped some day to incorporate North Korea into the Republic of Korea.

North Korean Aggression. In June, 1950, North Korean troops, supplied with Russian equipment and led by Russian-trained officers, crossed the 38th parallel and attacked South Korea. This unprovoked assault was regarded by many in western Europe and the United States as the signal that the "cold war" was moving into the stage of widespread military hostilities.

United Nations Action. The Security Council of the United Nations (with the Russian delegate absent) branded the North Korean invasion as an act of aggression and approved the use of force to punish the aggressor. The United States furnished the bulk of the United Nations' forces in Korea, but Great Britain and other members of the UN gave military, naval, and air support under the supreme command of General Douglas MacArthur.

Chinese Intervention. By November, 1950, the United Nations forces had broken the North Korean attack and had driven the invaders in retreat across the 38th parallel. Meanwhile, Communist China had moved large troop concentrations to the Manchurian border. Early in December, 1950, these troops crossed into Korea apparently with the determination to defeat the United Nations' forces and drive them from the Korean peninsula. General Mac-Arthur wanted to launch an all-out counteroffensive against the Chinese Communists, attacking them on Chinese territory.

The Dismissal of MacArthur. Frequent disagreements between General MacArthur and the Truman administration over the way in which the war in Korea should be conducted, caused an open rupture in April, 1951, when the President relieved the General of his command for disobeying an order to clear policy statements through the Defense Department. On his return to the United States, MacArthur was hailed by some as a hero, but many seemed to agree with President Truman that the real issue was the subordination of the military to civil authority and that the drastic action was needed in order to prevent the Korean fighting from developing into a third world war. MacArthur was replaced in Korea by General Matthew B. Ridgway.

Deadlock in Korea. In June, 1951, after the Communist troops had been checked by the UN forces, Russia suggested that it would be possible for discussions between the antagonists in Korea to lead to a cease-fire. Negotiations between two truce teams began promptly but dragged on month after month with each side trying to check the other's diplomatic moves. The issue on which the truce talks seemed deadlocked was that of forcible repatriation of prisoners of war, the UN insisting that such prisoners should be free to choose whether or not they wished to return to the country for which they had been fighting.

THE RETURN OF THE REPUBLICANS TO POWER

United under the leadership of Dwight D. Eisenhower, the Republicans gained a substantial victory—the first in twenty-four years —in the presidential election of 1952.

The Political Campaign. "Time for a change" proved to be an effective slogan for the Republicans, who succeeded in holding the internationalist wing of the party without losing the isolationist voters in the Middle West.

THE NOMINATING CONVENTIONS. Both major party conventions were exciting because the delegates were unusually free to reach decisions as the proceedings developed.

Eisenhower and Nixon. The Republicans nominated General Eisenhower after a spirited revolt of many delegates against the supporters of Senator Robert A. Taft of Ohio, who seemed to have control of the convention committees. Senator Richard M. Nixon of California, who was presented as a fighter against Communist infiltration in the civil service, received the nomination for Vice-President.

Stevenson and Sparkman. Equally dramatic were the proceedings of the Democratic convention in which the willing candidates— Kefauver of Tennessee, Russell of Georgia, Barkley of Kentucky, Harriman of New York, Kerr of Oklahoma—lost to Governor Adlai Stevenson of Illinois, who insisted that he was being drafted. For its vice-presidential candidate, the convention turned to Senator John Sparkman of Alabama, hoping thus to overcome the disaffection of some of the Southern Democratic leaders.

THE ISSUES. Governor Stevenson, with rare literary skill, tried to fix the voters' attention on the costly struggle which would be required to overcome the threats of war, poverty, and tyranny. He could not overcome the personal popularity of General Eisenhower, or escape the Republican charge that the Democrats had condoned corruption in executive departments. Perhaps the most effective oratory of the campaign was Eisenhower's simple promise: "I will go to Korea." Voters hoped he could thus end the war.

THE ELECTION RESULTS. The Republican candidates received 442 electoral college votes to 89 for their opponents. The landslide proportions of this victory did not carry over to the congressional vote, however. The Republican majority in the House was large enough to provide for party control, but the Republican margin in the Senate was dependent upon Senator Wayne Morse of Oregon, who had supported Stevenson as an "Independent Republican" and who later defected to the Democratic camp. To be successful, the administration's legislative program required support from conservative Democrats as well as from Republicans.

The Eisenhower Administration. President Eisenhower sincerely hoped to elevate the "tone" of politics, for he had strong faith in his countrymen's ability to make the right choices if they had the facts.

THE CABINET. The Eisenhower cabinet included several supporters of Senator Taft, named in an effort to repair the damage which had been caused by the fight in the nominating convention. The new cabinet position of Secretary of Health, Education, and Welfare went to Oveta Culp Hobby of Texas, who became the first woman of her party to serve as a cabinet member. John Foster Dulles, a New York lawyer and close friend of Governor Thomas E. Dewey, was named Secretary of State at a time when international problems were acute. (He had previously been an adviser to the Truman administration. See p. 227.)

BIPARTISAN SOCIAL LEGISLATION. The Eisenhower administration disappointed those conservative Republicans who wanted a frontal attack on the New Deal and Fair Deal laws. Actually the moderates in both major parties had accepted the principle that the federal government is responsible for the welfare of its citizens.

The Extension of Social Legislation. Legislation signed by President Eisenhower in 1954 added almost ten million persons to the lists of those who were entitled to receive Social Security benefits and increased the payment levels. In 1955 the minimum wage in covered employment was raised to $1.00 an hour.

Civil Rights. The issue of extending equality of public treatment to Negroes divided the nation along sectional rather than party lines. President Eisenhower and his advisers were joined by many Northern Democrats in the movement to extend civil rights. After long congressional debate a bill was passed in the summer of 1957 which empowered the federal government to seek court orders, if necessary, to guarantee the individual's right to vote in any state in the Union. A bipartisan Civil Rights Commission was appointed by President Eisenhower to examine abuses of civil rights and to make recommendations for new legislation.

EQUAL EDUCATIONAL FACILITIES. In May, 1954, the Supreme Court, presided over by Chief Justice Earl Warren, former governor of California, handed down a momentous decision of the segregation issue in the public schools. This ruling reversed a decision of 1896 (*Plessy* v. *Ferguson*) that "separate but equal" facilities were constitutional.

Brown v. *Board of Education of Topeka* (1954). In this case the Court unanimously held that the maintenance of "separate but equal" schools for Negroes—which was the practice in seventeen states—violated the Fourteenth Amendment. "Separate educational facilities," said the Chief Justice, "are inherently unequal."

Enforcement of "Desegregation." Implicit in the ruling was the Court's understanding that enforcement would require careful planning over a considerable period of time. The Eisenhower administration encouraged the several states to work out their own plans.

The Little Rock, Arkansas, Episode. In September, 1957, the Board of Education of Little Rock was prepared to admit to high school eight carefully selected Negro students. Governor Faubus, insisting that violence would break out if the students were admitted to classes, used the Arkansas National Guard to bar them from the school building. President Eisenhower responded by ordering federal troops into Arkansas to protect the students as they carried out their studies in the school year 1957–1958. He maintained that the action of Governor Faubus violated the law of the nation.

Progress of Integration. In a number of Southern states legislation was passed to allow the governors to close schools under orders to integrate. During 1958–1959, schools in Little Rock and in several Virginia communities were closed by such action. However, decisions by state and federal courts required the reopening of some of these schools on an integrated basis. Progress toward integration was most notable in border states such as Maryland and Kentucky. Schools in Washington, D. C. (where a separate Supreme Court decision invoked the Fifth Amendment) were also desegregated.

Internal Security. The problem of internal security was a continuing one for both the Truman and Eisenhower administrations. As happened after the First World War, the threat of international Communism aroused the American people to take drastic measures against individuals and groups considered subversive. Feeling against such people was heightened by disclosures of Soviet espionage during the war and by the conviction of former State Department official Alger Hiss, charged with handing over secret documents to Communist agents.

THE SMITH ACT. In 1940 Congress enacted a law providing for the registration of aliens and making it a crime for any person to advocate the overthrow of the government by force or to belong to a group that advocated it. Eleven leaders of the Communist party were convicted under this act in 1949.

McCARRAN ACT. In 1950 Congress passed the Internal Security Act (McCarran Act), over President Truman's veto. This law required the registration of Communist and Communist-front organizations. It also provided for the deportation of Communist immigrants and prohibited the immigration of anyone who had been a member of a totalitarian organization. (Certain exceptions were permitted by 1951 amendments for those who had been forced to belong to such organizations.)

McCARRAN-WALTER ACT. This act, passed in 1952 (also over Truman's veto), revised the immigration laws. It maintained the quota system but ended racial bars and gave priority to persons with needed skills and to relatives of United States citizens. It placed additional restrictions on the immigration and naturalization of Communists and Communist sympathizers.

INVESTIGATIONS. Former Communists, persons who had associated with Communists, and persons suspected of radical tendencies became the objects of public and private investigation throughout the country. Many of them were dismissed from their jobs on what seemed to be insubstantial evidence. The government "loyalty" investigation was extended to federal employees who for any reason could be considered security risks, and a number were dismissed on that ground, though very few were discovered to have been Communists. The most spectacular Red hunt was conducted by Senator Joseph R. McCarthy of Wisconsin, as chairman of a Senate committee on un-American activities. McCarthy's charges, which eventually included the Eisenhower administration, resulted in his being censured by a bipartisan Senate resolution for conduct unbecoming a senator.

SUPREME COURT DECISIONS. The Supreme Court upheld the constitutionality of the Smith Act on the ground that the Communist conspiracy was a "clear and present danger"; but it narrowed the application of the law to persons who had actually advocated forcible overthrow of the government. Other Supreme Court decisions (in 1957) held that the investigating powers of Congress were restricted to specific functions of Congress and that F.B.I. files used as evidence in loyalty cases must be produced in court.

The International Scene. Domestic policies in the United States were carefully watched by former colonial peoples of Africa and Asia, who were interested in the treatment accorded to minority groups and in democratic rights. American foreign policy in dealing with the Communists was set against the background of events at home.

NEGOTIATING WITH COMMUNISTS IN EASTERN ASIA. Native Communist parties became more active in almost every Asiatic country after the victory of the Chinese Communists in 1949.

The Korean Armistice. President Eisenhower quickly put into effect his campaign promise to visit Korea. Though not directly related to the truce negotiations at Panmunjon, his military inspection signified the desire of Americans to end the war. A truce was finally signed in July, 1953, fixing a line of demarcation between the Northern Communist state and the Southern republic and providing for repatriation of war prisoners on a voluntary basis.

Dividing Indo-China (Vietnam). In July, 1954, the pressure of Vietnam Communist forces led to a conference held at Geneva by the foreign ministers of nineteen nations, including the United States. This conference settled upon the 17th parallel as the dividing line between Communist North Vietnam and Southern Vietnam, which became a republic.

MILITARY ALLIANCES. In their efforts to limit indirect, as well as direct, Soviet aggression the leaders of the Western democracies formed new alliances, though they continued to give full support to the United Nations.

ANZUS. In 1952 the United States, New Zealand, and Australia signed the ANZUS treaty, pledging close co-operation in mutual defense plans.

SEATO. The United States took the lead (1955) in forming the South East Asia Treaty Organization. This was not a firm military alliance like NATO, but its members—the United States, the United Kingdom, France, New Zealand, Pakistan, the Philippine Republic, and Thailand—agreed to work together for security against external aggression.

Mutual Security Treaty with China. In 1954 the United States signed a treaty with Nationalist China providing for mutual aid in the defense of Formosa and the Pescadores. When, in 1958, Quemoy and other offshore islands were shelled from the Communist-held mainland, the United States convoyed supply ships to these islands.

THE SUMMIT CONFERENCE (GENEVA, 1955). In an attempt to ease international tensions, the leaders of the United States, Great Britain, France, and the Soviet Union met in a Summit Conference at Geneva, Switzerland, in July, 1955. The Soviet Union was represented by Nicolai Bulganin, who was premier following the death of Stalin in 1953 until he was replaced in 1958 by Nikita Khrushchev. President Eisenhower made a daring proposal for mutual aerial inspection of military installations in all parts of the world; but, since this proposal was unacceptable to the Soviet Union, the Conference merely generated for a brief time a spirit of good will.

THE MIDDLE EAST. With the waning of British and French influence after the Second World War, the United States was confronted by heavier responsibilities in the Middle East.

Arab Nationalism. The intense nationalism of Arab peoples formerly under European domination, created difficult problems. Arab leaders, especially the Egyptian dictator, Colonel Nasser, soon learned that they could play the Soviet Union against the United States and thereby win concessions from both sides.

The Suez Crisis. Secretary Dulles, trying to forestall Soviet influence in Egypt, had promised that nation financial aid in building the Aswan Dam to secure electric power from the Nile River. However, in 1956 Nasser's request for a large loan was turned down by the United States and Great Britain. Thereupon, Nasser quickly seized and nationalized the Suez Canal. Without informing the United States of their plans, Israel, Britain, and France successfully invaded the Canal area. When Britain and France blocked action by the Security Council, the General Assembly of the UN acted promptly, with both the United States and the Soviet Union pressing for a withdrawal of foreign forces from Egypt. The withdrawal

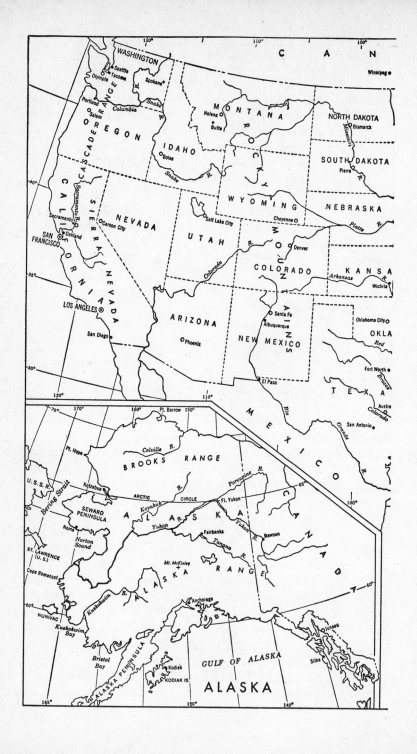

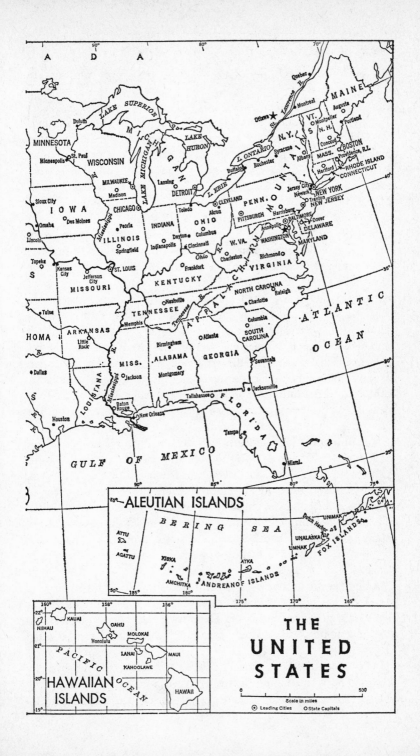

was made, and a United Nations Emergency Force was sent to patrol the area.

The Eisenhower Doctrine (1957). President Eisenhower acted quickly after the Suez crisis. He asked Congress to (1) grant funds for economic and military assistance to help Middle East nations preserve their independence, and (2) permit the use of United States armed forces to resist armed Communist aggression in that area. This Doctrine was approved by joint resolution of Congress in March, 1957.

Lebanon and Jordan. In July, 1958, President Chamoun of Lebanon asked the United States to protect his nation against subversive aggression. President Eisenhower immediately sent military forces and called for a meeting of the UN Security Council. At the same time Great Britain landed troops in Jordan at the request of King Hussein. The United States and Great Britain insisted that the crisis be handled by the UN. When a Russian veto prevented action by the Security Council, the General Assembly was called into special session. There, in August, 1958, President Eisenhower proposed a basic plan for the economic and political stabilization of the Middle East under the supervision of the United Nations. A compromise resolution sponsored by the Arab nations was finally passed, and American and British troops were withdrawn from the area after calm had been restored.

Eisenhower's Re-Election (1956). Neither a heart attack in September, 1955, nor an operation for an intestinal ailment in June, 1956, could deter President Eisenhower from seeking a second term. He and Nixon opposed Stevenson and Senator Estes Kefauver of Tennessee. Eisenhower polled 457 electoral votes to Stevenson's 73. The overwhelming endorsement of the President, however, did not apply to his party. The Democrats recaptured both the House and the Senate and won a majority of the governorships that were at stake.

The Second Eisenhower Administration. After his re-election, President Eisenhower began to exert pressure on Capitol Hill for his legislative program. Since the Democrats controlled Congress, bipartisan support was necessary for those measures that were enacted into law.

PENTAGON REORGANIZATION (1958). The President secured virtually the bill he wanted, putting the Defense Secretary in direct command of the armed forces and giving him explicit authority to assign weapon development among the various services. The act also provided for a director of Research and Engineering (under the Defense Secretary) to be in control of defense research projects.

FOREIGN ECONOMIC POLICY. At President Eisenhower's request the reciprocal trade program was extended at periodic intervals. The longest extension—four years—was enacted in 1958. This law authorized tariff cuts up to 20 per cent below prevailing rates. The President was permitted to reject Tariff Commission recommendations for higher rates unless he was overridden by a two-thirds vote of both houses of Congress. President Eisenhower was less successful in his urging of an adequate mutual security program; the appropriations authorized by Congress for this purpose were usually below his minimum standards. However, the basic policy of granting economic, technical, and, if necessary, military aid to countries whose defense was deemed vital to the containment of Communism remained unchanged.

SOCIAL LEGISLATION. Amendments to the Social Security Act passed in 1958 raised the benefits and tax rates for old-age, survivors', and disability payments. They also increased the amounts of federal grants to the states for maternal and child welfare and public assistance projects. Aid to farmers was continued by means of flexible price supports for basic products (a departure from the Democratic policy of fixed supports). In 1958, Congress authorized the expenditure of $887,000,000 over a four-year period for education purposes. State school officials were asked to come to Washington to draw up plans for the use of these funds.

ECONOMIC RECESSION. During the fall of 1957 and the first half of 1958, the United States was confronted with the most serious economic recession since the Second World War. Retail sales and industrial production declined sharply, and the number of unemployed rose to more than five million in the spring of 1958. To help overcome the recession, the Federal Reserve Board reduced its discount rate and the margin requirements for stock transactions; Congress authorized large expenditures for public works, including interstate highway construction; and President Eisenhower urged increased consumer buying. By the end of 1958, the nation was well on the road to economic recovery.

Labor. The AFL and the CIO had merged in 1955 into a powerful fifteen-million member organization. During 1957–1958, investigations by a Senate committee disclosed corrupt financial practices by some high union officials. Under its Code of Ethical Practices, the AFL-CIO launched a house-cleaning drive and expelled some unions, including the International Brotherhood of Teamsters. Labor continued to benefit from cost-of-living wage increases and welfare programs that unions had secured from a number of industries. However, by November, 1958, nineteen states had enacted "right-to-work" laws, under which a worker could not be barred from a job for refusing to join a union.

Elections of 1958. The vote in the 1958 elections was a record one for a nonpresidential year. The Democrats won control of both the Senate and the House by the largest margin since the Roosevelt landslide of 1936. The Democrats also won most of the gubernatorial contests (with the notable exception of New York state).

New States. In 1959, Alaska and Hawaii were admitted as the forty-ninth and fiftieth states of the Union. Elections were held in each territory to complete the transition from territorial government to statehood.

KENNEDY AND THE NEW FRONTIER

President John F. Kennedy's inaugural address was a call to his fellow countrymen to join him in pushing toward new frontiers, both at home and abroad; but there was no escape from the persistent and perilous pressures at home and abroad.

A Narrow Victory. The presidential election of 1960 was decided by the closest popular vote since 1884 (see p. 43). The Democratic ticket had only 112,800 more votes than the Republican in a total of sixty-nine million ballots.

THE CANDIDATES. There were few surprises in the national conventions of the two major parties in 1960. The Democrats chose Senator John F. Kennedy of Massachusetts for President, and Senator Lyndon B. Johnson of Texas for Vice-President. The Republicans named Vice-President Richard M. Nixon as their standard-bearer, and Henry Cabot Lodge, United States Ambassador to the United Nations, as his running-mate.

THE CABINET. During the campaign Kennedy had promised the voters that he would name a "ministry of talent" as his cabinet advisers. Among his choices were men experienced in government and diplomacy: for Secretary of State, Dean Rusk, president of the Rockefeller Foundation; for Secretary of the Treasury, Douglas Dillon, who had been Under Secretary of State in the Eisenhower administration; for Secretary of Health, Education, and Welfare, Governor Abraham Ribicoff of Connecticut; for Secretary of Commerce, the popular governor of North Carolina, Luther H. Hodges. Adlai Stevenson assumed the heavy responsibility of Ambassador to the United Nations.

A Stalled Legislative Program. President Kennedy had serious difficulty persuading Congress to accept the program which he regarded as essential for the maintenance of American prosperity.

Presidential Proposals. During the first two years of his administration, the President suffered defeat in Congress on several major bills. He failed to secure enactment of (1) the so-called "medicare" bill, designed to provide hospital and nursing care for the elderly by means of an increase in Social Security taxes; (2) a comprehensive program of federal aid to education; (3) a plan for the creation of a Department of Urban Affairs; (4) a bill imposing stronger controls on farm production.

Congressional Resistance. There were several reasons for the refusal of Congress to follow the lead of the President. (1) Democratic leaders were not convinced of the need for new laws. (2) President Kennedy was reluctant to make a public appeal for his legislative program. (3) The chairmen of the major committees in House and Senate were unsympathetic with younger champions of the "New Frontier." (4) Kennedy lacked a close liaison with the veteran lawmakers in his own party. (5) In spite of the President's plea that the country move forward rapidly, most voters seemed to be in a "conservative mood."

Relations With Capital and Labor. In its attitude toward economic problems the Kennedy administration strove to encourage greater production of goods and services and to curb inflationary forces.

Clash over Steel Prices. When the United States Steel Corporation in April, 1962, announced an increase in the price of steel, the President intervened promptly to divert government contracts to steel producers who would not raise prices. This compelled "Big Steel" to cancel the proposed increase. At the same time the Kennedy administration explained that its action did not arise from any hostility to business enterprise but was an attempt to halt inflation.

Labor's Difficulties. Eager to stimulate the productivity of the nation's workers, Kennedy's advisers were concerned over the troubles within the ranks of labor. The leaders of the labor movement were also concerned over (1) the continuing dispute between AFL-CIO and the Teamsters Union, led by James R. Hoffa; (2) the rising rate of unemployment, especially among the less skilled industrial workers; (3) the need to retrain workers who had been thrown out of work by automatic machine processes; (4) the mounting disputes over hours and wages, resulting in labor-management conflicts such as the steel strike of 1959–1960, the strike of newspaper printers in Cleveland and New York City in 1962–1963, and the threatened walkout of railroadmen averted by the intervention of President Johnson late in 1963.

Continuing Struggle Over Civil Rights. Though measurable progress had been made toward school integration and toward safeguarding the right of all citizens to vote (see pp. 233–234), at the beginning of the Kennedy administration, Negro leaders insisted that much needed to be done in order to put an end to the Negro's "second-class citizenship."

Passive Resistance and Mass Demonstrations. City after city in the South felt the demand for an end to segregation in schools, stores, restaurants, bus stations, and all other public facilities. Many Negro leaders, following the example of Martin Luther King, Jr., an Atlanta clergyman, preached persistent pressure for civil rights by peaceful methods, such as boycotts, "sit-ins," petitions, and street demonstrations. Nonviolent protest, however, both North and South, degenerated into violent clashes between Negroes and their sympathizers on one hand and on the other hand, police authorities who claimed they were complying with local laws. President Kennedy, declaring that Negro protests must be moved out of the streets and into the courts, sent to Congress (June, 1963) a bill making illegal a long series of discriminatory acts and granting the Civil Rights Division of the Department of Justice more power to deal with discrimination practices. The bill was blocked by Southern legislators.

The March on Washington. In August, 1963, to arouse the American people and to dramatize the need for civil rights legislation, a gigantic march on Washington was organized by Negroes and supporters of their cause. More than 200,000 at the Lincoln Memorial heard Martin Luther King, Jr., describe his dream that his children might one day live in a nation where they would be judged not "by the color of their skin but by the content of their character." To some Americans the march was an attempt to intimidate Congress; to others it was a warning that time in which it would be possible to settle the civil rights issue by peaceable methods was running out.

THE CIVIL RIGHTS ACT OF 1964. The tragic assassination of President Kennedy did not destroy his program. President Johnson, a native of Texas, promptly gave his pledge to fight harder than ever for the most controversial part of the program, civil rights. Largely as a result of his leadership, Congress finally overcame a Southern filibuster in the Senate and passed the Civil Rights Act of 1964, just before the Fourth of July. One of its most important provisions was the attempt to speed up the process of voter registration in those states where few Negroes had ever been permitted to register.

CONFRONTATION AT SELMA. It was soon evident that the Civil Rights Act of 1964 would be effective only if the people of the United States decided to carry out its provisions in good faith. Crucial in the minds of many Negroes was the issue concerning registration of Negro voters. Selma, in Dalton County, Alabama, a community where Negro voters were few in proportion to the Negro population, was chosen as a place to test the willingness of local and state officials to abide by the federal law. What happened was a cruel travesty, arousing Americans to the brutal ways in which the right to assemble, the right to petition, and the right to register were being denied to white citizens as well as to Negroes.

The shocking spectacle of "man's inhumanity to man" at Selma spurred President Johnson to address the Congress on March 15, 1965, as he submitted legislation which the Department of Justice believed would give the federal government power to ensure nondiscriminatory procedures in all elections: federal, state, municipal. The bill was necessary, the President insisted, in order to enforce the Fifteenth Amendment to the Constitution, which 95 years before had conferred on the Negro the right to vote. It became law in August, 1965.

THE NEGRO SEEKS STATUS. For more than half a century after the Civil War, the Negro had lived in the shadow of his heritage of slavery. Though he had gained some job opportunities (p. 62) and enjoyed the sort of trade education which Booker T. Washington advocated, he had made slight headway in winning political rights or social recognition. It was not until the Second World War that he made any substantial gains along social and political lines. But the gains were slight compared to the goals which intelligent black leaders, such as W. E. B. Dubois, had set.

MODERATE LEADERS. There was disagreement among prominent Negro leaders, especially after 1965, concerning the best strategy in their campaign for black status in a predominantly white society. The National Association for the Advancement of Colored People (NAACP) frowned on violence, and its spokesman Roy Wilkins ably presented the views of the moderates. In the Southern Christian Leadership Conference, Martin Luther King, Jr., found it difficult to reconcile his nonviolent methods with the demands of those who advocated force to get results. In April, 1968, King was assassinated in Memphis, Tennessee, and his death deepened the sense of bitterness and hostility among blacks.

THE URBAN GHETTOS. Crucial to the Negro campaign for status was the fact that most of the black population had moved into the cities. By 1966 more than 69 per cent were living in metropolitan areas. Though they shared on a small scale in the national prosperity, their income level steadily fell behind that of the white urban population. Because of segregated housing in Northern cities, their school districts were also segregated. A powerful theme running through all black objectives was the desire to break out of the restrictions of the "ghetto."

MILITANTS. From 1964 to 1969 an unusual number of riots broke out in black areas of Northern cities. From New York and Newark to Cleveland, from Detroit to Chicago and Los Angeles, shooting and looting at times took over the city streets. The report of President Johnson's Commission on Civil Disorders found that some of these disturbances were instigated by white extremists and some were accentuated by police and National Guard inefficiency.

A DIVIDED NATION. The disturbing *Report of the Commission on Civil Disorders,* issued in 1968, asserted that the nation was "moving toward two societies, one black and one white—separate and unequal." This problem remains. But legal and social gains were being made, and there was a new pride among blacks. On many a college campus black students emphasized the importance of their own heritage by insisting on courses in black history and culture.

PRELUDE TO THE GREAT SOCIETY

Although President Kennedy had little success in persuading Congress to give him the legislation which he desired, he was quick to point out that in 1963 the United States was enjoying a period of prosperity which provided a firm basis for future planning.

The Assassination of the President. On November 22, 1963, the American people were stunned by the news that President Kennedy had been fatally wounded by an assassin's bullet while riding at Mrs. Kennedy's side in an open automobile in Dallas, Texas. For the fourth time in the nation's history martyrdom had come to its chief executive during his term of office. Vice-President Johnson quickly took the oath of office and firmly guided the country during the sorrowful days of mourning for the late President. The grief of all Americans was made more painful by the shocking slaying of the alleged assassin, Lee H. Oswald, before he could be brought to trial.

Presidential Transition. President Johnson understood the political aspects of his high office better than had most of his predecessors in the presidency. So adroit was his handling of relations between Capitol Hill and the White House that he secured from Congress legislation which it had declined to enact while Kennedy was president.

LANDSLIDE OF 1964. Lyndon B. Johnson of Texas was elected President and Hubert H. Humphrey of Minnesota was chosen Vice-President by the largest popular vote in the nation's history. Johnson's 61.2 per cent of the total vote topped Franklin Roosevelt's 60.8 per cent in 1936 and Warren Harding's 60.4 per cent in 1920. Senator Barry Goldwater of Arizona, the Republican candidate for President in 1964, received only 52 votes in the electoral college against 486 for President Johnson.

PLANNING FOR UTOPIA. In winning a presidential term in his own right, President Johnson spoke with emotion of the "Great Society." He seemed to promise a renewed attack by all the forces of government on poverty, disease, ignorance, and war. His ability to translate his Utopian hopes into reality depended upon congressional enactment of a program that could be enforced.

An Obedient Congress. For two years after he entered the White House, Johnson had little difficulty in securing from Congress the legislation he requested. Bill after bill was enacted almost in the precise form that the President's advisers had suggested.

War on Poverty. In August, 1964, the House and Senate by large majorities passed an anti-poverty bill, and a year later by a narrow margin doubled the appropriations in the original bill. Additional legislation provided relief for the underprivileged in distressed areas. A billion-dollar program of relief for the eleven-state Appalachian region was authorized in March, 1965. Federal grants to distressed areas other than Appalachia totaled more than $665 million in 1965. In addition, Congress enacted a low-cost housing program for a four-year period at an estimated cost of $8 billion.

Enhancing Education. Students in elementary and secondary schools, in colleges and universities, received the benefit of governmental generosity either directly in the form of scholarship grants, or indirectly through loans and grants to the educational institutions they were attending. The details of such appropriations were complicated and often controversial; but the result was a remarkable increase in the resources available for student training from the kindergarten to the graduate school.

Controversial Medicare. In spite of widespread questioning of the role of the federal government in providing medical care, and the outspoken opposition of many of the nation's doctors, Congress finally enacted a law (Medicare) providing medical and hospital care for the aged under the auspices of the Social Security system. The law became effective on July 1, 1966. Federal assistance was also extended to state medical-aid programs that met the requirements of the federal government.

A Discontented Congress. The spirit of co-operation which marked the early years of President Johnson's administration began to wear thin in 1965. A year later the congressional elections gave the Republicans a gain of 47 seats in the House and four in the Senate. The Ninetieth Congress paid less attention to legislative proposals from the White House. It did, however, enact (1) a bill creating a Department of Transportation; (2) a program for demonstrating new plans for the rebuilding of cities; (3) a bill establishing safety standards for automobiles; and (4) a bill increasing the federal minimum wage to $1.60 an hour effective in 1968.

The Twenty-fifth Amendment. In the spring of 1967 the United States amended its Constitution for the twenty-fifth time. The new amendment provided means for the Vice-President to assume the office of Acting President when a President becomes incapacitated, and the method whereby the President resumes his office if he recovers. It also authorized the President, whenever the office of Vice-President falls vacant, to appoint a new Vice-President who would take office when confirmed by a majority of both houses of Congress. Thus a constitutional gap in procedure, which had troubled the nation for almost two centuries, was filled.

FROM JOHNSON TO NIXON

After the Democratic reversal in the congressional elections of 1966, President Johnson's popularity declined rapidly.

The President Withdraws. At the close of a speech on the war in Vietnam, President Johnson on March 31, 1968, surprised the nation by saying: "I shall not seek and I will not accept the nomination of my party for another term as your President." Many political commentators believed that his decision resulted from his feeling that the voters were dissatisfied with his foreign policies, especially in Vietnam, and with his failure to quiet unrest and rioting in the larger cities of the nation.

An Unusual Campaign. Before his withdrawal as a candidate for re-election, President Johnson had been challenged in the Democratic primaries by Senator Eugene McCarthy of Minnesota and Senator Robert Kennedy of New York. Senator Kennedy had won the primary elections in several states before he was assassinated in Los Angeles, California, on June 5, 1968. His death opened the way for Vice-President Humphrey, who had entered the race as soon as President Johnson withdrew. After a bitter factional fight on the floor of their convention in Chicago, the Democrats nominated Humphrey for President and Senator Muskie of Maine for Vice-President. During the convention clashes erupted on the Chicago streets between demonstrators and police.

Nixon's Victory. The Republicans, in a convention that was well managed, quickly nominated Richard M. Nixon for President and Spiro T. Agnew, Governor of Maryland, for Vice-President. Profiting by his experience in the campaign of 1960 against John F. Kennedy, Nixon gave skillful direction to the Republican campaign. Although the margin of victory in the popular vote was slim—only 310,638 in a total vote of 72,245,000—Nixon and Agnew received 302 electoral votes to 191 for Humphrey and Muskie. George C. Wallace, former Governor of Alabama and retired General Curtis LeMay, received 45 electoral votes on a third-party ticket. When the electoral college voted, however, one elector pledged to Nixon switched to Wallace to give him 46 votes. This action underscored the demand that the whole procedure for choosing a president through an electoral college be reconsidered.

The Republican Revival. Although the Nixon victory increased the Republican membership of both the Senate and the House of Representatives, the Democrats still retained control of both houses. Nevertheless, President Nixon was hopeful that he would receive considerable Democratic support in his efforts to take the nation forward toward domestic harmony and international peace. His chief adviser in international relations, he announced, would be Secretary of State, William P. Rogers of New York, who had been Attorney General in the Eisenhower administration. Nixon's cabinet was largely composed of men with business backgrounds.

An Uncertain Nation. The leaders of the Nixon administration faced complex problems. From 1969 to 1973 they strove to overcome inflation in the economy, unemployment in the labor market, pollution in the environment, and frequent violence on college campuses and city streets. In August, 1971, Nixon suddenly imposed wage and price controls, which seemed to slow slightly the inflationary spiral. He reorganized the poverty program, recommended drastic changes in the welfare system, and proposed a guaranteed minimum income for every American family. His recommendations, however, were not implemented by legislation. He did persuade Congress to restructure the postal service and to share federal revenues with states, cities, and towns, thereby curtailing a number of federal domestic programs. Adroitly, he moved toward more liberal policies on domestic issues without abandoning his conservative principles; but he disappointed those who desired more progress in enforcement of civil rights legislation and in school desegregation.

A Strange Election. Through a combination of remarkable good luck, shrewd political timing, and bold moves in foreign policy President Nixon won a second term by an overwhelming popular majority.

THE NOMINATIONS. Minor challenges early in 1972 to the renomination of President Nixon and Vice-President Agnew by the Republican party were so easily turned aside that popular interest was fixed on the contests in the Democratic primaries. Senator George McGovern of South Dakota, promising reforms both in his party and in the nation, won a surprising victory over other leading contenders —Senator Muskie of Maine, Senator Humphrey of Minnesota, Senator Jackson of Washington, and Governor Wallace of Alabama. His supporters—among them many young, minority, and reformist groups—worked so effectively that they secured a majority of the delegates to the national Democratic convention, revised the party rules, took over control of the convention, and nominated the ticket of McGovern for President and Senator Thomas Eagleton of Missouri for Vice-President. Governor Wallace, partially paralyzed after being shot at a campaign rally, declined to repeat his third-party movement of 1968.

DEMOCRATIC TROUBLES. Senator McGovern's campaign quickly lost the enthusiasm and momentum that had marked it while he was fighting for the nomination. Soon after the convention adjourned, party leaders were stunned by the news that Senator Eagleton had received shock treatment for mental depression during the 1960's. Reluctantly, McGovern agreed to select another vice-presidential candidate, and the Democratic National Committee finally chose R. Sargent Shriver, former director of the Peace Corps. In trying to gain the support of veteran party leaders, most of whom had opposed his nomination, McGovern lost some of his influence with the young reformers who had hoped that he would rebuild the Democratic party along more liberal lines. In handling such issues as unemployment, tax reform, amnesty for draft evaders, abortion, drug abuse, and crime, he gave many voters the impression of indecisiveness.

REPUBLICAN STRATEGY. Stressing the heavy pressures of his presidential duties, Nixon spent little time "on the stump." He tried to blunt Democratic charges concerning inflation, unemployment, corruption in the federal government, the break-in and bugging of the Democratic Watergate headquarters, and favoritism to Republican special interests. In turn he charged that McGovern would embark on unsound economic programs, would reduce the United States to a second-rate power, and would end the war in Indo-China so rapidly that American prisoners of war would be left in North Vietnam and the government of South Vietnam would collapse. For many voters the war issue seemed to be resolved when the Hanoi, Saigon, and Washington governments announced simultaneously on October 26, 1972, that they were ready to sign a tentative cease-fire agreement as a prelude to a more permanent peace settlement.

PRESIDENTIAL VICTORY. The balloting in November, 1972, gave Nixon a large majority. He lost only one state, Massachusetts, and the electoral District of Columbia. When the Electoral College met in January, 1973, one of the Republican electors in Virginia cast his ballot for the Libertarian third party, so that Nixon had 520 votes, McGovern 17, and John Hosper, one vote. Far from losing its strength in the nation, the Democratic party did well in state and municipal contests and gained two more seats in the Senate. Perhaps the strangest feature of this strange election, was the fact that only a little over half (55 per cent) of the eligible voters bothered to cast ballots.

NIXON'S REORGANIZATION. As he began his second term, Nixon regrouped his "team." Promising to reduce the size of most departmental staffs, he made numerous administrative changes. Generally the appointments emphasized the declining power of cabinet officials and the growing influence of White House aides in the Administration.

INTERNATIONAL AFFAIRS

Though the conflict between Communist and non-Communist nations continued during the Eisenhower, Kennedy, and Johnson administrations, the government of the United States was persistent in its efforts to prevent international tensions from breaking out in military hostilities. However, the United States did become involved in a long and costly war between opposing forces in Vietnam.

Disarmament Negotiations. Bases for disarmament proposals by United States representatives to the United Nations were: (1) the establishment of an effective inspection system; (2) a suspension of nuclear tests; (3) a ban on the manufacture of atomic weapons; and (4) a transfer of some nuclear materials to industrial use. The primary difficulty in negotiating on these points was the unwillingness of the Soviet Union to agree with the Western powers on methods of international inspection. In an attempt to reach some accord on this issue, as well as on the future of Germany (which had remained a crucial problem since the Second World War), discussions and meetings were held in 1959 to pave the way for another Summit Conference.

Collapse at the Summit. President Eisenhower worked to prepare the way for a Summit Conference in 1960 that would bring worthwhile results.

THE KHRUSHCHEV VISIT. In September, 1959, Khrushchev accepted an invitation to visit the United States, and Eisenhower used the opportunity to negotiate face to face with him. There were high hopes that the two men had laid the basis for a fruitful general meeting in Paris.

THE U-2 INCIDENT. A few weeks before the scheduled Summit

Conference on disarmament was to convene, a United States reconnaissance plane—U-2—was brought down inside the Soviet Union. Its pilot, Francis G. Powers, told his Russian captors that he had been mapping military targets. Khrushchev promptly demanded an apology from President Eisenhower. When he received no apology, he refused to negotiate with Eisenhower at Paris.

The Berlin Wall. In 1961 Khrushchev tried to intimidate President Kennedy by renewing his threat that the Soviet Union would sign a separate peace treaty with Communist East Germany. Kennedy's response was prompt and decisive. He obtained a build-up of American armed strength in Europe and asserted once more the right of the Western powers to stay in Berlin. The Soviet reply was in effect a confession of Communist fear that Germans in increasing numbers would flee from East Berlin to the western sectors of the city. A high wall was built across the city, and East Germany closed the border between the two parts of Berlin. Known to Berliners as the "Wall of Shame," it became a symbol of the danger that border clashes might finally lead to global war.

Communists in the Caribbean. In 1960 the Communist tactics of espionage, infiltration, and sabotage came close to the shore of the United States.

CASTRO IN CUBA. Premier Fidel Castro, who had led a successful revolutionary movement against the government of President Fulgencio Batista, began to turn to the Communist nations for economic and military support, as his policies became more dictatorial, and his anti-Americanism grew more virulent. The patience of the Eisenhower administration was commendable, but Castro forced the issue by a demand that the United States reduce the size of its embassy staff. Eisenhower replied by breaking off diplomatic relations (December, 1960).

THE FUTILE INVASION. Late in April, 1961, an invasion of Cuba by anti-Castro exiles, which had the approval and support of the United States government, ended in tragic failure at the Bay of Pigs along the Cuban coast.

CHECKMATE FOR KHRUSHCHEV. In 1962 Castro managed to secure from the Soviet Union arms, which he maintained were purely "defensive" weapons. When American aerial photographs indicated the existence of offensive missile bases, constructed by experts from the Soviet Union, President Kennedy ordered a naval "quarantine" of the island of Cuba and demanded the withdrawal of the Soviet installations. Khrushchev yielded, after securing a promise that the United States would not invade Cuba. Castro's activities in the whole Caribbean area remained under close American reconnaissance.

Chaos in the Congo. East and West were drawn into the baffling struggle for power in Congolese Africa, late in 1960, after Belgian colonial rule came to an end. The efforts of the UN, led by Secretary-General Dag Hammarskjöld, to establish order were thwarted by the encouragement which the Communist bloc gave to some African leaders. In the chaotic situation the United States strongly supported the UN.

Crises in the UN. Hammarskjöld literally gave his life trying to bring peace to the new Republic of the Congo, for he was killed in an airplane crash in Africa in 1961. The Soviet Union refused to accept a new secretary-general of the UN, demanding a committee of three, one of whom would be named by the Communist nations. At the same time the Russians declined to pay their share of the expenses incurred by the UN forces maintaining peace in the Congo. The first of these issues was settled in 1962 when U Thant of Burma was chosen secretary-general. The second remained unsolved. Since the United States insisted that no nation in financial arrears should be permitted to vote, the UN almost ground to a halt. In March, 1965, a special committee of the Assembly started work on a new plan for the support of UN activities, which was put into effect early in 1966 when the United States agreed to a compromise acceptable to the Soviet Union. It had become clear by 1967 that the United Nations could take no action on international disputes unless the United States and the Soviet Union were in agreement.

Quick War in the Near East. After months of accusations and recriminations between the government of Israel and that of the United Arab Republic, an Arab-Israeli war broke out in June, 1967. It could have been a prelude to World War III, but both the United States and the Soviet Union quickly indicated that they would not intervene in the conflict. Both of the great powers had supplied arms and other war materials—the Soviet Union to the Arab nations and the United States to Israel—and neither could hold its allies to a peaceful course. Israel's swift victory over the United Arab Republic and its allies gave an important diplomatic advantage to the United States, but its aftermath was a bitter quarrel over the status of Israel as a nation and the boundaries of the several Arab states in the

Middle East, and an accelerated arms race between the Arab nations and Israel.

Entanglement in South Vietnam. By 1960 Communist pressure in southeast Asia had made South Vietnam a danger spot, and the ensuing warfare continued throughout the next twelve years.

AN EXPANDING WAR. Vietcong guerrillas, strongly backed by Communist North Vietnam, infiltrated the jungles, determined to overthrow the anti-Communist government in the capital, Saigon. When President Ngo Dinh Diem asked for American assistance, an advisory mission was sent to South Vietnam to bolster the government and strengthen the military forces fighting against the guerrilla tactics of the Vietcong. Though American aid at first was limited to supplies, military equipment, and civilian and military advisers, the United States steadily became more deeply involved as North Vietnam, China, and the Soviet Union sent a growing stream of arms and ammunition to the guerrilla forces. In the early months of 1965, President Johnson approved air raids by American planes on strategic bases in North Vietnam, usually in support of the South Vietnam air force. American policy was twofold: first, to stabilize the government of South Vietnam on a more popular basis; and, second, to destroy the sources of aid to the Vietcong that were located in South Vietnam, Cambodia, and Laos. By 1967 there were 464,000 American soldiers in Vietnam.

PROPAGANDA AND PEACE TALK. On March 31, 1968, President Johnson, aware of the rising opposition in the United States to the prolonged war in Vietnam, directed that allied bombing of approximately 90 per cent of the territory of North Vietnam cease. The North Vietnam government responded in May by sending representatives to a conference in Paris to discuss with American delegates the possibilities of a peaceful settlement to the Vietnamese conflict. More than seven months were used by the representatives of North Vietnam in putting forward propaganda statements. Not until President Johnson ordered the cessation of all American bombing of North Vietnam territory on October 31, 1968, did the delegates begin to discuss proposals for peace. By this time there were delegates at the conference table representing the United States, South Vietnam, North Vietnam, and the Vietcong. President Nixon named Henry Cabot Lodge to head the American delegation, replacing Averell Harriman, who had spoken for the Johnson administration. In 1970 David K. Bruce was appointed to succeed Lodge.

CONTINUED WAR. While the peace talks dragged on in Paris, the first American troops were deliberately withdrawn from South Vietnam; but the thrust by United States forces into Communist sanctuaries in Cambodia, ordered by Nixon in May, 1970, aroused widespread opposition. In the ensuing demonstrations against the government's military policy, students at Kent State University were fired upon by members of the Ohio National Guard and four were killed. Carefully supervising a program of "Vietnamization," that is, training the forces of South Vietnam to assume full responsibility for military actions, the Administration steadily withdrew American troops until there were fewer than 25,000 in South Vietnam by January, 1973.

PROLONGED NEGOTIATIONS AND FINAL AGREEMENT. Though the peace talks in Paris were stalemated, the public discussions had been supplemented by private and secret meetings between Henry Kissinger, presidential adviser for national defense, and Le Duc Tho, chief representative of North Vietnam. Drama came in October, 1972, when a cease-fire agreement drafted by the negotiators seemed to have been accepted by all sides. President Nixon, however, insisted that the terms of settlement be clarified, and no truce was immediately reached. In December heavy American bombing of Hanoi and Haiphong was resumed and Hanoi finally agreed to continue negotiations. On January 27, 1973, a cease-fire in all Vietnam went into effect. The agreement provided: (1) all Americans involved in military combat would be withdrawn from Vietnam within 60 days; (2) the United States would remove or deactivate mines off the coast of Vietnam; (3) American prisoners of war held by North Vietnam would be turned over to American authorities within 60 days; (4) the United States and North Vietnam would respect "the South Vietnamese people's right to self-determination"; (5) President Thieu's government would remain in South Vietnam pending an election to be supervised by a "National Council of Reconciliation and Concord" composed of members from the South Vietnam government, Communists, and neutralists; (6) all aspects of the agreement would be supervised by an international commission with a 1,160-man force, consisting of troops from Canada, Hungary, Indonesia, and Poland; (7) an international conference, including the Soviet Union and China, would be convened within 30 days. In announcing the cease-fire agreement, Henry Kissinger said that he expected a cease-fire in Laos, to take effect within a short period of time, and eventually a "de facto" cease-fire in Cambodia.

TRYING TO LIFT THE IRON CURTAIN

President Nixon chose election year, 1972, to make his most strenuous efforts to raise the iron curtain between the Communist and the non-Communist worlds.

Visit to China. In February Nixon went to Peking to confer with Communist Party Chairman Mao and Premier Chou. After a week of private talks the representatives of both nations agreed to work toward improved relations, and Sino-American cultural and scientific exchanges were planned. Several months before these historic meetings the People's Republic of China had been admitted to the United Nations (1971) and Taiwan (Nationalist China) had been expelled. In Peking Nixon and Chou agreed that their two nations would continue in contact with each other so that they might arrange further joint ventures.

Summit Meeting in Moscow. Though hostilities continued in Vietnam, where Hanoi was being supplied with Russian arms while its ports were mined and its military areas again bombed by the Americans, President Nixon was welcomed in Moscow in May, 1972. After discussions between Communist Party Secretary Brezhnev and the President the two nations agreed to co-operate on environmental and health projects, to lower trade barriers, and to collaborate in space exploration. More important was the signing of two treaties to limit the growth of nuclear arsenals. Finally Nixon and Brezhnev pledged themselves to work for an era of peaceful coexistence which might eventually lead to total disarmament.

Decreasing Tensions. These new approaches of the Nixon administration toward the Soviet Union and toward China gave greater significance to the efforts of other nations to penetrate the iron curtain. Negotiations had begun late in 1971 to ease the tensions between South Korea and North Korea. Treaties of amity and commerce between the German Federal Republic and the Soviet Union were ratified by the Bonn partliament in May, 1972. East German restrictions on communication with West Berlin were modified. Late in 1972 a general East-West security conference was proposed in several European capitals.

PENETRATING OUTER SPACE

The race into outer space gained momentum because of the "cold war" between the Communist world and the free world.

Missiles. After 1957, the United States moved rapidly to perfect both defensive and offensive space missiles. In 1960 the *Polaris,* which could be fired more than a thousand miles from a submerged submarine, was successfully tested. The next year the American arsenal was increased by the huge *Minuteman,* which could travel to a target more than 6,000 miles away at a speed of 15,000 miles per hour. Even more spectacular was the *Nike-Zeus,* described as an antimissile missile. In 1962 the Department of Defense claimed that such a "bullet to hit a bullet" had intercepted an intercontinental missile in a special test.

Orbiting the Globe. Project Mercury was the name of the United States program to put a man in space. After years of careful calculation and experimentation, American scientists won the applause of their fellow countrymen for several achievements. (1) In 1961 naval commander Alan B. Shepard, Jr., was literally fired 115 miles above the earth from the launching site at Cape Canaveral, Florida. (2) A year later, Lieutenant Colonel John H. Glenn, Jr., of the Marine Corps orbited the earth three times. (3) A few months later, Lieutenant Commander M. Scott Carpenter confirmed Glenn's observations in a similar orbital flight. (4) After many frustrating delays, in March, 1965, Major Virgil Grissom and Lieutenant Commander John W. Young circled the globe three times in a two-man space capsule, which they could maneuver from one type of orbit to another. In January, 1967, it was estimated that the United States and the U.S.S.R. had sent more than 2,250 satellites into orbit, of which approximately 500 were still on their orbital flights.

Reaching for the Moon. In January, 1967, a tragic fire aboard the Apollo I, on the launching pad at Cape Kennedy took the lives of Virgil Grissom, Edward White, and Roger Chaffee. There was intense national grief, and a long delay in plans for the lunar projects; but late in December, 1968, the Apollo VIII carried three dauntless men—Colonel Frank Borman, Captain James Lovell, and Major William Anders—on the most fantastic voyage of exploration in human history. During 147 hours the trans-lunar space ship sailed from the earth to the moon (more than 238,000 miles), orbited the moon ten times, and returned to earth—to be recovered in the Pacific Ocean only 7,000 yards from the carrier *Yorktown*.

A Boundless Horizon. "One short step for a man, one giant leap for mankind." With these words Neil Armstrong stepped onto the surface of the moon in July, 1969. He and his companions in the Apollo XII, Edwin Aldrin and Michael Collins, brought back scientific data of immense value from the moon's surface. Between July, 1969, and December, 1972, five more landings on the moon were successful. The last flight in the Apollo program was made by Eugene Cernan, Harrison Schmitt (geologist), and Ron Evans. Cernan and Schmitt roamed over miles of lunar terrain. As they rocketed back to earth, Cernan said: "We leave as we came and, God willing, we shall return with peace and hope for all mankind." Even if the people of the United States could not understand all the technical and scientific aspects of the moon flights, they did realize that humanity had been given the "vision" of a new universe.

EXAMINATIONS *

Mid-Term Examination
(One Hour)

1. Identify and state briefly the economic significance of each of the following terms. (Choose six.)

    (1) Alabama claims (84)
    (2) "Black Friday" (34)
    (3) Boxer Rebellion (97)
    (4) "Carpetbag governments" (8)
    (5) Crédit Mobilier (34)
    (6) Granger cases (32)
    (7) Hepburn Act (106–107)
    (8) Treaty of Washington (84)
    (9) McKinley Tariff (55–56)
   (10) Northern Securities case (105)

2. Answer either (a) or (b).

(a) "The most important result of the Civil War was the victory of industrial capitalism over agrarian capitalism." Do you agree with this statement? Why? (8–13)

(b) To what extent were the policies advocated by the Progressives (1910–1912) similar to those championed by the Populists (1890–1896)? (69–70, 116–118)

3. Answer either (a) or (b).

(a) Discuss the various theories of labor organization which were tested by the leaders of American labor between 1865 and 1910. (59–64, 105)

(b) Why did President Cleveland believe that American tariff policies were responsible for the "trust problem" in the United States? How did he propose to deal with this situation? (55–57)

* The figures in parentheses refer to pages in the Outline where information relating to each question may be found.

Final Examination
(Three Hours)

Answer any eight questions.

1. Trace the role of the farmer in American politics from the days of the Patrons of Husbandry to the Farmer-Labor party of the 1920's. (31–32, 69–70, 158–160)

2. How do you explain the fact that no "third party" has been able to win political control of the federal government since the Civil War? (31, 34, 69–70, 76–77, 116–117, 153)

3. In what ways did the basic philosophy of Woodrow Wilson's "New Freedom" differ from that of Theodore Roosevelt's "New Nationalism"? (104, 125–127)

4. Compare and contrast the attitudes of each of the following toward (a) the tariff and (b) the regulation of business enterprise during his presidential administration:

   (1) William McKinley
   (2) William Howard Taft
   (3) Warren G. Harding

   (77–80, 113–115, 151–152)

5. For more than seventy years (1861–1933) the Republican party was usually in control of the national government. How do you explain this? Why did the party fail to elect its candidates for president between 1932 and 1952? (33–45, 150–154, 170–172, 173, 182–183, 201–202, 223–224)

6. By 1914 Europe was divided into two armed camps. Name the principal powers in each camp and explain why the United States was finally drawn into the world war which broke out between them. (133–138)

7. How do you explain the participation of the United States in the creation of the League of Nations and its subsequent refusal to become a member of the League? (142–146)

8. Compare the social and economic effects of the depression of 1929 with the conditions that followed the panic of 1893. (74–75, 166–167, 169–170)

9. If you had been President of the United States in 1950, would you have responded to the Communist aggression in Korea along lines

similar to those followed by President Truman? Explain your policy fully. (230–232)

10. What do you consider the most pressing problems of the United States today? What do you think should be done to solve them? What help in the understanding of these problems does the study of American history provide? (217–259)

PRESIDENTS AND SECRETARIES OF STATE

1.	George Washington	1789–1797	Thomas Jefferson	1789
			Edmund Randolph	1794
			Timothy Pickering	1795
2.	John Adams	1797–1801	Timothy Pickering	
			John Marshall	1800
3.	Thomas Jefferson	1801–1809	James Madison	1801
4.	James Madison	1809–1817	Robert Smith	1809
			James Monroe	1811
5.	James Monroe	1817–1825	John Q. Adams	1817
6.	John Quincy Adams	1825–1829	Henry Clay	1825
7.	Andrew Jackson	1829–1837	Martin Van Buren	1829
			Edward Livingston	1831
			Louis McLane	1833
			John Forsyth	1834
8.	Martin Van Buren	1837–1841	John Forsyth	
9.	William Henry Harrison	1841	Daniel Webster	1841
10.	John Tyler	1841–1845	Daniel Webster	
			Hugh S. Legaré	1843
			Abel P. Upshur	1843
			John C. Calhoun	1844
11.	James Knox Polk	1845–1849	James Buchanan	1845
12.	Zachary Taylor	1849–1850	John M. Clayton	1849
13.	Millard Fillmore	1850–1853	Daniel Webster	1850
			Edward Everett	1852
14.	Franklin Pierce	1853–1857	William L. Marcy	1853
15.	James Buchanan	1857–1861	Lewis Cass	1857
			Jeremiah S. Black	1860
16.	Abraham Lincoln	1861–1865	William H. Seward	1861
17.	Andrew Johnson	1865–1869	William H. Seward	
18.	Ulysses S. Grant	1869–1877	Elihu B. Washburne	1869
			Hamilton Fish	1869
19.	Rutherford B. Hayes	1877–1881	William M. Evarts	1877
20.	James A. Garfield	1881	James G. Blaine	1881

21. Chester A. Arthur	1881–1885	James G. Blaine	
		F. T. Frelinghuysen	1881
22. Grover Cleveland	1885–1889	Thomas F. Bayard	1885
23. Benjamin Harrison	1889–1893	James G. Blaine	1889
		John W. Foster	1892
24. Grover Cleveland	1893–1897	Walter Q. Gresham	1893
		Richard Olney	1895
25. William McKinley	1897–1901	John Sherman	1897
		William R. Day	1898
		John Hay	1898
26. Theodore Roosevelt	1901–1909	John Hay	
		Elihu Root	1905
		Robert Bacon	1909
27. William H. Taft	1909–1913	Philander C. Knox	1909
28. Woodrow Wilson	1913–1921	William J. Bryan	1913
		Robert Lansing	1915
		Bainbridge Colby	1920
29. Warren G. Harding	1921–1923	Charles E. Hughes	1921
30. Calvin Coolidge	1923–1929	Charles E. Hughes	
		Frank B. Kellogg	1925
31. Herbert C. Hoover	1929–1933	Henry L. Stimson	1929
32. Franklin D. Roosevelt	1933–1945	Cordell Hull	1933
		E. R. Stettinius	1945
33. Harry S. Truman	1945–1953	E. R. Stettinius	
		James F. Byrnes	1945
		George C. Marshall	1947
		Dean Acheson	1949
34. Dwight D. Eisenhower	1953–1961	John Foster Dulles	1953
		Christian Herter	1959
35. John F. Kennedy	1961–1963	Dean Rusk	1961
36. Lyndon B. Johnson	1963–1969	Dean Rusk	
37. Richard M. Nixon	1969–1974	William P. Rogers	1969
		Henry Kissinger	1973
38. Gerald R. Ford	1974–	Henry Kissinger	

STATES, TERRITORIES, AND DEPENDENCIES

States

Original thirteen states indicated in capital letters

State	Settled	Area Sq. Mi.	Entered Union
Alabama	1702	51,060	1819
Alaska	1783	571,065	1959
Arizona	1580	113,575	1912
Arkansas	1685	52,499	1836
California	1769	156,573	1850
Colorado	1858	103,884	1876
CONNECTICUT	1635	4,899	1788
DELAWARE	1638	1,978	1787
Florida	1565	54,252	1845
GEORGIA	1733	58,274	1788
Hawaii	c.500	6,415	1959
Idaho	1842	82,708	1890
Illinois	1720	55,930	1818
Indiana	1733	36,185	1816
Iowa	1788	56,032	1846
Kansas	1727	82,048	1861
Kentucky	1775	39,863	1792
Louisiana	1699	45,106	1812
Maine	1624	31,012	1820
MARYLAND	1634	9,874	1788
MASSACHUSETTS	1620	7,867	1788
Michigan	1668	57,019	1837
Minnesota	1805	80,009	1858
Mississippi	1699	47,223	1817
Missouri	1764	69,138	1821
Montana	1809	145,736	1889
Nebraska	1847	76,612	1867
Nevada	1850	109,788	1864
NEW HAMPSHIRE	1623	9,014	1788
NEW JERSEY	1664	7,531	1787
New Mexico	1537	121,510	1912
NEW YORK	1614	47,939	1788
NORTH CAROLINA	1650	49,067	1789
North Dakota	1780	69,457	1889
Ohio	1788	40,972	1803

State	Settled	Area Sq. Mi.	Entered Union
Oklahoma	1889	68,887	1907
Oregon	1838	96,248	1859
PENNSYLVANIA	1682	45,007	1787
RHODE ISLAND	1636	1,058	1790
SOUTH CAROLINA	1670	30,272	1788
South Dakota	1794	76,378	1889
Tennessee	1757	41,762	1796
Texas	1686	262,840	1845
Utah	1847	82,339	1896
Vermont	1724	9,276	1791
VIRGINIA	1607	39,838	1788
Washington	1845	66,709	1889
West Virginia	1727	24,079	1863
Wisconsin	1670	54,705	1848
Wyoming	1834	97,411	1890

Territories and Dependencies

	Acquired	Area Sq. Mi.
Guam	1898—ceded to U. S. by Spain	209
Puerto Rico	1898—ceded to U. S. by Spain; became a self-governing Commonwealth, 1952	3,421
American Samoa	1899—annexed by treaty with Germany and Great Britain	76
Canal Zone	1904—leased in perpetuity from Panama	553
Virgin Islands	1917—purchased from Denmark	133
Midway, Wake, and other Pacific islands		42

SELECTED REFERENCES FOR
ADDITIONAL READING

Books designated by an asterisk (*) have been reprinted in paperback.

CHAPTER I: BUILDING A NEW NATION

General Surveys:
Bowers, C. G., *The Tragic Era* (1929)*
Buck, P. H., *The Road to Reunion, 1865–1900* (1937)
Dunning, W. A., *Reconstruction, Political and Economic* (1907)*
Fleming, W. L., *Sequel of Appomatox* (1919)
Stampp, K. M., *The Era of Reconstruction* (1965)*

Special Studies:
Beale, H. K., *The Critical Year: A Study of Andrew Jackson and Reconstruction* (1930)
DeWitt, D. M., *The Impeachment and Trial of Andrew Jackson* (1903)
Horn, S. F., *Invisible Empire: The Story of the Ku Klux Klan* (1939)
McPherson, J. P., *The Struggle for Equality: Abolitionists and the Negro in the Civil War and Reconstruction* (1964)

CHAPTER II: AN EXPANDING ECONOMIC SYSTEM

General Surveys:
Fite, G. C., *The Farmers' Frontier* (1966)*
Hough, Emerson, *The Passing of the Frontier* (1918)
Nevins, Allan, *The Emergence of Modern America* (1927)
Riegel, R. E., *America Moves West* (4th ed., 1964)
Shannon, F. A., *The Farmer's Last Frontier* (1945)
Webb, W. P., *The Great Plains* (1931)*

Special Studies:
Atherton, Lewis, *The Cattle Kings* (1951)
Branch, E. D., *The Hunting of the Buffalo* (1929)
Dick, Everett, *The Sod House Frontier, 1854–1890* (1937)
Moody, John, *The Railroad Builders* (1919)
Pelzer, Louis, *The Cattlemen's Frontier* (1936)

Schlesinger, A. M., *Rise of the City, 1878–1898* (1933)
Webb, W. P., *The Texas Rangers* (rev. ed., 1965)

CHAPTER III: STALEMATE IN POLITICS

General Surveys:
Binkley, W. E., American Political Parties (4th ed., 1963)
Fish, C. R., *Civil Service and the Patronage* (1905)
Josephson, Matthew, *The Politicos, 1865–1896* (1938)*
Sparks, E. E., *National Development, 1877–1885* (1907)
Stanwood, Edward, *A History of the Presidency* (1928)

Special Studies:
Agar, Herbert, *The Price of Union* (1950)*
Ford, H. J., *The Cleveland Era* (1919)
Haworth, P. L., *The Hayes-Tilden Disputed Presidential Election* (1906)
Howe, G. F., *Chester A. Arthur* (1934)
Nevins, Allan, *Grover Cleveland* (1932)
————, *Hamilton Fish: The Inner History of the Grant Administration*
    (2 vols., 1936)
Ross, E. D., *Liberal Republican Movement* (1919)
Thomas, H. C., *The Return of the Democratic Party to Power* (1919)

CHAPTER IV: PRIVATE ENTERPRISE AND PUBLIC REGULATION

General Surveys:
Hacker, L. M., *The Triumph of American Capitalism* (1940)*
Hendrick, B. J., *The Age of Big Business* (1919)
Kirkland, E. C., *Industry Comes of Age: Business, Labor, and Public
    Policy, 1860–1897* (1961)
Tarbell, I. M., *The Nationalizing of Business* (1936)

Special Studies:
Allen, F. L., *The Great Pierpont Morgan* (1949)*
Carnegie, Andrew, *Autobiography* (1920)
Cochran, T. C., *Railroad Leaders* (1965)
Holbrook, S. H., *The Age of the Moguls* (1953)*
Josephson, Matthew, *The Robber Barons* (1934)*
Moody, John, *The Truth about the Trusts* (1904)
Nevins, Allan, *John D. Rockefeller* (1940)

Sharkey, R. P., *Money, Class, and Party* (1959)*
Taussig, F. W., *Tariff History of the United States* (1931)

CHAPTER V: THE STATUS OF THE INDUSTRIAL WORKER

General Surveys:
Beard, M. R., *The American Labor Movement* (1920)
Dulles, F. R., *Labor in America* (3rd ed., 1966)*
Ely, R. T., *The Labor Movement in America* (1905)

Special Studies:
Adamic, Louis, *Dynamite: The Story of Class Violence in America* (1934)
David, Henry, *History of the Haymarket Affair* (1936)*
Gompers, Samuel, *Seventy Years of Life and Labor* (2 vols., 1925)
Handlin, Oscar, *The Uprooted* (1951)*
Higham, John, *Strangers in the Land* (1955)*
Powderly, T. V., *Thirty Years of Life and Labor* (rev. ed., 1890)
Witte, E. E., *Government in Labor Disputes* (1932)

CHAPTER VI: THE WEST IN REVOLT

General Surveys:
Buck, S. J., *The Agrarian Crusade* (1920)
Destler, C. M., *American Radicalism, 1865–1901* (1946)*
Fine, Nathan, *Labor and Farmer Parties in the United States, 1828–1928* (1928)
Hicks, J. D., *Populist Revolt* (1931)*
Hofstadter, Richard, *The Age of Reform: From Bryan to F. D. R.* (1955)*
Pollack, Norman, *The Populist Response to Industrial America* (1962)*
Unger, Irwin, *Populism: Nostalgic or Progressive* (1964)*
Woodward, C. V., *Origins of the New South, 1877–1913* (1951)*

Special Studies:
Coletta, P. E., *William Jennings Bryan* (1964)
Croly, Herbert, *Marcus Alonzo Hanna* (1912)
Glad, P. W., *The Trumpet Soundeth: William Jennings Bryan* (1960)
McMurray, D. L., *Coxey's Army* (1929)
Simpkins, F. B., *The Tillman Movement in South Carolina* (1926)
Woodward, C. V., *Tom Watson, Agrarian Rebel* (1938)*

CHAPTER VII: THE PATH TOWARD EMPIRE

General Surveys:

Bemis, S. F., *A Diplomatic History of the United States* (5th ed., 1965)
Griswold, A. W., *The Far Eastern Policy of the United States* (1934)*
Leopold, R. W., *The Growth of American Foreign Policy* (1962)
May, E. R., *Imperial Democracy* (1961)
Pratt, J. W., *America's Colonial Experiment* (1950)
Weinberg, A. K., *Manifest Destiny* (1935)

Special Studies:

Bradley, H. W., *The American Frontier in Hawaii* (1942)
Cline, H. F., *The United States and Mexico* (1963)*
Dulles, F. R., *Prelude to World Power* (1965)
Freidel, Frank, *The Splendid Little War* (1958)
Millis, Walter, *The Martial Spirit: The Spirit of the Spanish-American War* (1931)*
Munro, D. G., *Intervention and Dollar Diplomacy in the Caribbean, 1900–1921* (1964)
Nichols, J. P., *Alaska* (1924)
Perkins, Dexter, *History of the Monroe Doctrine* (rev. ed., 1955)*
Pratt, J. W., *The Expansionists of 1898* (1936)*

CHAPTER VIII: THE ERA OF THEODORE ROOSEVELT

General Surveys:

Beale, Howard, *Theodore Roosevelt and the Rise of America to World Power* (1956)*
Blum, J. M., *The Republican Roosevelt* (1954)*
Chamberlain, John, *Farewell to Reform* (1909)*
Croly, Herbert, *The Promise of American Life* (1909)*
Faulkner, H. U., *The Quest for Social Justice* (1931)
Howland, Harold, *Theodore Roosevelt and His Times* (1921)
Rhodes, J. F., *The McKinley and Roosevelt Administrations* (1922)
Sullivan, Mark, *Our Times*, Vols. III and IV (1935)

Special Studies:

Bowers, C. G., *Beveridge and the Progressive Era* (1932)
Dennett, Tyler, *Roosevelt and the Russo-Japanese War* (1922)
Filler, Louis, *Crusaders for American Liberalism* (rev. ed., 1961)*
Goldman, Eric, *Rendezvous with Destiny* (1952)*
Hechler, K. W., *Insurgency: Personalities and Politics of the Taft Era* (1940)

La Follette, R. M., *Autobiography* (1913)

Morgan, H. W., *William McKinley and His America* (1963)

Mowry, G. E., *Theodore Roosevelt and the Progressive Movement* (1946)*

Noble, D. W., *The Paradox of Progressive Thought* (1958)

Pringle, H. F., *Theodore Roosevelt* (1956)*

———, *The Life and Times of William Howard Taft* (2 vols., 1939)

Roosevelt, Theodore, *Autobiography* (1913)

Shannon, David, *The Socialist Party of America* (1955)*

CHAPTER IX: WILSONIAN LIBERALISM

General Surveys:

Link, Arthur, *Woodrow Wilson and the Progressive Era, 1910–1917* (1954)*

May, H. F., *The End of American Innocence* (1959)*

Paxon, F. L., *The Pre-War Years* (1930)

Special Studies:

Blum, J. M., *Woodrow Wilson and the Politics of Morality* (1964)*

Dodd, W. E., *Woodrow Wilson and His Work* (1921)

Commager, H. S., *The American Mind* (1950)*

Forcey, Charles, *The Crossroads of Liberalism* (1961)

Link, Arthur, *Wilson: The Road to the White House* (1953)*

Walworth, Arthur, *Woodrow Wilson: American Prophet* (2nd ed., 1965)

White, M. G., *Social Thought in America* (1949)*

Wilson, Woodrow, *The New Freedom* (1913)*

CHAPTER X: IN THE FIRST WORLD WAR

General Surveys:

Bailey, T. A., *Woodrow Wilson and the Lost Peace* (1947)*

Hoover, Herbert, *The Ordeal of Woodrow Wilson* (1958)

May, E. R., *The World War and American Isolation, 1914–1917* (1959)*

Millis, Walter, *The Road to War* (1935)

Paxon, F. L., *American Democracy and the World War* (3 vols., 1936)

Seymour, Charles, *Woodrow Wilson and the World War* (1934)

Sullivan, Mark, *Our Times,* Vol. V (1933)

Special Studies:

Chafee, Zechariah, *Free Speech in the United States* (1941)*

Fleming, D. F., *The United States and the League of Nations* (1932)

Garraty, J. A., *Henry Cabot Lodge* (1953)
Murray, R. K., *Red Scare* (1955)*
Peterson, H. C., and Fite, G. C., *Opponents of War, 1917–1918* (1957)*
Preston, William, *Aliens and Dissenters* (1963)*
Rudin, H. R., *Armistice, 1918* (1944)

CHAPTER XI: THE PROMISE OF NATIONAL PROSPERITY

General Surveys:
Allen, F. L., *Only Yesterday* (1931)*
Faulkner, H. U., *From Versailles to the New Deal* (1950)
Goldman, E. F., *Rendezvous with Destiny* (1952)*
Leuchtenburg, W. E., *Perils of Prosperity, 1914–1932* (1958)*
Sullivan, Mark, *Our Times,* Vol. VI (1935)
Wish, Harvey, *Contemporary America* (4th ed., 1966)

Special Studies:
Bagby, W. M., *The Road to Normalcy: The Presidential Campaign and Election of 1920* (1968)*
Chase, Stuart, *Rich Land, Poor Land* (1936)
Galbraith, J. K., *The Great Crash, 1929* (1955)
Hicks, J. D., *The Republican Ascendancy* (1960)*
McKay, K. C., *The Progressive Movement of 1924* (1947)
May, H. F., *The Discontent of the Intellectuals: A Problem of the Twenties* (1963)*
Mecklin, J. M., *The Ku Klux Klan* (1924)
Merz, Charles, *Dry Decade* (1931)
Mitchell, Broadus, *Depression Decade* (1947)*
Sinclair, Andrew, *Prohibition* (1962)
Soule, George, *Prosperity Decade* (1947)*
White, W. A., *A Puritan in Babylon: The Story of Calvin Coolidge* (1930)*

CHAPTER XII: ECONOMIC CRISIS AND THE NEW DEAL

General Surveys:
Burns, J. M., *Roosevelt: The Lion and the Fox* (1957)*
Moley, Raymond, *The First New Deal* (1966)
Rauch, Basil, *History of the New Deal, 1933–1938* (1944)*
Schlesinger, A. M., Jr., *Age of Roosevelt* (3 vols., 1957–1960)
Wecter, Dixon, *The Age of the Great Depression, 1929–1941* (1948)

Special Studies:

Bernstein, Irving, *The New Deal Collective Bargaining Policy* (1950)

Black, J. D., *Parity, Parity, Parity* (1942)

Cronon, E. D., *Labor and the New Deal* (1963)*

Graham, O. L., *An Encore for Reform: The Old Progressives and the New Deal* (1967)*

Jackson, R. H., *The Struggle for Judicial Supremacy* (1942)*

Roosevelt, Eleanor, *Autobiography* (1961)

Sherwood, R. E., *Roosevelt and Hopkins: An Intimate History* (rev. ed., 1950)

CHAPTER XIII: THE IMPACT OF WORLD POWER

General Surveys:

Beard, C. A., *President Roosevelt and the Coming of War* (1948)

Churchill, W. S., *The Gathering Storm* (1948)

Langer, W. L., and Gleason, S. E., *The Challenge to Isolation, 1937–1940* (2 vols., 1952)

———, *The Undeclared War, September, 1940–December, 1941* (1953)

Nevins, Allan, *The New Deal and World Affairs* (1950)

Rauch, Basil, *Roosevelt: From Munich to Pearl Harbor* (1950)

Special Studies:

Bemis, S. F., *Latin American Policy of the United States* (1943)*

Divine, R. A., *The Illusion of Neutrality* (1962)*

———, *The Reluctant Belligerent* (1965)*

Dulles, F. R., *China and America* (1946)

Feis, Herbert, *The Road to Pearl Harbor* (1950)

Griswold, A. W., *The Far Eastern Policy of the United States* (1938)*

Tannenbaum, Frank, *Ten Keys to Latin America* (1962)*

CHAPTER XIV: THE SECOND WORLD WAR

General Surveys:

Buchanan, A. R., *The United States and World War II* (2 vols, 1964)*

Burns, J. M., *Roosevelt: Soldier of Freedom* (1970)

Churchill, W. S., *The Second World War* (6 vols, 1948–1953)*

Feis, Herbert, *Roosevelt, Churchill, Stalin* (2nd ed., 1967)*

Fuller, J. F. C., *The Second World War* (1948)

Millis, Walter, *Arms and Men* (1956)*

Wilmot, Chester, *The Struggle for Europe* (1952)*

Special Studies:

Ambrose, S. E., *The Supreme Commander: The War Years of General Dwight D. Eisenhower* (1970)

Baxter, J. P., *Scientists against Time* (1946)*

Eisenhower, D. D., *Crusade in Europe* (1945)*

Feis, Herbert, *The Atomic Bomb and the End of World War II* (rev. ed., 1966)

Lord, Walter, *Day of Infamy* (1957)

Morison, S. E., *Two Ocean War* (1963)

Pratt, Fletcher, *War for the World* (1951)

Smyth, H. D., *Atomic Energy for Military Purposes* (1945)

Wohlstetter, Roberta, *Pearl Harbor: Warning and Decision* (1962)*

CHAPTER XV: THE QUEST FOR PEACE AND SECURITY

General Surveys:

Baker, D. G., and Sheldon, C. H., *Postwar America: The Search for Identity* (1969)*

Gatze, Hans, *The Present in Perspective* (3rd ed., 1965)*

Goldman, E. F., *The Crucial Decade and After: America, 1945–1960* (1960)*

Knapp, W. F., *History of War and Peace, 1939–1965* (1967)

Quinn, E. G., and Dolan, P. J., eds., *The Sense of the Sixties* (1968)*

Spanier, J. W., *American Foreign Policy since World War II* (3rd ed., 1968)*

Special Studies:

Bennett, Lerone, Jr., *The Black Mood* (1964)*

Clark, Ramsey, *Crime in America* (1970)

Cooper, C. L., *The Lost Crusade: America in Vietnam* (1970)

Fall, Bernard, *The Two Viet-Nams* (2nd rev. ed., 1967)

Feis, Herbert, *The Atomic Bomb and the End of World War II* (rev. ed., 1966)

Graham, Frank, Jr., *Since Silent Spring* (1970)

Lens, Sidney, *The Military-Industrial Complex* (1970)*

Novak, R. D., and Evans, Rowland, *Lyndon B. Johnson* (1966)*

Report of the National Advisory Committee on Civil Disorders (1968)*

Schlesinger, A. M., Jr., *A Thousand Days* (1965)*

Silberman, C. E., *Crisis in the Classroom* (1970)

Sorensen, T. C., *Kennedy* (1965)*

White, T. E., *Making of the President, 1960* (1961)*

———, *Making of the President, 1964* (1965)*

———, *Making of the President, 1968* (1969)*

INDEX

"Arsenal of Democracy" p. 199

"Reparations"

Kellogg-Briand 193

Muckrackers – pg. 108

Panama Canal – pg. 120

Theodore Roosevelt – pg. 104, pg. 118

Russian-Japanese War p. 130

Wilson. Democratic / pg. 129.

pg. 130   p. 134 – Lusitania

pg. 134 "He kept us out of war."

14 Points p. 142

Harding – pg. 150

Jazz age – p. 154.

Immigration – pg. 161

163 – Sacco – Vanzetti

Depression – p. 170

TVA – P. 175

Social Security – p. 179; Collective bargaining 180

The "Nine Old Men" p. 183